THE
PHOENIX PARK
MURDERS

THE
PHOENIX PARK
MURDERS

CONSPIRACY, BETRAYAL & RETRIBUTION

SENAN MOLONY

MERCIER PRESS

WHAT YOU NEED TO READ

MERCIER PRESS
Douglas Village, Cork
www.mercierpress.ie

Trade enquiries to CMD Distribution
55A Spruce Avenue, Stillorgan Industrial Park, Blackrock, County Dublin

© Senan Molony, 2006

ISBN: 978 1 85635 511 7

10 9 8 7 6 5 4 3 2

A CIP record for this title is available from the British Library

DEDICATION
To my son Tomás

Mercier Press receives financial assistance from the Arts Council/
An Chomhairle Ealaíon

Printed and Bound by J. H. Haynes & Co. Ltd, Sparkford

Contents

Prologue

Earl Spencer to Lady Spencer
6 May 1882; The Castle, Dublin

'Just in after certainly the best reception I ever got in Ireland.

'It was a lovely day, and the streets were crammed with people; pavements, windows, college parks, railings.

'The cheering was tremendous at times, and I would see many old friends at windows, etc. I heard once or twice Davitt's name; but I never heard a hiss; more often "Welcome back".

'At one window a great St Bernard gave a loud bark by command of his mistress.

'Old friends were very cordial indeed. I wish you had been in the procession. You would have had a tremendous reception!'

Earl Spencer to Lady Spencer
6 May 1882; Viceregal Lodge, Dublin

'We are in God's hands. Do not be filled with alarm and fear. I was alone and have no apprehension.

'God knows how I feel, this fearful tragedy – two such men at such a time. I dare not dwell on the horror, for I feel I must be unmanned.

'I am very calm.

'Do not, loved one, come unless you feel more unhappy in London than here. There is no danger really whatever.

'See dear Lucy if you can and tell her that I am not made of ice, but I dare not face what has occurred. God help and comfort her and all his relatives'.

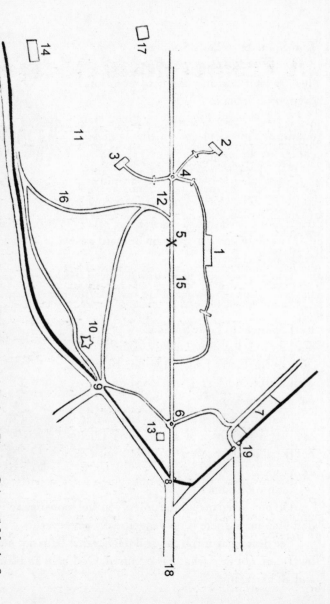

Phoenix Park, 1882 – 1. Viceregal Lodge 2. Under Secretary's Lodge 3. Chief Secretary's Lodge 4. Phoenix Column 5. Murder Scene
6. Gough Statue 7. RIC depot 8. Park Gate 9. Islandbridge Gate 10. Magazine Fort 11. Fifteen Acres 12. Escape Route
13. Wellington Monument 14. Hibernian School 15. Chesterfield Avenue 16. Road to Chapelizod 17. Mountjoy Barracks
18. Towards City 19. North Circular Road Gate.

A Tremendous Reception

IT WAS INDEED A 'LOVELY DAY' and many were taking advantage. Some of those enjoying the warm weather in the Phoenix Park later appeared 'extremely sunburnt'.

Others did not have the luxury of idleness. Saturday was not a day of rest but an ordinary part of the working week for thousands of Dubliners. They sweltered in coal yards and cooperages, sculleries and schoolhouses.

At Kingstown, now Dun Laoghaire, the honour guard at the pier had reason to curse their headgear and heavy tunics. They may also have cursed Earl Spencer, the freshly arrived lord lieutenant of Ireland, the visible embodiment of her Britannic majesty.

Except he was not yet visible and it had been hours now. His vessel, the mail boat *Ulster*, crossed from Holyhead in the dark and had been lying since seven o'clock under puffball clouds in soporific calm.

The men of the Rifle Brigade itched with impatience. It was now was past ten and still Spencer did not appear.

The boys' band of the Meath Industrial School had taken up position and was playing pleasing music, helping 'to lessen the tedium of the delay', as a stifling newspaper reporter rankled.

Kingstown yacht clubs, the coastguard and revenue stations, the Irish Lights office and Board of Works, were all decorated with bunting. Shortly after 11 o'clock, crowds began to take up positions on the slopes and barriers overlooking Carlisle Pier and the railway line by which the train to Dublin was to pass.

On board the *Ulster*, the Earl Spencer was taking a leisurely breakfast with Lord Frederick Cavendish, his new chief secretary for Ireland, who was accompanied by his curious younger brother Robert, an MP.

Freddy Cavendish had been to Ireland before when a third brother, Lord Hartington, was chief, but Bobby was looking forward to seeing the city for the first time. Mr Courtenay Boyle, private secretary, poured the tea.

Boyle had already indicated to the colonel in charge of landing arrangements that the lord lieutenant intended, despite his early arrival, to remain on board until the hour appointed for the State ceremony.

Thus two lines of Metropolitan police continued to peer fixedly at each other, chinstraps under impassive features, their uniforms framing the short distance from the landing stage to a platform beside the railway line.

The Irish state train, its engine handsomely decorated in festoons of evergreen and flowers, pulled up alongside this grand display of immobility at precisely twenty minutes to noon.

It had just brought down a viscount, a lord chancellor, master of horse, one joint chief commander of police, sundry military officers, some distinguished railway personages, and four aides-de-camp.

They joined the honourable Captain Crofton, harbour master, and other local dignitaries already arrayed beside the steamship, some discreetly consulting a fob from an inside pocket.

News was then conveyed that his excellency would be glad to receive a delegation in his cabin, and a representative sample thus ascended the gangway, respectfully doffing their hats as they did so.

Within a short time they returned and the large crowd brightened immeasurably. As the sun reached the meridian, the figure of Earl Spencer was finally seen on the upper deck, being greeted by 'a hearty cheer'. The viceregal flag on the mainmast was lowered, the guard of honour presented arms briskly and the regimental band could at last strike up *God Save the Queen*.

Spencer had seen it all before having been sent here in the same post in 1869, but to the whole party it was a delightful panoply. They remarked as much on eventually getting free of the handshakes and obsequious scraping and into the cool compartment of the train.

The Royal Salute from the guns of the *Belleisle* guardship had been the most gratifying pomp of all, the younger Cavendish thought. Dublin could hardly top Kingstown for this kind of grandeur, surely? His excellency thought it certainly would, resplendent himself in a black frock coat, with the star of the Order of the Garter on his breast and the badge of the same suspended from a ribbon around his neck. His top hat rested in white gloves, against his grey trousers.

The locomotive jolted, gliding the short distance to Westland Row. On the way hats and 'kerchiefs were waved in welcome, until seven minutes had gone by and the new administration of Ireland gained the city centre, detraining itself to fresh expressions of loyalty and happiness.

Flags of all kinds, but chiefly Union Jacks, bedecked the station. Here was the lord mayor, Charles Dawson MP, and members of the corporation in their robes, effusive and ingratiating. There were also prelates, concerned to pay homage to representatives of temporal power. Mr Frost, Chairman of the Dublin and Wicklow Railway Company, hovered in hope of an introduction.

Lord Frederick Cavendish, fawned upon and nodding in his turn, was surprised to see another army of children assembled. Six hundred boys from the Artane Industrial School, their band members well versed in hymns to imperial greatness, stood spruced at the ready.

Now they were silent but as the imperial express had come into sight, they too had invoked blessings on Queen Victoria through a rendition of the national anthem. Its closing notes were drowned in a protest of brakes, and the sea of heads remained uncovered.

His excellency bowed continuously, shook hands endlessly and was about to greet again when approached by the city marshal, J. P. Carroll, who presented him with the keys of the city on a crimson cushion.

Beaming countenances abounded. Spencer was urbanity itself,

returning the keys to the safe keeping of the lord mayor and city elders, who had looked after them so well for so many hundred years. He looked forward to seeing how Dublin had been behaving itself in his absence, he said. He was assured that the city retained her fondness for his excellency and was invested with even more pride at his renewed presence. The viceroy thanked their lordships, the reverend fathers and councillors, for their consideration. Through them, he thanked the citizens, many of whom had already given him a very kind reception. And not only to him, but also to the new chief secretary, the one who would be doing all the work (laughter), and he indicated Lord Frederick, whose brother animatedly began the applause.

Cavendish, forty-five, stroked his luxuriant black beard as the clapping died down. He intended to speak only very briefly, to echo the gratitude of the lord lieutenant for a reception as splendid as it was humbling, and to hope that both this happy day and their tenure of office would contribute to the peace and prosperity of Ireland.

Cheers were raised as his excellency and the party made their way to the street. Here was further tumult; the noise swelling to a height as Spencer boldly executed the surprise he promised Cavendish would see in the course of the morning.

Instead of climbing into the open car that waited at the steps, the viceroy met an officer holding a bay horse by its halter. He swiftly mounted, cast a smile at Freddy, regally held out his hat, and swept it before the crowd in acknowledgment of their lustiness.

The others took their seats in the phaeton, the councillors cramming hurriedly into other carriages, and then his excellency, with cavalry outriders, began the procession. He swung his horse towards Merrion Square with Napoleonic aplomb.

John Poyntz, the fifth Earl Spencer, was very well known in Dublin. But the pleasure which marked his arrival was not entirely due to familiarity. Much of it emanated instead from sheer relief. The streets had been just as crowded two days before to see the departure of Earl Cowper, the outgoing viceroy.

It was not so much Cowper, a supine figurehead, they were glad to see the back of, but his chief secretary, the man with responsibility for the day-to-day control of Irish affairs, a post increasingly synonymous with the ruthless rule of law.

'Buckshot' Forster was widely despised. The uncompromising force he brought to his job, implementing a policy of coercion against an impoverished peasantry, was seen to have curdled into simple cruelty.

The helpless Cowper had always known that Forster, his nominal underling, would hold the reins, but he disliked the fact his chief secretary never came to see him, never canvassed his opinion, or communicated his intentions. For months, the viceroy had been angling for a recall to England, but even this would prove to be in the gift of his subordinate.

Just four days before Spencer's triumphal re-entry to Dublin, Buckshot Forster waspishly tendered his resignation to London.

It was not the worsening security situation, nor the surfeit of state inflicted misery which had prompted his unexpected action, but exasperation at the government's decision to release that insufferable troublemaker, Charles Stewart Parnell.

If Forster had expected the prime minister to wheedle and plead for him to reconsider, he was to be very much surprised. Gladstone had at length formed an equally ill opinion of him as had the Irish people, and had been privately contemplating a change of direction.

Coincidentally, the day Forster's resignation became known, a leading Dublin newspaper, the *Freeman's Journal*, called for the wholesale replacement of the British apparatus in Ireland, marking 'a total change of measures and men here'.

As Forster stomped across the Irish Sea on 2 May in order to denounce in the Commons London's remote control of Ireland, Mr Parnell, the leader of the Ireland's constitutional nationalists, was released from Kilmainham jail with a number of fellow agitators. It was done on foot of of special orders, reluctantly conveyed by Dublin Castle.

But politics could wait for Spencer and Cavendish, the replacement emissaries. Look how smiling ladies hung from every window! Every house in Westland Row held little specks of lace that waved assiduously. Around the corner it was the same, crowds of spectators pressing on the pavement, the huzzahs reverberating, with 'just an occasional faint hiss', as the *Freeman* observed. Much had certainly changed in a few days.

The gaiety continued along Lower Merrion Street, the hats in the phaeton extended in returned goodwill, through Clare Street, to Nassau Street. Here, especially between Kildare Street and the end of Grafton Street, the gusts of acclaim were 'uninterrupted, and Earl Spencer, instead of raising his hat at intervals, kept his head uncovered'.

The band of the Dublin Metropolitan Police, drawn up at Kildare Street, played the national anthem yet again as the viceroy passed. At crowded Grafton Street the thoroughfares presented a 'very animated appearance', with flags strung across the street.

The students of Trinity College were said to be conspicuous by their absence, however, 'with the exception of a few efforts to renew very stale practical jokes, such as throwing little bags of flour at some of the civic dignitaries'.

The Countess Spencer was anxiously looked for, but she was not accompanying the lord lieutenant, at least not yet. Instead the fêted few were all men. Many spectators were particularly curious to get a glimpse of their new chief secretary, the unknown quantity.

At College Green, there was a sudden surge of anxiety. People broke through the ranks of the soldiers lining the route and crowded around the horse on which the viceroy was mounted. They exulted, waving their hats, but the dragoons closed rapidly in on them to press his excellency along.

The nervous moment passed, and looking back Lord Cavendish could see the soldiers regaining control, shoving shoals of pedestrians back up onto the path.

Turning left at the Bank of Ireland, once the setting for no less a thing than an Irish parliament, the cavalcade met with further deep drifts of the public. Here it was the turn of the band of the 97th Regiment to play the imperial dirge so often heard before. When the figures of significance had passed, they launched from the anthem into the more spirited *St Patrick's Day*.

It was now a short distance to Dublin Castle, the obdurate seat of British prestige in Ireland. Dame Street was profusely decorated with banners across the street, the first emblazoned with *Quis Separabit* ('who shall separate us?'), a motto associated with King William III, victor at the Boyne, whose equestrian statue strutted beneath.

The usual drunks mocked proceedings at the rear of the crowds. A parade of perhaps five inebriates, loud in their denunciation of Buckshot Forster and wishing all that was bad to Britannia, was later suspected by some, a trifle irrationally, of what was to follow.

The words 'Welcome to Erin' were picked out in green and gold letters on a scroll spanning the entrance to Anglesea Street. Ahead and above hung lines of flags, from the Munster Bank to Jury's Hotel opposite.

The band of the 13th Regiment was stationed halfway along Dame Street, and they did not disappoint. 'They played the cortege past in the same manner as at College Green'. Earl Spencer 'seemed amused and not a little gratified at the genuine welcome'.

Everywhere the footpaths and all available windows were occupied. A recorder of the event at street level said remarks passed among the crowd were most complimentary, 'although sometimes scarcely appropriate to the occasion, or couched in the most cordial language'.

One ruffian asked the open carriage: 'Is Lord Cavendish here?' and got no reply. He asked again: 'Who is Lord Cavendish, please?' and was ignored afresh. He scampered close by as they jolted along: 'Lord Cavendish, please?'

Courtenay Boyle shot at glance at Freddy, who decided to humour the man, raising his hat: 'I am Lord Frederick Cavendish'.

The man stopped, took him in with a long look, and answered mysteriously: 'Thank you, that will do'.

The carriage rolled on.

This *Céad Míle Fáilte* considerably impeded the progress to the Castle, and its gates were not reached until a few minutes before one o'clock. Spencer clattered in, gratefully replacing his hat on his pate. The phaeton followed, turning left past City Hall and up the slight incline of Cork Hill to enter beneath the statue of Justice, her back famously turned on the city.

They could now breathe a sigh of relief. Spencer dismounted and waited to be joined by Cavendish. They shook hands with each other, then with waiting officials.

The most important here was Thomas Henry Burke, the permanent under secretary. Unlike the transient placemen of various administrations, Burke was the ever-present. His thirteen years of experience in a vital post had been relied on by many a grateful viceroy and chief secretary, particularly Spencer in his first lieutenancy.

Burke and Lord Frederick Cavendish now shared a particular moment of greeting, as Castle potentates buzzed around the viceroy. The chief and under secretaries would be expected to form a close bond. Burke had remorselessly done Forster's bidding, now he would see to Cavendish, and control him if he could.

Sir Bernard Burke, the Ulster king-at-arms and the gentleman usher were already conducting his excellency through to the Castle's inner sanctums. In the presence chamber Spencer was received unctuously by the lords justice, the duke of Leinster, the master of the rolls, and by Sir Thomas Steele, the general commanding the British army in Ireland.

Spencer's private secretary was on hand to produce the queen's commission appointing his Master to office, and Spencer and his entourage were escorted to the privy council chamber. Everyone else flocked behind.

The formal swearing-in was to take place before the assemblage could settle down to a fine luncheon. In this next high-beamed room were honoured guests, even more aides-de-camp, someone called a pursuivant of arms, numerous gentlemen-in-

s, the Dublin herald, the chamberlain, the
ntroller of the household, his steward, and
ously titled.

he viceroy's entry. Thomas Henry Burke
sly translated himself from the courtyard
nd was now bearing the sword of state.

the duke of Leinster, and the commander
into their important seats. Other privy
lord chancellor, the lord chief justice, the
of judges did likewise.

Earl Spencer stood on the right of the lords justice and delivered with a flourish his letter of appointment signed by her majesty. This was handed in turn to the clerk of the crown, who read it aloud in full.

Dr Kaye, QC, clerk of the council administered the oath of allegiance. Mr Burke then surrendered the sword of state, and his excellency gravely accepted it. The duke of Leinster stepped forward and invested Spencer with the collar and insignia of the ancient Order of St Patrick. He was now the lord lieutenant, and with bells on.

Lord Frederick Cavendish was called forward in his turn and sworn in as chief secretary in the same manner. Outside, a rocket tore up from the castle yard to announce the completion of the ceremony. Within a few seconds they heard the dull rumble of a fifteen-gun salute from the Phoenix Park.

A recessional phalanx was formed and the new viceroy returned to the presence chamber where he ascended the throne. Another rocket leapt skyward to mark this step and the signal was met by no fewer than three salvoes from a twenty-one-gun salute in the Park.

Some formal presentations were made to his excellency in the chamber, while most witnesses privately hungered. These addresses were quickly concluded, a gong rung, an announcement made and the hordes could repair to the gilded trough at last.

The guests having departed heartily fortified in all respects, Earl Spencer had a little time to write a note to Charlotte, his beloved wife. It had all been perfectly wonderful thus far, but the business was just starting. He was about to have a detailed presentation on the state of the country.

Spencer, Cavendish, and their officials were now met with Under Secretary Burke, that steady old hand, and his senior assistants. It was 2.30 p.m. Also present were the lord chancellor, Hugh Law, Dublin Castle law officer John Naish and Superintendent John Mallon, chief of detectives of the Dublin Metropolitan Police, standing in for the invalided Colonel George Hillier, head of the force.

Burke's assessment of the agrarian outrages, continued killings, and attempted assassinations of landlords was gloomy in the extreme. The situation had worsened considerably since Parnell and the other Land Leaguers were held without trial under emergency provisions. Now that they had been let out, there was perhaps hope for improvement.

Lord Cavendish and Spencer both laid great stress on the bill agreed in London two days ago to strengthen the courts against the intimidation of witnesses and jurors. Lord Frederick sat in cabinet in his new role, unlike the viceroy. He promised there would be new regulations for special magistrates to defeat the cowardly tactics employed by those intent on terrorising their fellow man and discouraging the production of evidence.

The meeting dragged on. Many points were raised, some refinements suggested. Proposals would have to go next week to the solicitor general. As they closed their work folders at 5.20 p.m., Thomas Henry Burke was pleased at the workmanlike approach of the new administration. It was all very promising.

A Walk in the Park

At six minutes past 6 o'clock the same day, 6 May 1882, it rained in the Phoenix Park. It was a 'flying shower', said witness Patrick Tobin, but it probably prompted Lord Frederick Cavendish to take his umbrella.

Lord Cavendish, Earl Spencer and even Burke all had official residences in Dublin's vast green amenity. The viceregal lodge (now Áras an Uachtaráin), designed by Nathaniel Clements Burton and built in 1751, was by far the most impressive.

Cavendish would occupy the chief secretary's lodge nearby (now the American ambassador's residence), while Thomas Henry Burke had long been ensconced in the under secretary's lodge (currently the Phoenix Park visitors' centre).

After the situation briefing the new men had gone to see their workplaces and to meet their individual staff. Cavendish quite liked his room overlooking the quadrangle of the upper Castle yard. He was still settling in when he spotted Spencer below, crossing the steaming cobbles to meet his escort for the trip to the park.

That reminded him that he hadn't seen his brother in quite a while. Bobby had melted away with the luncheon guests, but he presumed he would see him later at the viceregal lodge for the big dinner that was planned. He checked his watch. He was suddenly feeling rather tired.

Cavendish finally dismissed his last public servant. He was sure that Burke was still busying himself somewhere, but now Freddy was starting to feel that he had been cooped up long enough – from cabin to compartment, to carriage, and finally here in the Castle itself.

If he was to work off that long lunch and make room for the big meal to come, he had better get in some exercise. Glancing out the window, he saw a hansom cab waiting below, and his heart sank. There had been that spot of rain, but now it was glorious sunshine again. He certainly didn't want to retreat to another dark interior.

Lord Freddy stuffed his remaining official papers into a pouch. He left his private office and crossed the hall to the office of the superintendent of messengers. A clock on the wall said 6.30 p.m., and Superintendent Steele vouchsafed that he would be very glad to have the pouch sent on to the viceregal lodge.

Cavendish called out a last goodnight and descended the staircase. Already he felt warm in his coat. He had just remembered Earl Spencer's stunt of earlier in the day, the matter of the horse. He too would forego the formal transport.

What nicer way to get to know his new patch? A stroll home along the north quays, looking at the Liffey. He knew the route from past visits to his brother during his time in the park. There was no danger – he was not remotely known to the commoners of Dublin. Besides, it would do a body good. Not going to be many chances in this job for long nature rambles like those he took at home with Lucy.

He loosened his tie, being off-duty. Striding across the dried cobbles, he saw his official horse and car begin to jingle into movement towards him. He waved them off, jabbing towards the street with his umbrella: 'It's all right, thank you. I am just going to walk'.

And out he went, a redcoat saluting smartly from a sentry box. Once outside, a dark policeman simply stared. That was quite all right – dare say they would all learn to recognise him in due course.

Thomas Henry Burke, three weeks away from his fifty-third birthday, was married to the job. It was epigrammatic in Dublin Castle that the lord lieutenant danced, the chief secretary rode to hounds, and the under secretary slaved.

Opinions of Burke varied which was a good indication that very few knew the man. To the *Times* of London he was 'extremely cautious and reserved', to others austere, even aloof. Perhaps the loneliness of his single life had engendered a certain shyness. But there was no doubt that he was ramrod straight in carrying out what he saw as his duty and his greatest fealty was to the law.

From Knocknagar in Co. Galway, he was scrupulous in remitting money to his aged mother, the widow still living in the home place, where Fanny Burke had a certain standing as the niece of Cardinal Wiseman. Like Caesar's wife, she was beyond reproach.

But Burke also owned land in the area, being the eldest son of the late William Burke. And he was certain that he should receive his rents. When a certain tenant applied for an abatement – pleading illness for past arrears – Burke applied the statute.

The Land League complained that the man was paying £31 and five shillings for 'a miserable piece of bogland', which was five times above its value. But Burke had no trouble obtaining a court judgement, with £20 costs. The unfortunate man was evicted and his twenty sheep seized and sold. Thus the cost of Burke's recourse to the majesty of the law was defrayed. One posthumous account would praise the under secretary as 'a stranger to intrigue', but perhaps the quality of mercy was also alien.

Still, the Victorian ethic was for hard and fast rules and Burke was the instrument of the system. His name as under secretary often appeared at the bottom of proclamations banning public demonstrations or warning inhabitants of a particular area that a curfew would be imposed in light of nocturnal lawlessness.

If Burke appeared haughty, as was often claimed, he was also said to be 'a gay and cheerful companion' and 'much loved by his intimate friends', even if they were few in number and largely ignored. The *Times* noted that he allocated 'hardly any intervals for recreation', being 'unremitting in his attention to his official duties'.

This then was the man who had climbed from the bottom rung, junior clerk, to the highest post ever occupied by a Catholic at the Castle. He had served for more than thirty years, over a dozen as the number two in the Irish civil administration, the highest permanent functionary in the land. He liked to think that he did not make mistakes.

Thomas Burke, having burned the office oil until 6.40 p.m., thought he should perhaps go home. He was not worried about keeping anyone else late this Saturday evening, for he always 'walked about at all hours, without fear and unarmed'.

He closed up, turned down the wick of the lamp, locked his office door, and popped the key in his pocket. He pulled on his trademark grey gloves. They matched his entirely grey suit. A witness later referred to his 'peculiarity of dress', but meant that he was a striking figure.

Only last July Burke had been first noticed, and then widely recognised, as he stood on the fringes of a huge meeting in the Phoenix Park. Ten thousand Land Leaguers were there. Burke had wandered out from his lodge and down to the Nine Acres to watch proceedings, standing close to a man from the Castle. The latter had a difficult task, taking notes of the speeches in the pouring rain.

Now Burke bustled out of the Castle, blinking in the sunlight, not hearing the respectful valedictions as he strode. He turned towards Christchurch, and was soon in Thomas Street.

To the urchins of the Liberties he was a wondrous sight. 'Give us a tanner, mister', some cried after the brisk figure, whose stick occasionally flicked detritus from his path toward the gutter. It was force of habit; he brooked no obstruction, and always expected to reach Kingsbridge in fifteen minutes.

Yet another figure from Dublin Castle was being drawn to the Phoenix Park that evening. John Mallon, the chief of detectives, liked to get his hands dirty. If Burke was a stranger to intrigue, Mallon was its closest familiar. He was due to meet an informer.

Mallon scowled in the glare as he faced west. Entering by the impressive granite piers, he began a slow ascent of the steep incline to the Gough monument. Several times he was tempted to rest, but that would mean a delay. His eye fell on some of his darling Dubliners, more than a few swigging from flasks or brazen bottles. Breaches of the park bye-laws all over the place. *The obedience of the citizens is the happiness of the city* ran the Latin motto of this magnificent metropolis. A very unhappy place, if that's the case.

Still, it was its very ferment – in all senses – that gave him his living. His empire was built on innumerable drunken squabbles to the topmost point of intoxicating plots for 'Irish freedom', whatever that meant. The gin-soaked abandoners of babies at the bottom of his keg, frothy anarchy at its head. And talk of treason everywhere between.

Mallon bumped into one of his detectives close to the turn for the Royal Irish Constabulary depot. The agent passed the time of day, stroked his moustache. Mallon mentioned that he was going to meet John Kenny at the back of the Zoological gardens. The man was suddenly doubtful.

'Shouldn't do that, Sir. There are some odd people around. I really think it must be dangerous. You are too well known'.

'Any of our acquaintances here?'

'Well, not really, but a lot of drunks. Let me come with you, Sir, or at least call in for some RIC on the way'. He patted his coat pocket significantly.

Mallon registered what it meant. He paused in momentary indecision. The agent took the revolver out of his pocket, offered it handle-first to his chief. 'You're close to home, Sir. I'll see to Kenny for you'.

Mallon looked at the gun, but shook his head briskly. 'Well, these new shoes are killing me', he admitted. They walked a hundred yards together toward the entrance to the RIC barracks, still within the park. There Mallon bade a farewell, and turned pigeon-toed towards his house on the North Circular Road. The agent turned left, in the direction of the rendezvous.

His chief halloed after him. Making a gesture with his thumb, Mallon also jerked his head towards the depot. 'Go in and get another man,' he said.

Nicholas Brabazon, a gnarled old driver, was stopped with his horse at the front of the cab rank on Parkgate Street, outside the Royal Oak pub. He hoped for some drinkers to emerge or for the rain to return, but there was little hope of either. Then his luck turned – around the corner of the bridge, on foot, came Mr Burke.

The under secretary arrived and climbed on his sidecar without a word, sitting onto the bench to the left, facing the road. Old Nick hoisted himself from the pavement into his 'dickie', the little box to the front.

'He said nothing,' Brabazon remembered later. 'I knew where to go. I knew he wanted to go to the under secretary's lodge. I drove him there many a time'.

They clopped along in silence. The bushes on the left, inside the park, gave way to a fine vista of the Wellington monument, the obelisk casting a long shadow. People still lazed on the extensive lawn at its base, though it was now ten minutes after seven. A dog ran after a ball. A man with a clay pipe shouted at his children.

The car reached the Gough statue, a bronze equestrian figure erected on a pedestal just two years before. Burke had been present at the grand unveiling, but he didn't care for it much. Their horse now nodded past the motionless steed. The car continued up the main road, Chesterfield Avenue.

A hundred yards further, and Burke gasped in recognition and commanded the driver to stop, 'just when you get to that gentleman there'. Lord Frederick Cavendish heard the wheels crunch close to his side of the road. He turned to find Burke looking down from on high. 'Good evening, my Lord Frederick! Shall I get down or would you like to get up?'

Cavendish broke into a broad smile of discovery. 'I think you had better get down. I am not up to your level yet'.

They walked together as Brabazon wheeled his car around to go back towards town. Burke put his glove back on, having fished in his pocket for a coin. The sun was on their faces, and off to the left a cricket match was yet underway, white figures on the green sward.

The men chatted. Cavendish may have said that he and Lucy liked to walk, wandering about Derbyshire and Yorkshire. She had not been at all anxious that he should take this job. Not many people come out of it well, she said. Lucy actually wondered, only half in jest, whether he would be called 'Buckshot Freddy'.

It is easy to imagine Burke seeking to reassure Cavendish on this point, something about sticks and stones, just as Lord Freddy had undoubtedly told his worried wife that he shouldn't mind whether he was called 'Caveman' Cavendish or anything else. In some ways such a sobriquet would be a sign that he was getting the job done.

A chap suddenly whizzed by on a tricycle. The gentlemen were said to have 'paid particular notice'.

'Good lord, look at that fellow!'

They strolled on. Burke 'always walked splendidly erect, and carried his cane sword-fashion on his shoulder'.

Another tricycle went past, then a horse and car. Traffic was light enough, but the last chukka had just ended on the polo ground opposite and there would be a little more movement soon. Men were dismounting, the few spectators drifting away. A horse in red socks was led towards the paddock.

'This land is called the Nine Acres', Burke might have said, indicating to his right. He was there for a big Land League meeting the previous summer, but it wasn't like this. The heavens had opened and it had been a wash out.

There was a good view here to the left, towards the Wicklow mountains. The cane may have flicked briefly in that direction. They walked, and Burke now linked his arm with Cavendish. 'You mustn't worry about this job', was the message, spoken or not.

A body of men was walking towards them. Just discernible was the Phoenix column in the distance, and beyond this next clump of trees was the viceregal lodge. The sun was a burnished red and Lord Cavendish felt momentarily the uselessness of the umbrella he had carried all this way. The figures ahead were dark against the light. He noticed a car and a driver a little further along. Mr Burke was conceivably saying that he thought that a place in the Park was the finest thing about this job. No other European city could boast a pleasure ground to match.

Perhaps it was the sight of the men ahead that turned the conversation dark again. Cavendish asked again about the political situation. They could just begin to see the boundary of the viceregal lodge.

There was later evidence that Thomas Henry Burke was telling Lord Frederick Cavendish the details of an attempt on the life of his predecessor, Buckshot Forster, when the men walking towards them arrived.

The pack was on them. Harmlessly, for the first three men scurried easily by. Then came four men in working coats. That fellow's eyes were bright as he stared. Two followed by two. Burke was used to getting the odd glare. He moved aside as he continued talking. The first two men passed, one brushing Cavendish on the outside, blocking his view across to the lodge.

Cavendish inclined his head to touch his hat in greeting as the last pair went by. A gruff voice, an imprecation; whirling movement, barging from behind. Assault! A flash of famished steel. Blows thumping his companion. Burke howling noiselessly, convulsing.

'Ah, you villain!' Cavendish thrashed with his umbrella. Dancing backwards, he twitched away from the hungry man in front, saw one knife and then another. Came a blade, running him through. No hurt, just cold. A vacuum in his warm body.

Burke down. His own umbrella gone. Staccato stabbing; jabbing, and the hatred. Staggering collapse. Wetness on his hands, sliding up in front of the diving gleam. The hard ground of the roadway, and the closing in of shadows. Darkness in the long-bright sun. Jerking movement, pain. Flitting shapes, descending silence.

In God's Hands

Thomas Foley and Patrick William Maguire were work colleagues at Monahan & Company in Henry Street. Both sporty, Maguire had the faster tricycle.

Foley did not quite ride up to the Phoenix monument, but saw Maguire go up to round it and come back. Foley was tired, and sat on his machine looking about. He heard the clatter of a car, and looking around saw a horse and passengers noisily taking the road to the left, leading to the Chapelizod Gate.

'We turned our machines to ride towards town, coming down the road very quickly. When just opposite the viceregal lodge we observed a man on the road lying on his right side, and a man on the footway about six or eight yards from him lying on his back'.

They were the men they had passed a few minutes earlier who had been walking arm in arm, apparently talking very pleasantly. The two gentlemen had seemed to take particular notice of the machines. Now they were sprawled.

Foley alighted, sprinted to the man on the road and stared at him. He then ran to the man on the footway and saw that he had his throat cut. Foley shouted: 'Maguire, it's a murder'. His friend cried: 'Stop you there; don't leave them. I'll go for the police'. He tore away as a boy ran up.

Foley went over to the man lying on the road and asked a question 'to see if he had life'. Lord Frederick Cavendish 'merely turned his eyes'. Getting no answer, Foley went back to the man on the footway. 'I took hold of his left hand, which was lying across his heart, to see if his pulse was beating, and he just gave his last breath into my face and the blood oozed up from his neck'.

Maguire flew down the main carriageway. He too had seen marks of blood on Burke's neck, while the man closest appeared quite dead. He panted as he raced towards the Gough statue, pedalling for all he was worth. He passed two men, sitting on a bench and shouted 'Murder!' and pointed backwards. He kept going.

A minute, or two minutes, clicked by hopelessly. He reached the statue, and then two Royal Irish Constabulary men miraculously appeared.

He called incoherently at them, loudly, his voice choked. They stopped. 'There's been a murder', Maguire blurted, before an odd question tumbled from his mouth: 'Are you on duty?'

The two RIC men looked at each other. This wild dervish was babbling. The older one turned back to Maguire: 'We are not.'

They turned to walk on, shooting him suspicious glances. Maguire begged: 'Please go to where the bodies are', and he pointed in the direction in which he had come. Seeing that the policemen were growing harder of hearing, he began pedalling again. Away from them. The policemen watched him leave, and then walked in the direction of their depot.

Maguire reached the park gate and accosted a metropolitan policeman. Breathlessly he told him, and the DMP man's reply was hopeful: 'I shall procure assistance'.

Maguire yelled, 'It's a matter of life and death!' and the policeman broke into a run to the gate lodge.

The tricyclist could hear the policeman inside, shouting at a colleague: 'Put on your uniform!'

They dashed out, climbed into a car, and whipped their horse desperately toward the scene. Maguire followed, flailing on his ungainly trike.

Alfred Walters and John Power were sitting under a clump of trees, caching the last rays, when Maguire flew by. The cry of 'Murder!' was unmistakable in its intensity. They rose immediately and rushed in the direction indicated. As they saw the cluster of figures, Power had the good sense to look at his watch. It was 7.28 p.m.

They joined Foley, standing at one body, with a youth at the other. Power stayed while Walters rushed across the road to the fence to the viceregal lodge to alert the people there.

The youngster had just been at that sunken fence to which Walters was headed. A seventeen-year-old draper's assistant with

Comyn's of College Green, Samuel Watson Jacob had been out bird-nesting in the park. His attention was attracted by what appeared to be a group of men sparring or scuffling. He saw the blows and two men fall.

Jacob had no idea that it was a murder; but seeing the men lie too long, he went towards them. 'When I came up, the two gentlemen were lying quite motionless. The blood was gurgling from the throat' of the man on the path. He had heard no noise 'except one gasp or moan' from the roadway man, just before he fell.

Power asked who did this. Jacob offered that he saw the assailants jumping off a car. He thought the car was in motion all the time. After the murders, the men jumped back on and drove off rapidly 'over there', and he pointed to the Phoenix column.

That was where Lieutenant Ferdinand William Greatrex had been at a quarter past seven. Now he was nowhere to be seen, because he too had rushed to fetch assistance. Greatrex later claimed to have been first at the bodies.

An officer of the Royal Dragoons, he had been walking his dogs. He turned at the Phoenix and began descending towards town when he saw a car and what seemed to be a drunken squabble about 200 or 300 yards in front of him.

'It was more like horseplay,' he later corrected himself. 'I thought they were larking about on the grass slopes, on the same side I was on'.

One of his dogs was very delicate and nervous, always running away. 'I turned to call her, and when I looked again there was one of the men apart from the others, striking another man and putting him down. The men got on the car and drove towards me.

'The car went along the road towards the Hibernian School. I was watching the two on the ground and wondering why they did not get up.

'I did not think much about it. I had no idea of anything in the shape of foul play, seeing the driver sit so unconcernedly in his seat. The car started at once when the men got up and drove off rapidly'.

He looked to see if he could see a number on the vehicle, 'as I thought it was rather a brutal thing to knock two men down that way. I looked round to see if there was anybody about, that we might catch the fellows.'

It began to look a bad business. He said as much to an old man behind him, who agreed. Greatrex said they would have to give information to the police. 'I suppose so', the old man replied doubtfully. Greatrex never saw him again.

The lieutenant hurried on towards the prone forms. He told the subsequent inquest: 'I found them both dead. No, the one on the road had his eyes a little bit open and appeared to be alive'.

The man in the grey suit was definitely dead. The one in the roadway was covered with dirt and dust. 'I thought he was one of the men who had attacked the gentlemen – and the gentlemen had shot him'.

Lord Frederick Cavendish 'was so dirty, and looked such a ruffian as he lay there', he explained. Greatrex must have thought the man got what he deserved.

He spotted a member of the Royal Engineers some distance away, darted over to him and told him what he had seen. The sapper [William Dawson] and Greatrex now abandoned the bodies and hastened towards the park gate.

After a couple of hundred yards, they met two constables. These may have been Maguire's flatfoots, for when Greatrex told them what had happened they astonished him by replying that it was 'no business of theirs'.

Perhaps mindful of what a bad impression this might create of officialdom, Greatrex later told the inquest he did not blame these idlers 'because two brother officers of mine have since told me that my story looked like a hoax'.

A little further on they met a mounted policeman and panted out the news. Increasingly tired they headed for the park gate. It was at this point, said Greatrex, that 'the gentleman on the tricycle', Maguire, passed in the same direction.

Two RIC men arrived at the scene from the viceregal lodge

and looked startled to find that Walters' report was true. Foley told them what he had seen. A gentleman in a trap now came rattling along the main road, and Foley, imbued with police powers, ran out and stopped him.

One constable climbed up into the trap, the man turned his horse and they galloped off to Castleknock to inform the police there.

Maguire then came up on his machine with the outside car and the police from town, uniforms freshly buttoned. By this time Colonel Forster from the viceregal lodge had joined the small but swelling throng. Colonel Caulfield, following him, cried out 'Good God' on recognising Cavendish.

To Forster it appeared that both men were dead. Foley asked this impressive officer if he knew who the murdered men were.

Colonel Forster flashed him a look of surprise that the questioner did not know. He pointed with his finger and said, 'the gentleman on the road is Lord Frederick Cavendish, the new Chief Secretary; and the gentleman on the path is Mr Burke, the Under Secretary'. Foley gaped.

Soldiers arrived as evening fell. The car that had brought the police was used to carry Mr Burke's body, the bewildered Foley climbing on to help hold it onto the car, being joined by Constable

153D and Sergeant 27A. Maguire also assisted. Colonel Forster directed that they should go to Dr Steevens' hospital at Kingsbridge.

A stretcher arrived, and soldiers carried the body of Lord Cavendish across the road to a second car. They left behind perhaps twenty people by now, two dust-sprinkled pools of blood, and a pair of abandoned tricycles.

Earl Spencer goggled with shock, having to be helped to an armchair. He gazed straight past those who assisted him, flustered maids going for whiskey in middle distance, a messenger at the back of the room finding no one to accept Lord Frederick's pouch.

'Poor Burke,' he cried. 'Poor Freddy'.

The word was that the chief secretary was 'dangerously wounded'. The guardroom had already been ordered to 'fall out', with couriers haring off to Mountjoy barracks. They reassured the earl that the hospital was on alert, doctors on the way.

'What shall I tell the prime minister?' moaned Spencer, before stiffening his resolve. 'Fetch a stenographer'. He waved away the whiskey.

Dear God, Freddy but a few hours in the country! He knew the crushing weight would be tenfold on Gladstone. Cavendish was more than his political son. He was married to the prime minister's niece. Lucy! Oh poor Lucy. She will be prostrated. The man she loves fighting for his very life …

The killings had actually been witnessed. Not by the viceroy himself, but by Colonel Caulfield, looking from the dining-room window, expecting to see a carriage, but witnessing a disgraceful fight. He told Courtenay Boyle there were brawling thugs across the road, to send out some police.

Dr Thomas Myles, the resident surgeon from Dr Steevens' Hospital, met the party carrying the body of Burke about 150 yards inside the park gate. At first, he believed that he could feel heart action in the cold, clammy wrist. But it was actually his own heart, palpitating fiercely. He saw the fixed pupils, the cut throat, and realised all instinct was gone.

Sending them on, he rushed for the man he was told was yet alive, if gravely wounded. Half a mile further on he met the party of guardsmen with Cavendish. This time he steadied the head and looked first in the eyes. The lolling jaw and glassy regard told him that this one too was dead.

At 8 o'clock that Saturday night, Acting Inspector John Bride rapped loudly at the door of Superintendent Mallon's home on the North Circular Road. He told him that Mr Burke, the under secretary, and his brother, had been murdered a mile and a half away.

Mallon's shock was compounded by confusion – why would Burke be with his brother when he should be dining with the lord lieutenant? 'I proceeded to the place,' he wrote, 'and ascertained that it was Lord Cavendish and Mr Burke who were murdered'. Mallon felt sick to the pit of his stomach, the congealed puddles in front of him a mockery and an affront.

'I gathered on the spot some meagre details, the most being that the assassins, four in number, had escaped on a car'. He ordered speedy telegraphs to all the seaports and every important centre of government in the United Kingdom.

He directed that detectives take cars to every Royal Irish Constabulary station around county Dublin. All men were to be called in. Foot patrols were to go out immediately in each district. Had all these persons had their statements taken? Yes sir, it was being done. Every detail must be procured, every item of description. This was the most appalling act that had ever struck the country and the police were already an hour behind. Mallon privately quailed at what that might mean.

He kept up a stream of instructions, proclaiming that all the city telegraph offices must be kept open the following day, Sunday, when they would usually close. Telegraphs to all RIC divisional headquarters down the country too.

Calculations raced in his head. All the latest trains for the provinces had left before the murders were reported. The perpetrators could not go far from Dublin. All night sailings from North Wall and Kingstown had already taken place.

Of course arrangements would have to be made to watch future departures from the city. That meant men at every railway station, main road and embarkation point. There was some suggestion that the escape vehicle was a hackney. Carriage constables were dispatched to look up every car in their respective districts.

The other available constables of G Division were sent to look up hotels and lodging houses.

Anyone of any suspicious character whatever was to be immediately arrested.

Inspector Kavanagh and some sergeants and constables had arrived at the hospital. They learned that the murdered gentlemen had been left draped with sheets in a darkened ward, still in their bloodied clothes. A servant from the viceregal lodge had identified the bodies.

The inspector ordered that the door be locked. He placed a man on guard there and two outside in the yard. Absolutely no one would be allowed to see the remains from this point on until the Coroner arrived in the morning.

He then found Foley and Maguire, standing around at a loose end. They were brought to the Bridewell to give all the information they held. He reassured them that Colonel Forster was taking care of their machines in the park.

Later, having given their statements, Foley and Maguire were driven back to the park with a detective on the same car that had brought one of the bodies to hospital. It was now after 10 p.m. and dark. The car was stopped at the park gate by jumpy policemen, soldiers covering all aboard with their rifles.

The detective spoke up and they were allowed to pass. On reaching the scene, they found constables guarding the ground on which the blood patches lay, but no sign of their tricycles. They were told Colonel Forster had ordered them sent to Bessborough Barracks.

The news was beginning to break in the city. It spread from the pubs just outside the park, pushing like a ripple along the quays towards the centre. It radiated north and south in the same way. Nobody could believe it. Many heard garbled versions, but the essential kernel was the same: two of the most powerful British administrators in Ireland had been hacked to death, and the deed done in the very sight of officialdom.

The disbelief centred in part on the fact that the bloodshed happened within half a mile of Royal Irish Constabulary head-quarters, within a nexus of official residences, less than a mile from Mountjoy army barracks (later the Ordnance Survey), and yards from where twenty-one fieldpieces had a few hours earlier trumpeted British military might.

It also resided in the fact that these two powerful personages were walking alone and without bodyguards. It might have been Burke's peculiar self-indulgence, but the last chief secretary had a file of threats against his life nearly nine inches thick at Dublin Castle.

The lord lieutenant would later wring his hands to Glad-stone: 'Freddy would not drive up with my Private Secretaries, but walked. Mr Burke drove part of the way ...'

The heightened police activity that night, the raiding of rooming houses, checkpoints on main roads, despatch riders flying about the city, signalled to many that something extraordinary had happened. Members of the public wandered into police stations to enquire what it was. Crowds gathered at newspaper offices for confirmation – and the lights burning brightly for special Sunday editions, never before published, told them it was true.

Dublin journalist J. B. Hall was at a performance of *Maritana* by the Carl Rosa Opera Company at the Gaiety Theatre. During the first act, two acquaintances came into his box in a state of great excitement and recounted the appalling news, 'the only definite fact being that the two men had been murdered, whether shot or stabbed was not mentioned'.

A question arose whether to have an announcement from the stage and the performance stopped. There were fears of a panic in the packed house and it was thought best to let the news percolate.

The artistes and the conductor were told between curtains, and the opera shortened as much as possible.

In another 'exhibition palace', a military band was playing *Turkish Patrol*. 'The last sound of the cymbals is scarce over when a young man rushes down the main aisle' to ask the performers to leave the stage. No explanation is given.

The audience is alarmed and rises from its seats in consternation. The hubbub starts immediately as the house lights come up and patrons empty to the outside air: 'England's two chief rulers in the country are slain the park'.

Opera-goer Hall never knew anything to exceed the wave of excitement which spread throughout the city, 'an excitement made all the more intense by the fact that the rumours that night were so indefinite, and in many respects so conflicting'.

All hands were turned to bringing out a midnight edition of the *Evening Telegraph*, in which Hall himself assisted. 'The available staff scurried hither and thither to collect what facts were to be gleaned', while 'from nearly every house one passed came people straining eagerly to gain tidings of what had really happened'.

The opera performers, including foreign artistes, were not immune. At Portobello Hotel at 1 o'clock in the morning, a strange spectacle presented itself. In the coffee room under a flickering light were a crowd of the Carl Rosa Company, and in their gala-garbed midst stood Snazelle, the great baritone, reading details aloud from the special paper.

Earl Spencer had been sending telegrams, 'dangerously wounded' in early ones soon replaced by stark messages of double death. They went to Lord Harcourt, the home secretary, and to the queen at Windsor, who was woken at midnight with the grim revision to earlier tidings.

Prime Minister Gladstone left a late dinner at the Austrian embassy still not knowing. 'Buckshot' Forster had heard it at a Whitehall soirée. Other prominent politicians received their telegrams at home, or at their club. All were stunned.

It fell to Lady Louisa Egerton, Freddy's sister, to break the news to Gladstone's niece. As the prime minister, pierced by pity, knelt in prayer with his wife on the hall floor of No. 10 Downing Street, Louisa was making her way to the Cavendish townhouse at No. 21, Carlton House Terrace.

Lucy had just said goodbye to her own sister, who left at close to midnight. Meriel Talbot had come for company's sake because she knew the first day without Freddy would be an empty one.

When the bell rang again, Lucy may have thought Meriel had left something behind. Instead it was her stricken sister-in-law, telegram in hand.

'As soon as I saw her face,' Lady Frederick Cavendish wrote in her diary, 'the terror seized me ... All my blessed joy of many years, wrecked in the darkness'.

The Day After

Who did this? It was not good enough to observe that it was four men on a car, clacking away unconcernedly while the machinery of state slept. The police had been at least half an hour behind in taking any action at all, and what they did do was useless.

Mallon had been up all night, but nothing could undo that initial inertia. There had been arrests in the early hours, but a moment's consideration of the reports showed that these were drunken Fenian sympathisers who exulted a little too much, or poor hapless tramps who could give no addresses.

The chief of detectives had only four main witnesses – Greatrex, Jacob, Maguire and Foley.

He read their statements again and again.

Jacob said the four attackers were dressed alike, with slouched hats, while the car was a red paralleled one and the horse 'a good goer'. Jacob could not identify anyone, but thought he would know the horse and car.

Foley and Maguire did not get a look at any faces either, but believed the car was red or brown-backed, and agreed that the horse was a fast one. They believed the time of the killing was about 7.25, or about ten minutes later than Greatrex.

The Royal Dragoon officer said the horse was bay, and a highstepper. He didn't notice the colour of any panel on the car, but he did offer the only descriptions the police force had to work with.

The driver, said Greatrex, looked of the middle age, with a bloated red face, about three days' growth of beard, and a black soft hat pulled down.

One of his passengers was of very sallow complexion, with a

pale sandy moustache and a thin beard, he said. He wore a shirt and long black tie, dark colour overcoat and soft hat. Greatrex thought he could identify this man. He wasn't sure of anyone else, except that the attackers appeared slight in stature, and to be 'rather respectable looking tradesmen'.

It wasn't good at all, thought Mallon. Just one eyewitness giving a description of two men, and that one eyewitness might be wrong in all respects. All that he could be sure of, from the separate statements, was that they had worn hats and had obviously carried knives.

The car seemed red or brown, and the horse might be bay. It was not much.

Thomas Foley had an intriguing line in his account. He 'nearly saw the registration of the car'. He saw the mark of the figures on the back of the car, but could not see what the figures were. 'The reason I looked at the car at all was because I thought I might have seen the new Chief Secretary,' he offered.

Greatrex had looked for a registration too, but hadn't seen one. Every car for hire in Dublin had to be approved by the metropolitan police and carry an identification plate. Had this been a hackney car or not?

Mallon ruminated on the point. Was it likely that the persons who carried out the whole affair would employ a registered car, the number of which might be caught at a glance? As a rule the car men were not mixed up much in politics, he wrote later.

Any number might be false, a simple ruse. The only certainty must be that a party of conspirators would not simply hire an innocent hackney to take them on a mission of murder. Of course, the driver had to be involved, even if he looked 'unconcerned'.

Mallon thought about the use of knives, which showed not only malice aforethought but also a degree of cunning. Gunshots would bring police and army from far and near in a much more rapid response.

Since it was an accident that the two victims had been walking together, perhaps it was an accident that they had both been killed.

Persons lying in ambush could not know that either man would be walking … surely they would have been forced to plan to intercept a car at the very least. If there was only going to be one bite at the cherry, as it were, who was the primary target?

Burke had been walking about unmolested for thirteen years, yet Cavendish was but a few hours in the country with all the problems of identification and prediction of movement …

Perhaps the post mortem examinations would yield further clues to what was doubtless a political conspiracy. Mallon was turning over these matters in his head between five and six in the morning when his detectives brought an important witness into his presence.

George Godden was a park ranger who had only learned of the killings at midnight. He slowly realised that he might have seen the perpetrators.

Godden lived in one of the deerkeeper's lodges at the Fifteen Acres, close to the Hibernian School. He told Mallon that the previous evening he had been returning home from a garden he worked in Chapelizod. He entered the park by the Chapelizod Gate. Having walked 300 yards, his attention was attracted by the noise of an approaching car. He saw it about 200 yards away, approaching very rapidly. There were two men on each side, and a driver in the box seat. He looked carefully at them all. It was twenty-five minutes to eight o'clock.

Mallon thought Godden 'a very sensible, steady old man' as he recounted that the horse was chestnut, of splendid action, and in thin but good working condition.

Then came a disappointment. Instead of the car being red or brown, Godden insisted it was olive green, picked out with white. Nor did it strike him as a hack car. At all events, he was certain it had no number on it.

Godden then gave descriptions that would be widely circulated, staying in the police gazette *Hue & Cry* for months to come. Mallon privately regarded these portraits as 'suspiciously accurate', given the distance involved and that the car layout would have presented some backs to Godden, but he printed them anyway:

Description of the four men wanted for the murder of Lord Cavendish and Mr Burke, the Chief and Under Secretaries for Ireland, on Saturday 6th inst. Between 7 and 8 p.m.:

1. About 35 years old, stout make, dark complexion, hair, whiskers and moustache recently clipped to give a bristling appearance. Narrow forehead, natural hollow or dinge on bridge of nose; wore a soft black jerry hat and dark clothes.

2. About 30 years, sandy hair, whiskers and moustache; brown faded coat, as if much exposed to sun, soft black jerry hat.

3. About 20 years, small dark moustache, no whiskers; soft black hat and dark clothes.

4. About 30 years, sandy hair and moustache, with beard on chin; wore dark clothes and soft black hat.

The height cannot be given of any, all being sitting on an outside car driven by a man between 35 and 40 years, red bloated face, with a few days' growth of beard on; dark or brown coat, supposed frieze, and low, soft black hat.

It was all he had to go on, but the superintendent became slightly more hopeful. He was already envisaging an identification parade of suspicious hackney cars, with his handful of witnesses to study cabs, horses and drivers.

Some of Dublin's citizens only learned of the killings at worship that Sunday, even though the cry of newsvendors could be unusually heard in every thoroughfare from before breakfast.

Prayers for the souls of the dead men were asked in all churches, and the revelation from the altar caused some ladies to faint with shock. In one, St Kevin's of Heytesbury Street, the priest himself fell dead 'in the act of speaking'. This sensation was all the more widely remarked upon because of the cleric's name – Fr Burke, although he was no relation.

Groups of men could be seen outside the various churches, discussing the gravity of the situation. A chronicler named Tynan, whose observations were jaundiced in the extreme, claimed that some expressed themselves approvingly of what had happened: 'Though in some cases they spoke guardedly, yet the smile of joy that lighted up their faces and flashed from their eyes revealed the depth of their feelings. There are peculiar mannerisms by which Irishmen convey their real sentiments to each other, even though their tongues speak differently …'

Another writer ascribed to the people a feeling of amazed indignation. This caused the temporary suppression of even personal sorrows – funeral processions passing through Sackville Street on their way to Glasnevin cemetery stopped at the newspaper offices to buy newspapers to devour in the mourning coaches.

The inevitable thrill of horror mutated into morbid fascination. At the crime scene, which the police could hardly secure, souvenir hunters actually dug up samples of bloodstained soil with trowels brought for the purpose.

One foreign gentleman, himself a few hours in the country, obtained a dark-stained pebble as a keepsake, the *Freeman's Journal* reported. Cavendish had died on the road, impossible and dangerous to excavate, but Burke's ground was more pliant. Soon there was a hollow at the spot where he had died.

The Dublin hackney drivers, under suspicion as a class, conveyed numerous visitors to the scene. Eventually the police were reinforced, the crowds were controlled, and to deter further relic-hunting boards placed where the bodies had lain. Yet the diggers were hardly deterred: they instead scooped out a deep cross in the ground to mark the spot.

'In the afternoon the whole town poured into the Phoenix Park', contemporary writer Tighe Hopkins put it. 'By four o'clock the people in thousands were struggling to advance a pace along the mile and more of road between the Phoenix gate and the Phoenix monument'.

Vendors set up refreshment stalls. Persons claimed to gullible groupings that they themselves had seen what really happened. Fresh rumours took legs – the viceroy himself had also been stabbed, but managed to get away. Two soldiers were dead and the authorities were suppressing the fact. A foreigner, a nihilist, had been captured. More killings were on the way, with several assassination gangs sent over from America.

The newspapers would in due course hear most of the rumours and rightly dismiss them.

Some, however, they printed. 'Another startling statement,' wrote the London *Times*, was that 'on Saturday Lord Chief Justice Morris and Mr Justice Barry, while walking together in the park, were accosted by a rough-looking fellow, who said, 'Michael Morris, the Chief Secretary and the Under Secretary have been murdered, and you are the next man spotted'

'Supposing the man to be a lunatic, they passed on without taking any notice and soon afterwards heard that the report of the murder was true.

'It is also stated that Mr Clifford Lloyd [a detested magistrate] has received notice that a number of men are on their way from America for the purpose of assassinating him'.

What the Dublin newspapers did not print that Sunday was

the fact that they had each received a card into their letterboxes late on the previous evening. The anonymous, black-bordered cards carried the legend: 'This deed was done by the Irish Invincibles'.

The newsrooms regarded the cards as a dastardly prank, the sort of thing dreamt up by the Trinity students who had earlier been throwing flour at the cavalcade. There was no such group as the ludicrously titled Invincibles, even if it was quick-witted of the students to get their cards out so promptly.

The police had not yet heard of these cards, although rumour would soon bring them to their attention. The same rumours suggested more fancifully that it had been intended to toss one of the tokens on the slaughtered corpses ...

Mallon had to deal in facts. He knew the getaway had been through the Chapelizod gate. His men were already making house-to-house enquiries, now that it was a decent hour, to try to establish the rest of the escape route.

The medical reports would give him a little more to go on. The city coroner, Dr Nicholas Whyte, arrived at the hospital where the bodies lay at about 11 o'clock. Whyte lost no time in empanelling a jury, with seventeen Dubliners, mostly from Aughrim Street, pressed into service.

The coroner had, as yet, no witnesses – the police were not ready to produce them – so he intended to open his inquest and adjourn for the rest of the Sabbath.

The jumble of jurors was sworn and Whyte addressed them:

Words are inadequate to describe the horror, indignation and shame with which I feel overwhelmed in proceeding to discharge one of the duties of my office on this day of rest. I have summoned you in order that I might be in a position to permit the removal of the remains of the two victims of this dastardly and cowardly assassination from this hospital to their respective residences.

Someone wanted control of the post mortems, his audience realised. Earlier Whyte had been dubious about his power of removing the bodies to the Phoenix Park lodges, because they lay technically out-side the city boundary and therefore beyond his jurisdiction. The authorities told him tersely not to worry about such technicalities; the enormity of the crime superseded all other considerations. The transfer was the express wish of the viceroy himself.

The coroner proceeded tell the jury of the courteous, gentle and unassuming manner of the under secretary. While the opinions of people might differ in other respects, they must all unite in saying that Mr Burke was a most inoffensive, unobtrusive official and that his murder and that of the chief secretary 'must bring disgrace and reprobation on an entire nation of an irremovable character'.

A door was then unlocked and the jury was invited to briefly view the remains of the two deceased gentlemen. Pressmen who passed through in their wake stated that they were 'horribly disfig-ured and mangled' with dagger stabs in the face, throat and breast. The inquest adjourned to the morrow, and the bodies were for-mally released.

The corpses were placed in temporary coffins and borne to the front of the building where two hearses were drawn up with an escort of mounted police. It became clear that the plan was to take both sets of remains to the chief secretary's lodge, but it also emerged that it would be impossible to do so via the main park gate because of the throngs now congregating there with the inten-tion of gawking at the crime scene. A detour was necessary.

The cortege moved off, crossed the Liffey, headed west along the river bank. It avoided the masses by entering the park at the Islandbridge gate. Then it turned left at the Magazine Fort, and proceeded down to an S-bend road close to the Hibernian School. This was where Godden had watched the murderers flee.

Ascending the hill by the Fifteen Acres, the convoy headed in the direction of the Phoenix column. At several spots along the way, small knots of spectators had gathered, but not a single head was uncovered as they passed, the populace presuming that these were empty coffins heading to the hospital.

The *Illustrated London News*, whose correspondent was in the cortege, put the apparent indifference down to the 'deep awe which must have fallen upon everyone', adding however that no one accustomed to the usual demeanour of an Irish crowd in the presence of the dead could fail to be struck by the circumstance.

Half a dozen police were at the gate by which the chief secretary would finally arrive at his official residence, while along its boundary were stationed at intervals detectives from G Division. The building itself looked gloomy and deserted, the blinds pulled down over every window.

Almost at the moment that the bodies were carried inside, a heavy thunderstorm burst overhead and maintained its torrent for half an hour.

The bodies were laid out on separate tables in the drawing-room, where the windows looked out over dark acres toward the mountains. On the table nearest the conservatory, the door of which was closed, the body of Burke was placed stark and ghastly in the gaslight.

It was said that his features retained a stamp of dignity, although they were scarcely recognisable through the blood that spattered them and filled the mouth. His neck and chest bore gashes as if inflicted by a butcher's knife.

On another table at the end of the room was the body of Lord Frederick, 'presenting an appalling spectacle' in the mirrored room suggestive of refinement, luxury and enjoyment.

The medical team stripped off their jackets, donned aprons, and took scalpels and saws in hand. The bodies, 'red with the blood of the victims, presented a sight which even those familiar with the terrors of the battlefield could not look upon without emotion'.

The examination was made by George H. Porter, surgeon to the queen in Ireland, assisted by two others and by Dr Myles, the surgeon who had first met the bodies.

Dr Tweedy, physician at Dr Steevens' hospital, carefully noted down the evidence, assisted in the observations by Dr Speedy, medical officer of the North Dublin Union.

Until the bodies were stripped, no adequate idea could be formed of the 'savage malignity' with which the homicides had been committed. Lord Cavendish was examined first, and was found to have suffered eight gaping wounds.

In his right armpit was a 'horrible gash', caused by a stab in the right shoulder. It was the fatal wound, cutting through arteries and vessels, and causing death by haemorrhage. The doctors noted that there was a very large pool of blood under his body when it was found in the park.

This victim also had two cuts on the right shoulder blade, two more above the second rib in the right breast, and a deep thrust in the centre of the back. There was a wound in the neck too, at the right side, and a wound opposite the second rib at the right side.

The left arm was 'almost severed' by a slashing blow which had cut through the bone. It was surmised that this could have been caused by a bowie knife. Cavendish, the evidence indicated, had raised that arm to protect himself.

Mr Burke had no fewer than eleven wounds. The most serious was in his throat, which was three and a half inches deep and had severed the jugular vein, causing death.

An horrific wound in the back, drawn downwards, pierced the breast and could have killed him on its own. There were three penetrations in the front of his chest, besides other wounds, such as three cuts to the fingers of his left hand.

The murderers were determined to complete their bloody task and they must have done it with amazing rapidity. Various theories were offered as to the separation of the two victims by so many feet, as they had initially been so close together. They thought it probable that Burke was first set upon, and Lord Frederick stabbed while attempting to assist him.

The deadly wounds in the case of Cavendish were administered from behind with 'furious violence'. The hacking indicated an insatiable bloodthirstiness, as any one of the principal blows would have served the full purpose of the assassins.

The medicals later concurred in their assessment to Mallon that the men had been killed with long and very sharp knives, of good temper. They may have been surgical knives, or boning knives made especially keen, or they might also have been bowie knives.

Mallon nodded gravely. The mention of bowie knives, coupled with the slouch hats of other descriptions, made him think of an American connection. That would point in turn to the exiled hot-heads of the Irish Republican Brotherhood.

Lord Spencer had come in from the viceregal lodge to the Castle, 'and was engaged all day in conference with the authorities of the Irish Executive in connection with this horrible affair'.

Communications in cipher had already been passing between the Castle and cabinet ministers all day. A large body of police were feverishly at work in the Castle, collating reports from hundreds of others out in the field.

The police told Spencer that they believed there were many persons involved in the plot and that the movements of the two unfortunate gentlemen had been watched from the moment they left the Castle.

The police were at every tavern associated with treasonous talk and anyone approaching was being subjected to stop and search. The officers were reading every scrap of paper found on their persons.

The viceroy was unlikely to have been impressed. He had stood only yesterday with the noble lord who took an oath alongside him, full of life and promise at the outset of a new career, and next he was lying on Irish dirt, a pitiable and shocking sight.

Spencer sat down to write a long note to Gladstone. He described how the men had come to be walking up the centre of the park, adding: 'I must have crossed the road riding either behind or in front of them within a minute of them. To give you an idea of the publicity of the place, a polo match was only just over and many people were walking towards the town. Four distinct people were within 200 yards of the scene of the murder; three of them saw the scuffle.

'Mr Burke defended himself as his gloves were cut; he was stabbed in the face, neck and other places. Freddy about the heart and also in three other places (I may not be quite accurate on these points). They both, the surgeon says, must have died almost instantaneously.

'Freddy's face I hear was as if he were asleep; poor Burke showed the agony of the struggle'.

Spencer turned to a worrisome aspect of the tragedy: 'I cannot give a good account of the police as protecting life and detecting crime. I will not condemn them, but I am disposed to think that it will be necessary to bring here some distinguished and experienced officer to … help the heads of the police in trying to ferret out the Secret Societies, Fenians or murderers which centre on Dublin.

'I shall not do this for two days, because in this special case he could be of no use and I should discourage the men now at work', he wrote and went on to ask that ministers should consider who they could send for this special work.

'You must help me in London. Sir Garnet Wolseley strongly recommended Brackenbury, now military attaché at Paris, who organised the Cyprus police. There are doubtless other men, but he must be of first-rate ability, power and good sense. He will have a difficult task to perform'.

Spencer said he was not going to order the arrest of Fenian suspects since there was little specific information about the case. 'If I cannot strike a telling blow I shall remain quiet, for it is weak to beat the air merely for effect.

'Troops are confined to barracks tonight and everything is ready for a row if night brings one. We hear that the turbulent element are very jubilant and inflammatory in language …'

This Hellish Crime

The night passed quietly, and the population awoke to a proclamation pasted in prominent places. It offered a reward of £10,000 to anyone who provided information leading to the arrest and conviction of the killers.

A further £5,000 was offered to anyone giving 'private information', designed to assist those with a fear of giving evidence in open court. And a free pardon was guaranteed to anyone on the fringes of the crime, other than the actual perpetrators, who came forward.

Spencer had been initially opposed to offering a reward. 'I found that no public reward has ever brought a bit of evidence. It is therefore a sign of weakness to offer it, a mere sop to opinion, and it generally helps to stifle evidence never very easy of access'.

His oblique references to Irish distaste for the paid informer did not find much favour in London, where it was believed that a proclamation would demonstrate the determination of the crown to run the matter to ground. It would also heap pressure on those responsible, and in their wider circle someone might crack. It was, in the final analysis, worth trying.

As it turned out, the decision was fortuitous. Parnell and the constitutionalists issued their own proclamation, often stuck up side by side with the Castle document, denouncing the murders as a blow 'which cannot be exaggerated in its disastrous consequences'.

The sheet added significantly: 'We feel that no act that has been ever perpetrated in our country during the exciting struggles of the last fifty years has so stained Ireland as this cowardly and unprovoked assassination of a friendly stranger, and that until the murders of Cavendish and Burke are brought to justice, that stain will sully our country's name'.

It was as well that the authorities were now making a parallel point, and politically the climate had never been better for the apprehension of suspects.

But if the viceroy was overruled on the offer of a reward, he at least succeeded on another front: London had canvassed his opinion on the return of 'Buckshot' Forster. The former chief secretary, on learning of the murders, had immediately made it known to Gladstone that he wanted to go back. The killers, he suggested, had acted because they felt 'the pressure taken off' because of his departure.

Gladstone had his doubts that more repression was in order, but when Spencer was routinely canvassed for his opinion, the viceroy reacted in horror. He told the prime minister he was clear in his mind that 'it would not be right for him to come'.

Forster's presence was not required, 'and he would weaken my hands, I think, if a blow struck by me were identical with what he would have struck. It would lose its force to some extent if associated with him just now.

'We all here feel agreed upon it. I have not time to expand my reasons'.

Meanwhile there had been reprisals of a sort. At Brighouse, in Lord Cavendish's Yorkshire constituency (North West Riding), a mob attack was made upon the Irish quarter of the town in response to the tidings of their MP's death. Many of the houses of the Irish community were 'wrecked, and their residents badly beaten, while the remainder have fled from the town'.

In Dublin, the inquest was reopened that Monday, one juror asking to be excused on grounds of delicate health and being duly refused. Evidence was given, the press scribbling down every last detail, and the panel finally retired. They returned after an absence of fifteen minutes. They gave as their verdict that Lord Frederick Charles Cavendish and Thomas Henry Burke were, 'on the evening of Saturday 6th May, 1882, in the Phoenix Park in the county of Dublin, feloniously and of malice aforethought, killed and murdered by some person or persons unknown'.

The newspapers that morning already had many of the existing clues, even talk of bowie knives and American slouch hats. It was tempting to indulge a vision of foreign radicals visiting terror on Ireland, just as the nihilists and anarchists were doing in Czarist Russia and elsewhere.

Foreign newspapers were less appalled than the *Freeman's Journal*, which black-bordered every single one of its columns that day. The *Marseillaise*, the only socialist evening paper of France, had declared: 'Thus it is no longer at simple landed proprietors that the musket balls of Ireland are aimed. They strike down the queen's delegates in broad daylight. We pity the victims, but the immense pity we feel for the horrible situation of the Irish people forbids us to show too much sympathy'.

Ireland, since the first day of the conquest, had been in a legitimate state of self-defence, the paper argued. 'If at the cost of a series of outrages she succeeds in casting off the terrible yoke which the sister island imposes on her, what friend of humanity would think of blaming her for it?' the editorial asked.

Superintendent Mallon knew it would not be Ireland that would be blamed if the crime could not be solved, let alone if a series of further outrages were to occur.

As it was, there were infuriatingly few leads. Colonel Boscawen had taken particular notice of a car with four men 'of the description given of the assassins' that passed him near Kingsbridge, heading towards the park before the murders.

This car had been traced to a public house at Chapelizod and then to Lucan, where it was satisfactorily established that the four men were working in a factory there. They had been spoken to, and were all right.

The getaway route was most important. If the assassins so desired, they might barely have made the 7.45 p.m. train for Cork, but there was no trace of the car coming towards Dublin once it exited the park at Chapelizod.

Enquiries in the suburb had turned up another youth, Joseph Code, who claimed to be an eyewitness to the flight. An eighteen-year-old van driver for Proctor the butcher, Code stated that at about twenty minutes to eight on Saturday night a car with four passengers had dashed across Chapelizod bridge from the park direction and nearly collided with him.

The driver seemed disposed to halt, he related, but the passengers would not consent. Code described the horse as chestnut, with good action, but the car was now brown or chocolate colour. He agreed with Godden that the driver had three or four days' growth of lightish beard.

While the inquest was going on, Mallon was personally interviewing two others who had come forward claiming they were present during the killings. William Meagle and John Fry were a brass finisher and boilermaker respectively, from the Inchicore Railway Works.

The men explained that they were penny-farthing bicyclists, although 'neither of us are experts'. They passed two men on tricycles on the main park road, Fry said, then a car waiting to one side. 'We saw two men attack two others, one of whom actually fell under Meagle's machine. One of the men attacked was dressed in grey and exclaimed, 'Ah, you villain!'

The driver of the car had his back turned and could not see

what was going on, they explained. It 'never occurred to them' that there was anything wrong, and they didn't hear of the murders until they read the papers on Saturday evening, a Sunday edition having issued early.

Fry said they never mentioned to anyone what had come to their notice 'until after breakfast today, when we told our foreman and he sent us here'.

The cyclists said they had passed on towards town after the incident. About fifty or sixty yards nearer to Gough's statue there was a cab on the opposite side of the roadway 'and just as we were passing it, four men got into it and drove into town'.

This was a departure in a completely contrary direction to that seen by other witnesses. It might have led Mallon to realise that there may have been more than one team of assassins involved, but instead he determined that the whole story was 'a make-up', or the men drunk.

Meagle and Fry promptly admitted that they had taken some drink that night. The superintendent then dismissed them, and later thought that they might actually have come to him as 'a plant, to confuse'.

If their story was true, he reasoned, the bicyclists should have passed over the dead body of Lord Cavendish. And it would mean that Jacob, Walters, Power, Foley and Maguire were not to be relied upon.

A valuable clue was thus lost, the police sifting instead through useless scraps offered by the likes of an auctioneer and his daughter, named Garland, who saw practically nothing. The eminent brewer, Mr Guinness of Farmleigh, had ordered his estate workmen Thomas Huxley, Patrick Murray and two others to give information, 'but their statements were of a general character and only related to time'.

There would be plenty of distractions. News was arriving of the arrest of William Ivory, labourer, at Milford Haven on Sunday night. The Waterford man had arrived by an Irish boat and was now on his way to a hearing at Haverfordwest magistrates.

He, like many others helpfully arrested in Britain, was wholly innocent.

Spencer had meanwhile received a reply from Gladstone. The prime minister wrote: 'Amidst all this grief and confusion, and with efforts little less than diabolical made in the *Times* [editorial] of today to fasten this hellish crime upon the Irish nation, it is a great comfort to me to thank you for your admirable letter, and to think that such a man as you are is on the spot and in supreme command. May the Almighty guide you, and carry you well through your arduous labour'.

He turned to the matters most pressing – executive appointments to replace Burke and the invalid police chief, Hillier, and the appointment of 'the successor to our dear Freddy'. Gladstone added: 'I am struck by your demand for an English eye to aid the police. I have repeatedly pressed this on Forster – but in vain. Indeed I do not remember that he ever accepted any executive suggestion from me'.

Emboldened by this support, Spencer wrote straight back: 'The case I have against the police is overwhelming. Today brings fresh evidence of incapacity and want of co-operation.

'I am obliged to see each head to ensure his knowing what the other has done or is doing. That of course cannot go on.

'I feel strongly that amendment of the jury laws alone is not sufficient to meet the present state of feeling. I would not act in a panic, but the very audacity of the crime will, if possible, still further paralyse juries, and that is an argument which would justify action now'.

Sending the letter out to be telegraphed at once, Spencer kept his pen in hand and next wrote to his wife, Charlotte:

'I went to see them last night. I dreaded it, but I never rejoiced more. Freddy looked so beautiful, his face unruffled, as if he never had a grief or had done a sin in his life.

'It remains a beautiful image in my mind. Even dear Tom Burke was good and noble in his looks, but it was painful ... I broke down hopelessly, but afterwards I felt quite a weight off my mind'.

That afternoon, between five and six o'clock, the body of Lord Frederick was removed from the chief secretary's lodge, leaving that of Burke behind. The Cavendish casket went on a gun carriage, with police stopping traffic at intersections along the North Quays. The remains and cavalry escort made their way to the North Wall for the voyage to Holyhead.

'All along the route to the boat the sad procession was received with marks of the utmost sympathy by the immense crowds that had gathered to pay a mark of respect to the deceased'. The body was enclosed in a lead coffin, the outer mahogany shell being panelled with rich black silk and velvet. It was carefully unloaded at the wharf as a detachment of dragoons drew their swords in salute.

The casket was carried aboard the London and North Western Company packet vessel *Lily*, and placed in a protective box on the deck. The breastplate gleamed with a legend that read: 'Lord Frederick Charles Cavendish. Second son of the Duke of Devonshire. Born Nov. 30, 1836. Died May 6, 1882'.

They covered it with a Union Jack. 'The steamer started almost immediately, and the saddened assemblage slowly dispersed'.

On Monday night, when the House of Commons met, MPs knew that Lord Frederick Cavendish would never again stand among them. In tribute to his memory, it had been arranged that both houses of parliament would immediately adjourn upon a formal statement being made by the prime minister.

The members gathered slowly and solemnly, adding 'the dignity of numbers to the occasion'. All wore mourning black, and some bore a private guilt with their grief. *The Graphic* remembered how many had mocked the appointment of Cavendish the week before: 'We have had, from time to time, many scenes in the House of Commons, not a few of a painful character. But the memory must go back a long way in search of a parallel to the one of Monday night.

'On Thursday the House learned with amazement that Lord

Frederick Cavendish had been appointed Chief Secretary, and that his seat was already vacant in view of the necessary re-election.

'What followed thereupon doubtless added a fresh pang to the sorrow that filled the land on Sunday. There was a consensus of opinion that Mr Chamberlain was the right man for the place. When, therefore, it became known that not only was Mr Chamberlain not appointed, but that Lord Frederick Cavendish was, there burst forth such a storm of derision and doubt such as rarely marks a ministerial appointment.

'Lord Frederick was known to everyone who had business within the House of Commons as an able, painstaking and courteous official, a man with a clear head for business, although of somewhat stammering speech.

'Mr Forster often had a difficulty in holding his own with the glib and adroit tongues of the Land Leaguers. The attorney general for Ireland is no match for them. What would happen when Lord Frederick, with his impetuous nature and his faltering tongue, came to the table was very clearly forecasted in men's minds.

'No bounds were fixed to the freedom of criticism, and Lord Frederick Cavendish, travelling to the scene of his duty by the Irish mail, might have bought all the newspapers in the country without finding himself cheered by one kind or encouraging word'.

Every area of the Commons was now crowded, including the gallery available to peers from the Upper House, even though the Lords was still in session. The gathering filled all available benches, with MPs standing in double rows along the side galleries and massing in a throng at the bar.

One of the most prominent figures was the Irish obstructionist MP, Joseph Biggar, dressed in deep mourning, even to black studs, and with his thumbs in the armholes of his waistcoat. With an 'unusually depressed' look on his face he stood in the centre of the crowd, his gaze occasionally wandering as everyone waited for the grim pomp to come.

Mr Gladstone came in at the very last moment, 'apparently shirking the task as long as was possible'. Unlike its usual mood when crowded, the House remained very quiet. So low were the tones in which men whispered, 'and so sad the prevailing look, that a stranger might have thought the bodies of the murdered men were actually in the chamber'.

Solemn silence pervaded while the premier drooped into his seat. It was done 'as if he could not have gone a step further', and he covered his face with his hands. The speaker proclaimed 'Order! Order!' although no quietening was necessary, and the uncle-in-law of the dead politician rose slowly to commence his painful task.

'At first his voice was scarcely audible. When he raised it a little it seemed as if it were only preliminary to hopelessly breaking down. He was literally crushed with grief, and instead of the eager animated figure with its aggressive mien which the House is accustomed to see stand at the table, it saw an old man with bent figure, eyes red with past weeping, and now filled again with tears, who spoke in a voice choked with sobs'.

There were few dry eyes in the assembly as Mr Gladstone laboured through his text.

He made an opening reference to Burke, offering tribute to his memory, but paused when this portion of his task was done. He resumed with the faltering remark 'But the hand of the assassin has struck nearer home', and then quite broke down.

MPs stood horrified and filled with pathos in the presence of their weeping prime minister. It appeared he would not be able to complete the duty. He managed it somehow, partly by being brief, and partly by avoiding reference to Lord Frederick by name.

Concluding his speech, 'and stepping for a moment into the more bracing atmosphere of politics', he announced that the tragedy of Saturday would compel the government to reconsider and recast their arrangements.

Without delay, a measure would be brought in for the preservation of peace and order in Ireland, and a bill to deal with the arrears question would immediately follow. It was a promise of firmness, but also a commitment to deal with the burning issue that lay behind innumerable evictions and the near despair of the peasantry.

In Dublin Castle at midnight, Mallon was still at work. His nominal chief had been replaced and someone was to come over from London to administer all police matters. The strain was enormous – and not just on himself and his senior men. All the 4,000 car owners in Dublin had been visited and asked to account for themselves.

The annual inspection of all licensed cars and cabs had been held only a few days before, and consequently the appearance of every horse and vehicle was fresh in the recollection of the policemen who checked them once again. They were able to proceed rapidly, he later minuted.

The cabs in the vicinity of the murders were all accounted for, having been brought to the park by gentlemen playing polo, which finished a minute or two before the murders were committed.

A list of only 100 'suspicious' cars had been drawn up. Mallon was determined to have his identification parade for the witnesses, whether they were looking for a brown, red, chocolate, olive green, or partly white vehicle. At least horses came in limited colours.

One more idea came to him in the early hours. He asked that the lord lieutenant's proclamation, with its rewards and promises of a pardon, be read to every single political prisoner or detained Fenian suspect, preferably while they were alone in their cell.

Chasing Shadows

The body of Thomas Burke left the chief secretary's lodge early the next morning, the hearse passing the Phoenix column and turning onto the Lamplighter Road, thus making its way by the park perimeter to the North Circular Road and thence to Phibsboro.

The coffin was of polished oak, with massive brass mountings, and it travelled by hearse past scattered knots of Dubliners. Policemen lined the route at intervals of fifty yards, each saluting in his turn as the remains went by. Civilians bared their heads.

It reached Prospect cemetery a little after 10 o'clock. The lord lieutenant and the cardinal archbishop of Dublin were represented at the obsequies in the mortuary chapel. Also present were the lord chancellor, lord chief justice, attorney general and other bigwigs, the setting rather less salubrious than Dublin Castle a few days earlier. The city coroner was among hundreds who walked the

short distance to the graveside to watch the body finally committed to the earth.

Meanwhile the police investigation was in danger of being similarly swallowed up. Arrests were being made in every major town, most often from excess of zeal or sheer anxiety not to make a mistake. Every idle suspicion of a member of the public was being dutifully indulged.

As Burke was being buried, the spree of detentions came full circle to the Phoenix Park. There, shortly before 11 o'clock, Acting Sergeant Roe, 27 D, had been studying two men sitting on a bench on the Castleknock side of the Phoenix Column. They presently got up and he followed. They stopped, sensing an odd atmosphere, and asked him if anyone had been got yet for the murders. The sergeant looked sharply at them for a long time without saying a word and one of the gas workers turned pale. They were promptly arrested.

It did not matter that they were released after an hour in the bridewell, as it was sometimes merely an exchange of one set of suspects for another. That same station, the same afternoon, played host to a car driver and a vehicle detained by a mob and forced into police custody.

The London *Times* welcomed the 'change of tone and habit among the lower classes' that saw a crowd of people gather around a hackney car with red panels and a number partly obliterated. The citizens insisted on a constable taking the driver and car to the station for identification – just when the gas workers were getting out.

The police were less likely than the *Times* to champion the public change from 'extreme reluctance to give any assistance to the police in such cases, lest they should be branded as informers', because such episodes were badly bogging them down.

The Castle was also inundated with reports from Britain of arrests and 'information received', neighbouring forces pestering with good intentions. The Americans wanted to know which ships to watch on arrival and had heard dark rumours about Fenians on the *Scythia*.

'Reports of arrests of different persons are flying about, but they turn out upon investigation to be unfounded, and some of them are supposed to be intended to draw police off the scent', opined one broadsheet.

Individuals were apprehended in Athlone, Clonmel, Galway, and a dozen other towns, in addition to those held in Preston, Southport and Glasgow. Two were taken into custody in Monaghan. 'The police do not feel sanguine that they are yet on the right track', the papers gossiped.

An arrest made in Maynooth might stand as an example. Charles Moore was a discharged soldier of the 43rd regiment who had arrived on the four o'clock train from Dublin and gone to an hotel. There he was sought out by police, no doubt on the clucking advice of someone who saw every stranger as a harbinger of death.

Moore's answers to questions were not satisfactory and the suspiciously large sum of eighty pounds was found upon this 'young man of rather reckless bearing'. He stated that he had just returned from America and was on his way to Co. Longford. Not feeling well, he had deemed it advisable to break the journey and make a short stay at Maynooth, he said. On being arrested, the prisoner fainted, which in itself was somewhat thrilling, if not wholly confirmatory. He was brought to Dublin by train the next day, his arrival at the broadstone terminus being met by a large crowd of people 'who showed their detestation of the terrible crime by the many violent expressions which they addressed to the suspected man'.

Moore was conveyed to the Castle and taken before the police magistrates. Here his interrogators had no difficulty accepting the ex-soldier's story and he was swiftly discharged.

Still the papers prattled: 'The police are indefatigable in their efforts to trace the assassins, and believe that with the unusual advantage which they possess of having popular sympathy on their side they will eventually succeed'.

A man was arrested in Limerick on suspicion of being involved in the assassinations. He had bought a new suit of clothes in the town, 'and bloodstains were observed at the time on his own ones.

He seems to be a foreigner. The old clothes are missing'.

At Tipperary a man who first gave the name of Harris and subsequently that of Pierce, was arrested on suspicion. He refused to give any account of himself.

Another, giving the name of Thomas Haybourne, was arrested at Castlebellingham, Co. Louth, and once more sent to Dublin for identification.

John Cloonan was arrested in Williamstown and removed to Tuam gaol. 'It is surmised that the prisoner was making his way to Galway or Limerick with the object of leaving the country by an emigrant ship'.

The hysteria continued unabated.

Trying manfully to rise above it all was the Castle hierarchy. Names of alleged culprits were pouring in from hundreds of public tip-offs and police resources were dangerously stretched. It was observed that 'a number of voluntary statements are made to the police, with probably the best intentions on the part of persons who profess a desire to help them, but in every instance they have only given useless trouble'.

Colonel Connolly, Captain Talbot, and other officials were engaged at the Castle in examining witnesses. It had been arranged for all the registered car-men of Dublin and suburbs to be paraded before the police, a system previously adopted 'after the terrible assault on Miss Jolly' by a lascivious car driver at Milltown.

A number of the crew of the *Belleisle*, the man-of-war which had thundered out a royal salute at Kingstown three days earlier, were meanwhile standing in the lower Castle yard with appliances for dragging rivers.

Their vessel had come upriver, 'having on board the most approved grappling irons', together with divers and willing young sailors. They took a launch to the Castle, asked there by 'detectives trying to recover a little of their lost prestige'.

It was rumoured that the desperadoes, when leaving the park, had killed the driver and horse, 'and in order to conceal and leave no trace of their crime, they threw car, horse and driver into the Liffey'.

The police were only following standard procedure in the hope and half-expectation that the murder weapons, merely, had been discarded in the nearest watercourse. The *Belleisle* seamen were asked to proceed at once to the Liffey at Chapelizod and to search towards the Strawberry Beds. This they did diligently for several days, without result.

Dr Charles Cameron, the city analyst, was meanwhile examining the cushions of a car driver, living on the south side of the city, who had been closely questioned for a time. Many a horse with foaming sweat on its flanks had implicated its owner that night, and this fellow was one. He stated firmly that he was not out for hire on Saturday, but was told in reply that neither would he be out for some time to come. His horse and car were in care of the police, and under scrutiny.

'It seems marvellous that with such extraordinary manifestations of sympathy and with such an unexampled unanimity in the condemnation of a horrid crime, no certain trace has yet been found of the five murderers', the press fussed.

'A horse and car cannot easily be removed without attracting attention, and yet no one seems to know anything about them'. But too many people, from the police point of view, thought they did.

Finding actual witnesses, not investigating unsolicited information, was still the focus. This day saw more statements given by those in the park at the relevant time, including that of a clerk in the General Prisons Board named Lewis, a carpenter named Guilfoyle of Lennox Street, and a painter called Woofington of Fitzwilliam Lane. This last individual turned out to be the old man referred to by Lieutenant Greatrex; the one who 'supposed' on the night that he should assist the police.

Overlooked was the statement of a man named Ladley of Marrowbone Lane. He had watched the polo match in progress that evening and had chatted with another spectator. The stranger then walked off and spoke to one of two men sitting on a bench, neither of whom Ladley knew. The game then ended, and Ladley walked home.

This vague and utterly unhelpful account was later to prove of prime significance.

On this third day after the murders, Mallon himself was engaged in the foot-slogging. Having attended Burke's funeral in the morning, he went out to Chapelizod, accompanied by PC Donohoe, to make his own enquiries.

He swiftly found another witness, one Edward Holohan. Holohan said that the car referred to by Joseph Code had passed him where the railway crossed the road at Inchicore. It had then been nine minutes to eight o'clock.

The horse was chestnut, of good action, he echoed. The car was chocolate colour, the driver and passengers apparently all of the one party, 'like cattle dealers returning from a voyage', and he imagined they were familiar faces, not foreigners. All were dressed alike, roughly but comfortably.

Holohan's sighting led to a Mrs White, the wife of the tramway head timekeeper at Inchicore. She said that a car with four passengers, like workmen, drove past rapidly at five minutes to eight.

A gardener named Ryan next said that the car with four passengers passed him at Richmond Hill at eight o'clock or a few minutes to it. Mr Such, of the firm of Such and Rudd, confirmed that a car with four dashed across Rialto bridge at about 8 o'clock. The rapidity with which they crossed over the bridge attracted his attention, but he could not identify anyone.

Mr Donald, assistant teacher in the Rehoboth school, saw a car with four passengers, the same as described by the others, pass the end of Rehoboth Lane (off South Circular Road) at about ten minutes or a quarter after eight. Mrs Matthews of Cork Street saw a similar car with the same number of passengers pass her house, coming from Dolphin's Barn, at about a quarter past eight.

Both Donald and Matthews said the horse looked jaded. All further trace was lost in Cork Street. Writing later, Mallon observed: 'Relying on the number of passengers, the general speed with which they travelled, the appearance of the car and horse, and the time noted at different points, it may fairly be assumed that the track that we traced to Cork Street can be relied upon.

'The only thing I heard advanced against it was that they would not have all four kept together. However it must not be forgotten that Cork Street was the first thickly populated spot met with.

'No stranger in Dublin could make his escape by the route without a hitch, and no better strategy could have been shown. Once over Chapelizod bridge there was no shortcut and the roads were a perfect maze afterwards'.

This local knowledge convinced Mallon that he was not dealing with Americans or foreigners. Witness Holohan also claimed to have seen the same car in the vicinity three weeks earlier, although he did not know to whom it belonged.

Mallon's interest in the escape route may have obscured some emerging details that were shedding light on what had happened back in the park.

He may not have liked Meagle and Fry, the penny-farthing riders who spoke of a car and passengers heading in the opposite direction to that of the murder vehicle. But a pattern was slowly emerging to suggest that Meagle was right, and that there were more men involved in the operation than initially imagined.

Joseph Gannon of Coolmine saw the horse and car facing the Phoenix before the attack, and four or five men standing under trees next to the road, their hands in their pockets. But he also saw the cab Meagle described opposite the polo ground, facing towards town, and there were men here also.

Joseph Powell of the Strawberry Beds was walking towards Dublin on Saturday evening, before the attack, to pick up a parcel of clothes. He saw four men against a clump of trees opposite the lord lieutenant's residence. A little further on he met a driver sitting on a car and he tossed him some remark about a pony that was passing.

Further down, towards the Gough statue, Powell too saw Meagle's car. The driver here was five feet eight inches, of stout appearance. He was fifteen to twenty yards from where a group of four men were standing about another clump of trees, 'two inside and two outside'.

They were all unremarkably dressed and appeared like tradesmen, either ironworkers or shoemakers. All of these accounts, faithfully recorded, might have added up to a two gangs theory. But it was hard to sift the telling detail from the dross.

Laurence Kavanagh, who worked in Mountjoy Barracks, offered further intimation of a careful conspiracy rather than an opportunistic attack by a single group. He passed the men under the trees across from the viceregal lodge. There were six or seven, he insisted, but 'two or three were dressed like gentlemen'.

The others were rough looking young fellows, about six or seven being 'together quite close'. There was a car and a shabby looking driver a few yards from them on the road. It struck the witness as 'strange to see the gentlemen and roughs together'.

About ten or fifteen minutes afterwards, Kavanagh said two gentlemen very quickly overtook him, heading in the direction of the city, 'as if walking a race'.

Curiouser and curiouser. But the crowning account would come from a French polisher named Sarah Hands, and her husband, Stephen, of Knockmaroon, who were out for a walk towards town on 6 May.

The couple were adamant that they saw four men lying on both sides of the road – eight men in all. The Hands connected the groups to each other in apparent purpose and attitude. Both sets of men were recumbent on grass slopes near their respective pedestrian paths, facing towards the road, as if lying in wait.

Sarah Hands was evidently a little unnerved, not least because of the striking appearance of one of those in the second group, closest to town. 'I think I would be able to identify this man. He looked up at us as we passed. He had a fierce appearance'.

Two groups of four ruffians, two drivers, and two gentlemen shuttling between the groups might add up to a twelve person assassination party. The police had to keep an open mind, even if

Mallon appeared to have adopted a casual attitude to these unusual accounts. He wrote in one report for London that a witness named Sarah Hands had 'turned up' that Tuesday, little knowing that she would eventually turn up trumps.

Both she and her husband would later identify the 'fierce-looking man', whose jail photograph would serve only to confirm his fearsome features.

At Westminster on Tuesday night, the British government announced the replacements for Lord Cavendish and Thomas Henry Burke.

The radical MP for Chelsea, Charles Dilke, had been asked to become chief secretary, but had refused the prime minister, finding some excuse. 'Dilke made a horrible mistake', wrote Gladstone to Spencer. Instead the promotion went to George Otto Trevelyan, forty-three, the secretary to the admiralty.

The man to replace Burke as permanent under secretary was Robert Hamilton, son of a Presbyterian clergyman on one of the Shetland Islands. Hamilton, a career civil servant, was likewise plucked from the admiralty buildings.

Lord Spencer also learned that evening that the organiser of the Cyprus constabulary, Sir Henry Brackenbury, had indeed been appointed to take charge of the Irish police forces and was leaving that night. There would furthermore be a new post of assistant under secretary for police and crime, to be filled by George Jenkinson.

Amidst all the new arrivals, the one that pleased Spencer most was a communication from his lady wife that she was leaving for Dublin the next night, accompanied by two London detectives. 'It will be the greatest comfort to me to be over the water,' the countess wrote. 'I do not in the least care how dull, or quiet, or prison-like the life is there. I shall be quite happy there, which I could not be here'.

But the main business of the British government that day was the introduction of a new Prevention of Crime (Ireland) Bill in direct response to the murders.

This measure intended to create emergency conditions to last for three years, the main provision being for the trial of serious crime – treason, murder, attempted murder, and attacks on dwelling houses – by special three-judge tribunals, sitting without a jury.

Extensive powers were also to be given to the police. They could search for arms without a warrant, and seize and suppress newspapers that spread sedition. In more general matters, any person failing to identify themselves could be arrested on the spot, and it would be an offence to be out after dark without reasonable cause.

Introducing the bill in the Commons, home secretary Sir William Harcourt thundered to MPs that night: 'All the body of Ireland is sound, but there is a frightful plague spot upon it and I firmly believe that the Irish, no less than the English nation, desires that it be removed.

'There is a cancerous sore on Ireland, and the House will anticipate that the great malady which corrodes and cripples its healthy frame comes from the baneful demon of secret societies and unlawful combinations.

'That being so, it is necessary that the surgeon's hand should cauterise and extirpate the disease, and to that operation I have to ask the attention of the House.

'Every jury man – we need hardly wonder and we can hardly blame him – looks with dread upon the levelled pistol at his heart, the dagger at his back, and the bullet of the rifle in his home at night ...'

And so he went on, eventually describing the intended legislation. Significant in the package was Section 16, which would empower any resident magistrate in any place to summons people to appear before him and give evidence on oath in relation to any crime.

This so-called 'Star Chamber' measure would eventually prove crucial to unlocking the mystery of the Phoenix Park murders.

'Various and Embarrassing'

Thursday 11 May saw the burial of Lord Frederick Cavendish at Edensor, near Chatsworth, the family seat. The entire cabinet and scores of MPs came down from London by special train, just as a dedicated train, windows draped in crêpe, had conveyed the body all the way from Holyhead.

The body had arrived the previous day at Rowsley and was conveyed on a hearse to the chapel at Chatsworth. There the body was on view to the inhabitants of the neighbourhood and 'those who knew the deceased gentleman pressed forward to see his remains'.

The coffin was covered with black velvet, national newspapers reporting that the features of the deceased bore a calm and placid expression, resembling sleep rather than death. The only scar visible was a slight one across the nose.

Over the body was hung a floral cross, composed of white azalea, mignonette, forget-me-nots, tea roses and maidenhair fern. The duke of Devonshire was the first of the family to enter the chapel after the arrival of his son, and at the sight of him completely broke down.

Lady Frederick Cavendish, accompanied by her two brothers, the Hon. Neville Gerald Lyttelton and the Hon. Alfred Lyttelton, also visited the chapel. A special messenger from the queen arrived with a splendid wreath.

The workmen of the estate were graciously permitted to view the body the next morning from 6 to 8 o'clock. Then Lucy braved the final leave-taking with her husband. The lid was closed on the coffin, and shortly thereafter began the biggest public funeral for the remainder of the nineteenth century until the death of the monarch in the next.

Seventy thousand mourners descended on the tiny Derbyshire hamlet, cramming into a churchyard dubbed 'the Dukes' burial place'.

Gladstone himself, bent in grief, carried a wreath of lilies. The harrowed face of Lady Lucy Cavendish, when it could be glimpsed between paroxysms of grief, was piteous to behold. The young widow, childless, was supported by her family and by Freddy's family in the moment of supreme loneliness.

Lord Spencer was at that moment receiving a letter in Dublin from the same Lucy and it left him very much affected. 'I shall be very glad,' she wrote, 'if there can be any means of letting it be known in Ireland, so as to have some good effect, that I would never grudge the sacrifice of my darling's life if only it leads to the putting down of the frightful spirit of evil in the land.

'He would never have grudged it if he could have hoped that his death would do more than his life. There does seem some hope of this, and you are doing all you can to keep down that most dreadful danger of panic and blind vengeance'. The lord lieutenant again shed tears.

No one told the widow of a police intelligence report that a meeting of Manchester Fenians, rejoicing at the blow struck against British pride, had heard a proposal that the body of Lord Frederick be removed from its grave. Special guards were posted thereafter at both Glasnevin and Edensor.

In Dublin, Mallon had finally conducted his identity parade of hackney cars and drivers at Dublin Castle. The entire procession turned into something of a public spectacle and the hundred-strong convoy drew the most boorish and lurid speculation from onlookers as to which one might prove to be the murder machine.

The exercise was an acutely observed failure in all respects. Greatrex the soldier saw horses and drivers, as did Jacob the bird-nester, Godden the park ranger, Code and Holohan of Chapelizod – and they collectively failed to identify any one of them.

Mallon later wrote that the descriptions given of the murder vehicle were 'various and embarrassing'. The horse could be any horse. Furthermore Godden's verbal portrait of one of the actual killers, impossibly exact, clashed hopelessly with a tally of the same man offered by Greatrex, casting doubt on all of Godden's guidance.

'From the different views expressed,' the superintendent wrote in August, 'I have no hesitation to say I think they [the witnesses] could not be relied on to identify any person'.

The fiasco of the parade left the car men of Dublin very anxious to remove the stigma they felt had been cast on them, with their leaders voicing a strong desire to see the assassins brought to justice.

'They desire to give public expression to their feelings, and have convened a meeting of the cab and car owners of Dublin and Kingstown to be held on Friday at the Phoenix Park, and a mass meeting of owners and drivers at the same place on Sunday next,' reported the *Times*.

One of the most mysterious facts connected with the crime was that they could not find the car used by the killers, the paper added, before wandering into further lurid speculation: 'It is also suggested that the woman, or the person in a woman's dress, who was seen at the spot with a basket, and who was or pretended to be intoxicated, was an accomplice. No trace of her has been found'.

It was an attractive newspaper angle – had the woman hidden bombs in her bundle to rescue any failing effort by her men friends? – and the basket woman was championed for a while as the key to the whole affair.

In fact, she had already been eliminated from the investigation. Some witnesses had indeed commented on the woman's odd behaviour, but she was simply in shock. She was Mrs Margaret Sharpe, wife of the gate lodge keeper at Knockmaroon.

Meagle and Fry, the bicyclists, said they had seen the woman

with a basket passing up at Gough's statue just after the attack. She was near the second group of men, close to the town gate, one of whom Fry even claimed to see brandishing a knife.

This point seemed to confuse Mallon, who imagined that Meagle and Fry were placing the killers close to the equestrian statue, hundreds of yards from where the assassinations had actually taken place. In dismissing them he reasoned thus: 'It is true that Mrs Sharpe, one of the gate lodge keepers, passed up, but it must have been near the Gough testimonial, as when the poor woman reached the scene of the murders the dead bodies were being removed'.

This latter part is not quite true. Mrs Sharpe was unable to give a coherent account of what she witnessed, but it appears she may have seen the killings, albeit at a considerable distance. The sapper William Dawson met her in the immediate aftermath, and she was babbling 'I will not be able to go home', or something to that effect.

'I did not know her, but imagined she had taken drink,' said Dawson. 'I afterwards heard the woman's name was Mrs Sharpe, Phoenix Park gate lodge, Knockmaroon'.

Mrs Ellen Brewster, Astagob, Strawberry Beds, had been drinking with her husband in Queen Street. Going home through the park, they saw the dead bodies, one on the footpath, and the other on the road. 'There were present two men who had bicycles, a man who appeared to be a working man, a sapper from Mountjoy barracks and a woman,' she said.

'My husband assisted to place the bodies on a stretcher and car. My husband was under the influence of drink and did not notice what I noticed'.

In her statement, Mrs Sharpe denied meeting any person between the Gough statue and Phoenix column. All she could recall was seeing the dead bodies of Lord Cavendish and Mr Burke. 'Mr Burke's body was lying on the path along which I passed. I then became weak and cannot remember having seen any person 'til I met my daughter at Phoenix column'.

Her daughter Mary said she left home at 7 o'clock. 'I went along the road leading to Phoenix column, which also passes the Chapelizod park gate lodge. Between the column and Hibernian School, I met a car, which I believe was not a hack car, with three or four men upon it. I did not notice the driver.

'The horse appeared rather small, and dark in colour. They were driving at a rapid pace, and the men appeared very much excited. They were not affected by drink, as they looked very closely at a dog which I had with me. I saw a crowd of persons at the bodies when I reached the Phoenix column'.

If Mary Sharpe saw the fleeing murderers when walking to meet her mother, it is likely that her mother was in a good position to see the attack itself, strolling from the Gough statue to the Phoenix.

This is no small point, as Mrs Sharpe had confirmed the evidence of Meagle and Fry, who saw a separate gang of four men, one of whom was apparently carrying a knife and who climbed aboard a second car in the aftermath of the slaying, riding off towards town.

If Meagle and Fry had been believed, and support for their two-gangs tale was to be found elsewhere, the police would have had many more avenues for enquiry. Witnesses were few in the Chapelizod direction, but more plentiful towards the city.

Only when the police did look in the direction of the second gang – but not until after Christmas – did they find individuals to identify some of the conspirators. Meanwhile the trail had gone cold and the superintendent only had cards, surrendered by several newspapers, claiming the deed in the name of the Irish Invincibles.

The missed opportunities were not yet beginning to tell against the investigation, with the newspapers withholding judgment until time had worn on.

'The Dublin police are indefatigable in their efforts to trace the assassins,' cried the *Graphic* on 13 May. 'The general body of the people of all grades and classes likewise exhibit a fervent anxiety for the capture of the guilty parties, and in spite of the harsh criticisms which have been made in some quarters as to the genuineness of their apparent horror and detestation of the crime, we are disposed to hope at least that the atrocious criminals may before long be brought to justice, and the honour of the country cleared of the foul stain which now blackens it'.

The people were indeed feverish in their efforts to distance themselves from the crime. Deputations from the lords mayor and corporations of Dublin, Cork and Belfast waited on the lord lieutenant to express their revulsion. Similar delegations came from the great towns of Ireland, the chambers of commerce, senate of the university, and public bodies like the Queen's College of Physicians.

Their collective loyal addresses expressing abhorrence of the hideous crime filled many folders at the viceregal lodge. It was said that there was not a guild of bricklayers nor a band of shipwrights who did not dutifully submit their own 'spake'.

Dublin car men, when they had their open air meeting in the Phoenix Park on Sunday 14 May, were if anything more outraged. Resolutions were passed unanimously by the 500 drivers present, emphasising that they felt 'in common with the citizens of Dublin and Irishmen of every shade of religion and politics, intense horror, detestation, and condemnation of the perpetrators of the dark and demoniacal crime that was committed in this beautiful park on Saturday week last, and hope that the efforts of the authorities will be soon crowned with success in capturing the assassins and bringing them to justice'.

In addition, there were further offers of reward. A public subscription was started in Cork for a subsidiary reward to the huge amount offered by the lord lieutenant. Sums of £1,000 were commonly broached, a number of British newspapers getting in on the act, and $5,000 was offered by the San Francisco branch of the Land League.

Repentance sprouted. Rev. Mr O'Boyle, parish priest of Saintfield, Belfast, had published a letter withdrawing certain terms used by him at a meeting of nationalists in Belfast on the eve of the slaughter.

In his speech the reverend gentleman said that Dublin Castle was 'a nest of vipers', that a 'rotten, foul atmosphere rested around it', and that it would be 'well for England and the Empire if it were reduced to ashes'.

He also referred in uncomplimentary terms to the Irish lord chancellor. 'He now expresses regret for having used such violent language'.

None of this was helping the police, and the *Illustrated London News* soon began wondering at the lack of progress, a detached surprise that would soon be expressed in more direct and cutting terms: 'It had been supposed that the metropolis in Ireland, the headquarters of Irish society, was in some degree, compared with the West and South, an abode of civilisation, with a humane, honest and orderly population.

'It might have seemed impossible in Dublin that a band of worse than savage manslayers, after perpetrating their monstrous deed in the middle of the park in broad daylight, should drive away in a hired public vehicle ... and elude pursuit, no positive information being given two weeks afterwards concerning their movements.

'The deep disgrace which has fallen upon Dublin, by the exhibition of such gross indifference to the most heinous of crimes, if not tacit connivance on the part of those, few though they may be, who must have known more of the circumstances than they choose to reveal, is felt by every respectable citizen'.

The police were still processing plenty of respectable citizens who had been locked up in the course of the continuing hysteria.

Michael Smith of Rathcline, Co. Longford, returned from America on the day before the killings, to visit relatives. He nonetheless found himself spending his holiday lodged in Longford gaol.

Smith was said to be 'dressed in the manner described by those who saw the occupants of the car in the Phoenix Park on Saturday. The slouch hat and American appearance of the prisoner first of all attracted attention'.

Find the Americans became the next piece of mischief. Octimus Deacon of Loughton, Essex, wrote to the authorities on 25 May 1882, to suggest that responsibility lay with war vessels of the United States Navy, which had been lying for some time at Plymouth.

'US sailors on leave could get away from the Irish coast unobserved, and no suspicion would attach to them when they reached Devonshire waters.

'Is it possible that the murderers came from out their crews? Probably the officers of the vessels would give every information as to whether any of their men have been away for a few days, or have deserted whilst in English waters. If it is stated that the authorities will 'leave no stone unturned' to find the murderers, here is a stone which may be worth turning …'

This informant was combining the 'American' atmosphere of the crime with the official police description of the culprits, which terminated with the claim that 'the men had the appearance of sailors or well-to-do artisans'.

Stephen Harris of Birchington, Kent, wrote to Earl Spencer, perhaps unconsciously tapping into a growing, if unspoken, feeling that the Irish police were dim of intellect: 'I see in the *Kentish Express* a reward is offered for information which may lead to the perpetrators of the crime in Ireland. Would you allow me to suggest a plan that I think would lead to their apprehension and also would discover secret societies?

'It will seem strange if I say that you can find them out by steam.

'Sir, you know that all letters come through the post office and the post office is under Government, then all letters that come from America or any other part of the world addressed to suspected persons could be opened by steam. If you put a letter over a cup of hot water a few minutes you will be able to open it, read it and then close it again, and they will be none the wiser'.

Spencer must have sighed heavily at that one, and wished the envelope had never been opened, whether by steam or no. But correspondence continued to pour in.

Rev. Dr Hogg, rector of Broomfield, Carrickmacross, Co. Monaghan, communicated his belief that a man named Patrick 'Bird' Finnegan was central to the plot. While the Bird was said to have died some years ago on his way out to America, it was also now being suggested that he had 'faked his own death for the purposes of being all along an active skirmishing agent'.

Rev. Hogg added: 'Contradictory rumours are afloat as to his being alive, and it is very possible that he may not be dead. He left the county so deeply in debt that he was immediately declared bankrupt on his departure'.

His housekeeper had twice distinctly seen the Bird alive and well and back in his old locality, he added. A police file had to be opened on this nonsense and local police activity generated to see if the theory remotely held water. A pathetic report on file notes that beyond mere rumour and suspicion, 'there is no information whatever to connect this Finnegan with the park murders'.

'Dear Sir,' wrote another tipster, this time anonymously: 'There is no use to try to find these murderers in Dublin. Save your time and look for them in some of your convents in Galway city'.

The cranks grew ever more weird. A letter posted on 10 May at Bristol, addressed to the chief of constabulary, Dublin, was stamped 'Received' the next day. It was from a resident of King's Square, who wrote: 'Sir, Dreaming is not much to go by, but I dreamt last night the number of the car used for the murderers' purpose was 1600'.

No such plate had been issued. Another letter claimed the number of the car was 104, but this was anonymous, and it was not as if there was a shortage of people denouncing named hackney drivers.

One police detective submitted a lurid tale to his superiors that summer which he heard from 'a most respectable' informant of his personal acquaintance. The story was that Laurence Farrell, a car owner, drove four men to his home in Cook Street at about 7.30 p.m. on the evening of 6 May last.

'Subsequently there was a bonfire in the yard belonging to his house and it is believed that the cushions of his car were those burned. Since the above, Farrell has procured new cushions for one of his cars.

'It appears that Farrell's horse and car were, with others, inspected by the D. M. Police. He had quite a different horse under his car from the one driven by him on 6 May. It is alleged that Farrell's wife is addicted to drink and when drunk talks of blood money and imagines that she sees the late Lord Frederick Cavendish and Mr T. H. Burke'.

Constable William Nelson, based at Santry station, informed his superiors on 12 May of a rather more hopeful lead:

'I beg to report that I have received information that four men corresponding to the description of the murderers of the Chief & under secretaries were seen drinking in the public house next to Bruce's boat shot in Great Britain Street on the evening of the murder about 6 o'clock.

'The public house I believe adjoins Cole's Lane. The car, in which was a bay horse, remained at the door; the driver, who also corresponded with the description, sitting in the dickie.

'They drew the informant's attention to them by the suspicious way they were going in and out and repeatedly feeling their breast pockets, so that he came to the conclusion that they were up to no good. They came out of the public house about 6 and a half o'clock, and drove rapidly away in the direction of Capel Street'.

All these stories and hundreds more had to be checked, leading to such statements from detectives as these in surviving files from the investigation:

'The man named in annexed … is well known as a simple harmless man in Kingstown.'

'John Merriman [of Ballinamuck] is not at all a reliable informant. He is fond of drink and is not in a position to get or give information'.

Another letter was sent to Earl Spencer, the lord lieutenant, from Liverpool. This one claimed that the Dublin Metropolitan Police was infested with secret Fenians. 'The police force is accused of having a great many members of the Fenian brotherhood. The way they recognise each other is by placing the first finger to the lips.

'I am informed that they meet in caves along the Irish coast, and in one locality in an excavation in the earth. You may not be disposed to credit these statements, but I would urge upon you the necessity of organising a search by steamer for these caves, which are entered by means of a boat'.

Spencer passed on these 'vague suggestions' to a police force in which he had lost almost all faith.

Strange Tales

John Mallon and G Division of Dublin Castle had the names of some of the actual principals in the assassinations within a short time. Unfortunately, those names were bound up with those of hundreds of other suspects, most well known to police, with nobody to tell who had actually carried out the deed.

Criminal touts and snouts had turned out thousands of snippets of pure gossip, although no one claimed to know anything of the so-called 'Irish Invincibles'. At the same time however, Mallon knew, in common with everyone else, that these murders were completely out of the run of the usual Fenian outrages.

Michael Davitt, the founder of the Land League, wrote privately that the weapons used were foreign to Irish crime. He declared: 'There is not one instance in the long list of outrages in Ireland where the dagger was used. The shotgun and the stick have always been the weapons employed, and the knife or dagger has been unknown.

'Had the perpetrators of the crime been Irishmen, they might have feared to employ the gun or revolver because of the attention they would attract, but in that case they would have used bludgeons'.

Davitt's reasoning had been separately adopted to link the crime not only to America, but also latterly to continental secret societies. It was claimed that socialists in France were anxious to establish a connection with the Irish agrarian struggle, and one Frenchman had publicly declared in early 1882 that 'something would happen in Ireland before long which would astonish the world'.

It was pointed out that the dagger had been favoured in Italy – where oath-bound criminal enterprises such as the carbonari had long been engaged in quasi-political self-improvement. Perhaps it was the drift away from the American angle that caused the prominent US-based Fenian O'Donovan Rossa to try to drag the matter back towards Ireland. He stated publicly in a political propaganda sheet that he personally knew the assassins. O'Donovan Rossa said they were members of the Irish Republican Brotherhood (IRB), an official name for the Fenian movement, which organised itself almost openly in the United States.

But Davitt, recently released from jail and back in Ireland, was scornful of such sideline commentary. He wrote: 'O'Donovan Rossa never knew anything about the assassination before it took place. It was as much a surprise to him as it was to everyone else, and he has not the slightest or remotest idea who did it.

'If he had, he could no more keep the knowledge to himself than a hen with one chick can help clucking. That he should say he does is not wonderful. He has been feeding the readers of his paper for so long upon paper exploits that he is forced to grab at a *bona fide* crime whenever he gets a chance'.

Mallon himself was meanwhile reporting to a judicial friend that he 'very much doubted if, as was universally assumed in England and suspected by many in Ireland, the outrage was the work of the Fenians'.

But if not them, then who? Davitt's labyrinthine analysis, based on the Ciceronian principle of *cui bono*, which asked who could possibly benefit from any particular deed or misdeed, led him into absurdity: 'Who had a motive in this case – the landlords or the people? For the Irish the assassination turned their victory into defeat; for the landlords it brought back that coercion which is their only hope.

'The landlords of Ireland, through the machinery of the Castle, control the police. They have what the people have not – plenty of money. They could obtain an accurate knowledge of the proposed movements of Lord Frederick Cavendish. Who, then, could have aided in the escape of the murderers as effectively as the men who could not only give all the information needed, but could furnish the money and control the police?

'I am not afraid to leave the answer to any man of common sense'.

On Friday 19 May, there was another claim of responsibility for the crime, and the most brazen to date. The leading Dublin daily, the *Freeman's Journal*, printed a startling confession to the murders by 'one who had taken part in them', and occupied the whole of their main news page in doing so.

The anonymous author claimed that the sole intention of the gang had not been murder, but to abduct the new chief secretary and to hold him hostage against the plight of the Irish peasantry. Burke had resisted, and was dragged separately away and knifed to death.

Lord Frederick, grabbed to one side, and told he was to be kidnapped, had supposedly replied: 'Gentlemen, this is a very uncongenial Irish reception. I decline to accept your offer. I have my duty to attend to'.

The stilted character of the conversation did not prevent the story from causing an enormous flap in the Castle. The lord lieutenant himself was on to them, asking what was being done. The exclusive was quickly exposed as a hoax, being followed by a letter, purporting to come from the author, stating as much.

The *Freeman's Journal*, whether taken in itself or not, in irritation suggested it had been forced into its own investigation by the incompetence of the civil authorities:

'Up to the present moment, no real capture has been made. The policemen have run their heads against brick walls and have made arrant fools of themselves on account of their endeavouring to save their honour and to give satisfaction to their superior officers', the paper harangued – without a trace of irony.

'They have set the hearts of unfortunate car drivers, publicans, lodging-house keepers and all who may have worn billycock hats or jerry hats, palpitating, ready to burst in, on account of the examination to which they have subjected them, and all to no purpose'.

Nature and newspapers abhor a vacuum, but Mallon and the various English police emissaries had to do their best to ignore the pressure besetting them on all sides. The superintendent of detectives admitted: 'Failing assistance from the persons who were in the park, I had to work on private information'.

He later boasted that by the week following the murders he had been told the names of four of those later convicted of the crime, and the surname of another perpetrator. But his informants were also conjuring every name in existing Castle files and many another besides.

The police did not know that they had traced the escape back to the city based on very unreliable sightings for the latter part of the journey. It could not be 'fairly assumed' that the trace to Cork Street was to be relied upon, as Mallon thought. The car and assassins had instead gone to Terenure and returned to the city another way.

Nonetheless, it is a quirk of fate that the supposedly last verified sighting of the car got Mallon thinking along accurate lines. Concentrating on the Cork Street clue, Mallon developed a theory about one of its native sons, a prominent nationalist named James Carey.

'Carey is a native of the locality, and several of his confederates reside there', wrote Mallon in one of his reports. 'An informer told me in November 1880 that Carey was head of the Vigilance Committee belonging to that neighbourhood'. It was also believed that he had also been involved in the abortive Fenian rising of 1867.

His being a Fenian naturally clashed with the detective's averred doubt that the Fenians were involved. Yet Mallon was capable of maintaining multiples strands of thought, even if some were contradictory. A policeman must keep an open mind.

Developing his theme, Mallon mused about Carey's employment at 'one or two dispensaries' and in the School of Medicine in Peter Street. He could therefore 'have procured the knives'.

Mallon observed: 'He was a pushing fellow and could get hints on anatomy. It was the opinion of the surgeons engaged in the post mortem that the person who inflicted the wounds knew something of anatomy'. Just six years later, in 1888, the same sort of conjecture featured prominently in the baffling crimes of Jack the Ripper.

This line of thinking might only illustrate the nebulous nature of the swirling allegations, which whispered on the wind the names of a legion of suspects. The dispensaries, school of medicine, College of Surgeons and city hospitals were missing no knives. Mallon had Carey watched in any case, but only when someone could be spared for surveillance.

It was all a question of resources. Orders had come down that no line of investigation was to be overlooked for fear of the possible cost. Money for underworld information and the cultivation of possible informers would be provided without stint. Police overtime was available to all units, even if the miserable of pay rate was not to be improved.

Mallon's chief shortage was of bodies and brains. The authorities had dictated the kind of blanket coverage that spread resources far too thinly. Not only were all the ports being watched day and night, but so too were coaching halts and every single railway station in the entire country.

It was only on 16 June that a senior officer in the Dublin Metropolitan area asked for a relaxation of the watch at intermediate stops between main railway stations. Ten days earlier had come a plea for the easing of the intensity of police enquiries in all areas, 'owing to the great strain put upon the force in protecting judges, official authorities etc.'

Six days after the double murder the inspector general of the Royal Irish Constabulary had directed that each sub-inspector relieve from duty and set apart for the Phoenix Park assassinations investigation 'two of the most intelligent men at each of the stations in his district'.

The RIC's jurisdiction consisted of all areas not falling under the aegis of the Dublin Metropolitan Police, with the most intense focus of investigation naturally occurring within the capital. By 6

June, a senior RIC officer wrote: 'I would take the liberty of suggesting that only one intelligent man at each of the [police] stations mentioned be in future employed' on the special inquiry.

Dublin Castle itself was anxious to have as many detectives as possible on the streets, but it was still being bombarded with letters filled with all manner of 'private information'. Most annoying of all must have been those cloak-and-dagger anonymous informants who asked for police responses to be given them through the codeword 'Alpha' or 'Y' in the classified advertising sections of the London *Times*. While extra civil servants were seconded to the Castle to act as readers of this material, many detectives felt that the sheer scale of the data-logging was virtually defeating itself. Master ledgers were opened for information and witness statements relating to the scene of the crime, descriptions of horses, cars, drivers and passengers, and for suspect individuals and their movements.

But the reality was that not enough cross-checking or referencing could be done in a paper-based system to enable the collating or retrieval of material that seemed to fit together. It was thus impossible to see the woods for the trees, not to mention the reams of paper.

Mallon had to rely on human intelligence first, and let the corroborative detail come later. He was frustrated that there were still massive demands on police man-hours in the effort to prevent the perpetrators from leaving Ireland when they had so clearly already gone to ground.

The effort, in this respect, went beyond a coastal cordon into the realms of the ridiculous. It might have impressed the man who suggested that the police use boats to scout out Fenians in caves, for instance, to learn that the law had graduated to ocean-going steamships.

Dublin Castle not only carefully checked all departing passengers, but also despatched spies on every mail boat sailing from Dublin in order to listen to gossip in the saloons, hopeful that distance from shore might loosen the tongues of escaping emigrants.

They also sent agents on transatlantic voyages from Queenstown when particular advance tip-offs, no matter how unlikely, were received.

One drunk promised to send money back from the United States to have a series of Dublin Castle agents assassinated. 'He was cheered by the passengers', the solemn surveillance report records.

Constable Denis Ryan reported on 26 May: 'I beg to state that in compliance with instructions, I proceeded on 22nd inst to Liverpool via Dundalk. I placed myself in conversation with a number of emigrants who were en route for America and who expressed themselves thus – that they were not to be bribed by the Castle money.

'While on board during the night I heard several of them to say that it was well known to many on board who murdered Lord Cavendish and Mr Burke. I also heard many of them denouncing secret societies, that it was too open a thing, that the Castle spies got into their secrets by giving drink and money. But now they had a new plan and it was doing well.

'Naturally I did all I could to discover this scheme, but failed to make anything of it'.

Perhaps the policeman's clumsy methods had given him away and the emigrants were enjoying themselves at his expense. But they were going to enjoy themselves in the saloons in any case, as constable James Howard illustrated from his separate sailing: 'Another man recited some verses, putting in the words Gladstone, Buckshot, Parnell and Davitt. I could not catch the verses as there was great cheering and shouting of 'To hell with them and the Government' every time Gladstone and Buckshot were mentioned'.

Assistant constable John Flaherty begged to state that he proceeded on duty on board the steamer *Windsor* from North Wall to Liverpool. There were about sixty emigrant passengers on board and five or six cattle drovers and he and a colleague conversed and mixed with them.

'One emigrant named Patrick Duignan from Co. Roscommon, who was under the influence of drink, addressed the passengers at intervals during the night. He denounced Buckshot Forster and the Irish tyrant landlords.

'He also said this was his last promise to his friends when leaving, to send home from the lands of liberty 100 dollars to have Buckshot and all his bloody officials and spies shot down. That he would do it if spared, and it was the duty of every Irishman to do the same.' The passengers received Duignan's sayings with cheers.

One could imagine pairs of police officers quite enjoying this line of duty, even if all it produced was bar talk and tired constables. It might have better suited the short-handed Mallon if the British had instead listened to a man named Spong.

He had written to Gladstone on 12 May, urging that Ireland itself be quarantined, with a ban on travel between districts and a ban on travel to and from the country.

Amid a series of planned searches and raids around the country, one at Maynooth College and seminary produced much criticism. The Castle had been receiving many anonymous notes stating that the murder car had driven there and was still secreted in the grounds.

A large force of police descended on the college and swept through its buildings and outhouses, despite the protests and remonstrations of the reverend fathers. But it quickly became clear that the letter-writing campaign against the college was entirely groundless.

Suspicion for the 'malicious motive' fell on one Patrick Maguire, who had been dismissed from his post as a house steward for drunkenness eight or so months before. Maguire had sent a solicitor's letter to the bursar, Rev. H. B. Somerville over his sacking.

Detectives obtained the original handwritten job application from Maguire, dated May 1881, and discovered similar handwriting to the anonymous tip-offs. Ironically, Maguire had written: 'If appointed I shall do every thing in my power to give entire satisfaction'.

Allegations of any sort could not be dismissed, given the enormity of the crime. Nor was the time wasting confined to Ireland.

One prisoner in Liverpool jail implicated another inmate in the crime following his own release..

Joseph Dickson, jailed for failing to pay a fine, identified as a conspirator an Irishman named John Ryan, who was serving a month in jail for the unpromising crime of stealing a pitchfork.

Dickson told of a conversation they had struck up in prison, when he had opined that the Phoenix Park killers would never be caught, and that they were probably Irish-Americans. Ryan had replied: 'Nothing of the sort. They are all Irishmen, and not one of them has left the country'.

The pitchfork thief then went on to 'reveal' that two of them were publicans in Dublin, one a farmer in Waterford, and two others farmers in Tipperary. He claimed the assassins had changed their clothes in Moore's pub, near St Stephen's Green, burning what they had been wearing in the back yard of the premises. It was all hogwash.

American police meanwhile were fruitlessly meeting all Atlantic steamers, scanning faces and documents in accordance with an earnest request from the British government. Monies had been advanced by London for the suborning of informants within the Irish Republican Brotherhood, and finding the results discouraging, the government had even turned to the famed Pinkerton detective agency.

William Knight of Smithfield Street, Birmingham, wrote to Prime Minister Gladstone after reading of the 'strange tales given by the two bicyclists (one of them actually stating that he had to turn his machine out of the way of the murderers)' which had 'caused the idea in my mind that they were either the assassins or participants in the crime'.

Suspecting witnesses was nothing new, but this particular delusion was passed on from Downing Street to Dublin and can hardly have increased Mallon's already low opinion of the statements of Meagle and Fry.

The sensations kept on coming. An Irishman walked into the office of the British consul in Puerto Cabello, Venezuela and confessed that he was one of the assassins of Lord Frederick Cavendish and Mr Burke. He gave the name of several accomplices. The man was promptly arrested, the foreign office in London excitedly alerted, and the prisoner sent under heavy escort to Caracas.

The confessor said his real name was Michael O'Brien and he had sailed from Swansea to South America under the name of William Westgate. He was conscience-stricken, having committed the murders for monetary consideration, and deeply repented his act.

O'Brien asserted in his deposition to the consul that he was employed by influential persons. 'His statement is that the price of the deed was £20, paid to each assassin, and he says that £20 is worth more to an Irishman than an Englishman's life', the Press Association reported.

This heady cocktail from the other side of the world briefly excited the newspapers. The *Western Mail* reported that a man giving the name of Westgate had indeed joined the sailing vessel *Gladstone*, 297 tons, at Swansea in May, shipping as a 'pier-jumper'.

It discovered that he had lodged for two days at the Museum

Hotel, where the landlord described him as dark complexioned and close to six feet in height. O'Brien rarely went out and 'seemed to shun both conversation and company'.

He had disclosed that he was a native of Dublin, and the landlord's wife had taken pity on him since he was badly dressed. She supplied him with a suit of clothes, and now regretted having inadvertently helped to disguise him and to dispose of incriminating apparel.

But O'Brien's story was itself badly dressed up, and was disregarded by Dublin detectives as soon as they had sight of his deposition. Nonetheless, he was sent home in chains, via Jamaica, on board her majesty's ship *Fantôme*.

By that stage however, Superintendent Mallon had been hearing from another prisoner.

Solid Progress

James Mullett was a prominent publican. His premises, opposite the rival Brazen Head on Lower Bridge Street, Dublin, was a known den of disloyalty. Mullett had been lodged in Kilmainham Jail since 4 March in connection with the murder of a police informer named Bernard Bailey.

Bailey had gone drinking in Macken's pub in High Street one Saturday night (25 February 1882) in order to 'get a few shillings' from a person he was to meet there, according to his wife. Towards 11 o'clock, a police constable passing through Cook Street in the city heard groans coming from a place called Skipper's Alley.

He found Bailey lying unconscious on his back, bleeding profusely from bullet wounds in the head. Removed to Jervis Street hospital, resident surgeon Dr Chance pronounced life to be extinct.

The deceased was found to have two bullet wounds in the head, one ball entering on the left side of the neck, behind the ear, piercing the brain. The other struck on the right cheek, 'shattering the jawbone and greatly disfiguring the face'.

The newspapers immediately linked Bailey, a forty-five-year-old with his own bacon-curing business, with passing information that had led police to a 'Fenian magazine' in Brabazon Street and Cross Kevin Street the previous December.

Commenting on his murder, the *Times* reported: 'It is strange that a tragedy of this nature could have been enacted in the midst of a densely populated centre without the neighbours hearing something of it'.

Bailey had lived with his family in a house in Francis Street which also provided the lodgings of two brothers named Whelan with whom he had previously quarrelled.

They gave him a heavy beating of that occasion, 'and on the police refusing to intervene, he threatened to be revenged'. Immediately afterwards Bailey informed the police that arms were concealed at a storehouse owned by the Whelans in Brabazon Street.

Police Inspector Marshall and his men raided the premises that same night and took possession of a quantity of arms, ammunition and dynamite, including a dozen hand grenades. Also found was a book with entries relating to the arms and affairs of the Fenian organisation, mentioning Mullett the publican.

Since December, Bailey had been under police protection, but at his own request it was withdrawn after two months – a week before his killing.

The Whelan brothers had been arrested and returned for trial on a charge of treason, yet the authorities had been obliged to abandon the case and release the prisoners. They were re-arrested on Bailey's murder, while Mullett joined them in Kilmainham under emergency powers legislation by dint of his mention in the seized papers.

A reward of £500 was offered for information leading to a conviction in the Bailey murder, or a sum of £400 and a free pardon to anyone involved who confessed all they knew and was not the actual killer. This touting for information alarmed Mullett in particular. The thirty-five-year-old publican vigorously protested his innocence of any involvement, not knowing that he had been separately named as a Fenian plotter by an informer named William Lamie. A valuable asset to Dublin Castle, Lamie had given details of the secret society branch to which he belonged, citing Mullett as a leading light.

Now, many weeks after his incarceration, Mullett wanted out of jail. No charges had ever been brought against him, but his business was suffering and there was a danger the banks would foreclose over loan repayments that he had not met. He asked to see John Mallon.

Mullett's proposed deal was uncomplicated: he swore that he had nothing to do with the Bailey killing and wanted to be released. In return he would tell what he knew or had heard in relation to a plan to assassinate the under secretary. But his co-operation was to be kept secret, and no bribe on earth would make him give evidence in court.

It was now 29 June. Mallon listened as Mullett cited James Carey, Daniel Curley, Lawrence Rinkell and a car man named Fitzharris as the principals in the bloodletting in the Phoenix Park. Mallon considered the information significant, even though Mullett had been behind bars for two months before the assassinations.

He acceded to Mullett's release, realising that he had little evidence in any case with which to connect him to Bailey's demise.

Surveillance, previously very loose, intensified on Carey. Here was a man who had originally been a bricklayer but was now a prosperous builder, engaging many workers on his own account. Carey's friend Daniel Curley, also named by Mullett, was a carpenter ten years younger, and the pair had often worked the same jobs. Curley was godfather to Carey's child.

Superintendent Mallon wrote in August: 'Carey and Curley were always moving about with workmen and their movements on the sixth of May could not be fixed'. Yet his own prior suspicions of Carey had now been reinforced.

James Carey was more than respectable. A landlord operating twelve houses in Dublin – serving no fewer than eighty individual tenants – he was clearly a go-ahead individual, even if most of the properties were on long-term leases for which he had to pay the head rent.

Not just energetic in the private sphere, forty-five-year-old Carey was active in the community, leading a campaign to stop a Scottish contractor getting the job of overhauling the Dublin city sewage system instead of Irish workers. He was also prominent in the Home Manufacture Association, which had recently passed a resolution condemning the murders. And he was a diligent member of a eucharistic sodality of the Catholic Church.

Yet Mallon had an abundance of material suggesting Carey was a strong-arm enforcer in Fenian circles. Some of the suspect's more dubious skills had been forged in campaigning for the Home Government Association in a bitterly contested election in Dublin in 1870, but he had also developed a talent for oratory. It was clear that Carey would easily be able to harness a body of men to do his bidding.

The other persons named by Mullett were of little importance and Mallon was always wary of being gulled into misconception. The car driver named by the prisoner was fifty years old, whereas witnesses thought the driver of the killers from the park was a much younger man.

On 15 June the deputy head constable at G Division, Isaiah Dale, told Mallon that he had obtained intelligence that 'a man named Kavanagh owned the car in which the assassins escaped'.

This Kavanagh would closer fit the bill, being twenty-three. But there was nothing to link him with Curley or Carey or any known nationalist sympathisers, and Mallon later wrote to London: 'I think suspicion rests upon Michael Kavanagh [only] because he has been in America'. He had no car or horse like the one described, he emphasised.

Mallon was inclined to treat all names suggested as that of the getaway driver with the greatest doubt. He thus mistrusted both Mullet's nomination of Fitzharris and Dale's of Kavanagh, just as

Assassinated: Lord Frederick Cavendish [left] and Thomas Henry Burke [right]

The body of Lord Frederick arriving at Dr Steevens' Hospital, 6 May 1882 [below]

Fanciful French magazine drawing of the assassinations [top]

1882 photo of the actual scene [below left]; and the tie Cavendish wore [right]

Chief Secretary's Lodge.
Phœnix Park.
Dublin.

May. 7th 1882

Post mortem Examination on the body of Lord Frederick Cavendish –

Clothes

Coat Cut on Centre of back of Coat
Cut 4 Inches long over right Shoulder
2 Cuts on left forearm of Coat
3 Cuts on right side about Six inch
below Axilla

Trowsers Cover'd with mud particularly
Knees & covered with quantity of
blood on right side & back

Waistcoat Cut on back of collar
right side

Notes on the post mortem carried out at the chief secretary's lodge [top]

Park Ranger George Godden [left] and Detective Superintendent John Mallon [right]

A PROCLAMATION.

By the Lord Lieutenant General and General Governor of Ireland.

SPENCER.

WHEREAS Lord *Frederick Charles Cavendish*, the Chief Secretary, and *Thomas Henry Burke*, Esquire, the Under Secretary, to the Lord Lieutenant of Ireland, were brutally murdered in the Phœnix Park, in the County of Dublin, on the Evening of Saturday, the 6th May, 1882:

AND WHEREAS four persons are believed to have been concerned in the actual perpetration of these murders:

NOW WE, JOHN POYNTZ, EARL SPENCER, Lord Lieutenant-General and General Governor of Ireland, for the better apprehending such persons and bringing them to justice, are pleased hereby to offer a REWARD of

TEN THOUSAND POUNDS

to any person or persons who, within Three Months from the date hereof, shall give such information as shall lead to the conviction of the murderers:

And a further Reward of

ONE THOUSAND POUNDS

for such *Private* Information, within the same time, as shall lead to the same result:

And We are also pleased hereby to offer to any person concerned in or privy to the murders (not being one of the actual perpetrators thereof), who shall, within the same time, give such information as shall lead to the conviction of the murderers, a

FREE PARDON

and the *Special Protection of the Crown* in any part of Her Majesty's Dominions.

DUBLIN CASTLE, 9th May, 1882.

DUBLIN: PRINTED BY FREDERICK PILKINGTON, 87, 88, & 89, ABBEY-STREET, PRINTER TO THE QUEEN'S MOST EXCELLENT MAJESTY.

Spencer's Proclamation – with a reward equivalent to millions today – was posted up all over Ireland. It held out an early promise of resettlement for anyone who turned queen's evidence.

Stephen and Sarah Hands were vital witnesses [top left] as was the lad Jacob who had been bird-nesting in the park [top right]

The Prime Minister

Prime Minister W. E. Gladstone is shown addressing the Commons about the murders [centre] and [below, to extreme left] attending the funeral of Lord Frederick Cavendish at Edensor

Royal Irish Constabulary Office,

Dublin Casile,

12 May 1882

The Inspector General
directs that the Sub-
Inspector will relieve
from all duty and
set apart for making
inquiries relative
to the Phoenix Park
assassination two
of the most intelligent
men at each of the
stations in his district
which adjoin the
D. M. Police District

Cyclists Thomas Foley [top left] and Patrick Maguire [middle] were key witnesses. General order calling for 'intelligent' RIC men to probe the killings [top right]. John Fitzsimons [below left] found in his landlord's loft the knives demonstrated in court by Inspector James Smith [below right].

The assassination car [top left] which Alice Carroll [top right] saw being used in a separate attack on juror Denis Field [circled]. It happened [below left] outside Field's house in North Frederick Street [below right].

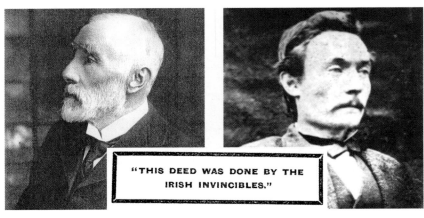

"THIS DEED WAS DONE BY THE IRISH INVINCIBLES."

John Adye Curran [top left] whose inquiry unlocked the plot of Joseph Mullett [right] and others. [Inset] Card left at newspaper offices, and a telegram to a Scotland Yard chief telling of the murders [centre]. Dublin's cab drivers protested the stigma of suspicion [below].

he did that of other candidates, such as Laurence Farrell, Tom Lyng and James Greeve.

One hackney driver named Nicholas Gorman was carefully investigated after reports that he had driven two gentlemen to the polo grounds on 6 May. It was established that his passengers were commercial travellers, whom Gorman had then taken to the North Star Hotel in Amiens Street. In any case, it appeared that he had left the park soon after six o'clock.

Thus Mallon was telling London as late as October in relation to Kavanagh and Gorman: 'Neither of these two car men would answer the description'. Yet one of them would eventually prove to be an ace in his hand.

On American Independence Day, 4 July, the superintendent of detectives suffered something of a personal blow. He learned that one of his leading subversive contacts, John Kenny, the man he had been due to meet at the rear of the viceregal lodge on the day of the park killings, had been savagely done to death.

The killing of Kenny happened at about 12.30 a.m. An altercation was heard in Seville Place in the northeast inner city, near the arches under the Great Northern Railway. One passer-by heard a sound like the stroke of a stick and a voice exclaiming: 'Oh don't! Ah don't!'

Immediately afterwards firearms were discharged 'two or three times'. Two citizens named Edward Ennis and Patrick Egan who lived in the neighbourhood, hearing the shots, ran down to the scene from nearby Amiens Street.

They found a man on his hands and knees. Kenny was unable to speak and was breathing laboriously. Leaving him in the charge of some new arrivals, the two men ran to Summerhill police station and reported the incident. All available constables at once hastened to the place, but Kenny was dead by the time they arrived. His body was removed to Jervis Street hospital.

The victim was a strongly built man, a little taller than average, obviously a labourer and rather poorly dressed. The holes made by bullets were easily discernible in his coat, according to police notes. He had also been wounded with a knife.

Kenny was wearing an old leather belt, with a brass buckle on it inscribed with the words 'God Save Ireland' and a harp. The initials A, L and O'B (Allen, Larkin and O'Brien, the Manchester Martyrs) were also engraved on it.

There were four bullet wounds in all, on the left shoulder and in the back of the head, and no fewer than seven puncture wounds on the left side and in the region of the heart.

The deceased was identified by his wife Sarah in the hospital mortuary the next morning. She told police that a tailor named Joe Poole had taken some whiskey with her husband on the night he died, and did so at their house in Cannon Place, off Oriel Street – about a stone's throw from the scene of the murder.

The men then went out together and her husband did not return. She would have to bring up their two children, a girl of eight years and an infant of five months, alone.

Large numbers of sightseers were at the scene of the tragedy the following morning, reported the newspapers, which did not hesitate to name Kenny as an informer. 'It is stated that the deceased was fired at two years ago on Burgh Quay, and that the attack then was made on him in consequence of there having been a suspicion of his having informed the police of some Fenian movements'.

A carpenter's gouge, with initials engraved on the handle, had been found at the scene of the murder. The seven puncture wounds around the heart were believed to have been inflicted with this instrument.

The victim, a docker, had certainly been singled out because of his secret work for the police. Something – perhaps the long accumulation of circumstantial evidence – had finally sealed his fate. Mallon knew that Kenny had recently been instrumental in supplying the details of some hidden weaponry.

The haul was pitifully small, and now Mallon wondered whether it hadn't been bait in a trap – the whereabouts of the material supplied to Kenny to see what happened.

A day or two later Mrs Sarah Kenny arrived back from burying her husband in Glasnevin to find three men sitting in her kitchen. They began to intimidate her, but she ran out into the street screaming for the police. She was later attacked, struck on the head with a candlestick, and denounced as an informer.

Ironically, John Kenny had been anxious to leave for England but was refused in his request for the financial aid necessary to do so, the House of Commons heard later. Mr Trevelyan, the new chief secretary for Ireland, told MPs that careful steps had now been taken for the protection of Mrs Kenny and her children.

Kenny did his police handler one last favour however. His killing gave Mallon the flimsy grounds on which to arrest Daniel Curley as a 'suspect', hopeful that the latter could provide a route to Carey. Curley would have to be carefully groomed, but perhaps it was possible.

The day after Kenny's death, Mallon ordered the apprehension of Daniel Curley, Thomas Caffrey and Joseph Poole, the latter two identified as having been drinking with the unfortunate Kenny on the evening of his death. Poole would later hang for the murder of Mallon's tout. Curley and the others were added to the swelling numbers of suspects lodged in Kilmainham Jail. 'Dapper Dan' made an unlikely prisoner, being well-spoken, well-dressed, and altogether too well-educated to be mixed up in murder.

Aged thirty-five, Curley kissed his wife Jane and explained to his children: 'These men have made a mistake. I shall be home soon', when arrested in the early morning. Taken away, he laughed richly when told he was believed to have played a part in the murder of John Kenny. He said he knew no such person and could prove he had been nowhere near Seville Place that night.

Curley was visited by his friend James Carey on his second day in jail. As Carey left Kilmainham, he was approached by police and told that he too was under arrest for the very same killings under the 'suspect' provisions of the Protection of Life and Property Act. Carey was apoplectic. He tried to fling off the hands laid upon him, told them not to be ridiculous. He was a respectable tradesman, he insisted, trying to walk on. He struggled as they grabbed him, hit out angrily, and had to be carried away bodily.

Prior to his arrest, a day or two after Kenny was shot, Carey was said to have remarked to a fellow nationalist: 'It would be a terrible thing to be shot as a traitor and to be really innocent; it is not so much the loss of life as the stain and degradation on your memory. And then, think of the infamous name which would be attached to your children and their posterity. It is too horrible to think of'.

Mallon may have hoped to impress Curley with Carey's arrest, to have sown seeds in the younger man's mind of how he might free himself from being drawn into a whirlpool of official revenge for the death of Kenny.

The superintendent was still pursuing his hope of a break-through in the Phoenix Park case, despite the loss of a key under-world asset. He would be content to let the men stew for a few weeks before considering his line of approach.

But on 29 July came a dramatic development that required no direct instigation. Mallon minuted the sensational breakthrough: 'I received information that Carey had the knives with which the murders were committed concealed in a house'.

A few days after Carey's imprisonment, one of his tenants, John Fitzsimons, who had noticed the landlord making secret visits to a loft in his tenement house in South Cumberland Street, decided to investigate what he had been doing.

Taking a table and chair – where Carey had always used a ladder to reach the loft and 'carry out repairs' – the old man hauled himself up into the same spot to satisfy his curiosity. He poked around and soon discovered, under a heap of rubbish, two surgical knives and a very fine and expensive rifle. Excited and alarmed at what the discovery might mean, Fitzsimons removed the weapons to a 'more convenient location' in the loft.

A fortnight went by while he considered what to do, turning over the temptations of reward in his mind. Then, on Saturday evening, 29 July, Mrs Carey and her son Peter came to the place with a stranger and a ladder. The stranger and the boy went up into the loft, the woman remaining below. After a while they descended, and the whole party went away.

Fitzsimons made up his mind immediately. He contacted the police. At 11 o'clock that night, Inspector James Smith and a constable from the Exchange Street station went to the house and found the two transfixing knives and a Winchester repeating rifle.

Mallon was elated when told of the discovery. The knives glittered brilliantly when produced to him, one from a case and the other from a sheath 'made by an amateur, likely for an illegal purpose, certainly not for professional use'.

He immediately saw that the knives were a model for the Phoenix Park killings – 'just the class of weapons that would inflict the wounds – long, extremely sharp, and nearly the same width'.

It was a bonus that they bore on their handles the maker's name – that of Weiss & Son, the famous cutlers of 62, the Strand, London. Enquiries would be started there once the weekend had passed.

Heartily congratulating Inspector Smith, a delighted Mallon ordered the weapons to be sent to Dr Cameron, the city analyst. There were stains that looked like they might be blood on one of the blades …

On the following Monday evening, the last day of July, Mrs Maggie Carey, her brother-in-law Peter Carey and his wife came to the house in South Cumberland Street. They asked Fitzsimons if the police had been there on Saturday night, as they had heard from another tenant. He confirmed that they had, but said he really didn't know anything more about it.

Events were moving at a quickening pace. Dr Cameron confirmed that the minute stains on one of the knife blades were blood, but all he could say was that it was the blood of a mammal, up to and including a human being.

The blades, eleven inches long, were seen by Dr Myles and Dr Porter. Both confirmed that the knives could have produced the injuries seen at post mortem. The weapons were surgical amputating knives, Dr Porter said.

At the shop of Weiss & Son, manufacturers of medical instruments, detectives were combing through recent sales records. It would prove a fruitless search, since the staff could remember no Irish person buying knives. It was further unlikely that any purchaser who was a member of an assassination conspiracy would have given a true name and address.

The investigation into the origin of the nine-shot Winchester rifle was doomed to a similar fate, although it was eventually linked by repute to a Fenian suspect named Larry Rinkell, now believed to have returned to the United States.

Mallon felt very close to the Phoenix Park conspirators. Carey was certainly involved. He arranged for his prime suspect, together with Curley and others, to be seen by his eyewitnesses from the evening of 6 May.

Lieutenant Greatrex, park ranger Godden and van driver Code, the latter nearly knocked down by the killers as they fled out the Chapelizod gate, were first shown pictures of the suspects. They failed to identify anyone.

Crestfallen, Mallon arranged for them to go to Kilmainham Jail to see the range of Fenian suspects without their knowledge. Still they could not positively pick out a single man, all of them completely different in any case to the original Godden descriptions.

Mallon was frustrated beyond bearing. James Carey had been seen by Fitzsimons at the loft where the weapons were hidden on the Monday after the Phoenix Park murders. Yet many other people had access to the same place, and the weapons were not found until Carey was nearly a month in jail. He would need a great deal more to solve the case.

Bungled Attacks

The summer waned and with it a sense of drift permeated the police investigation. Nothing very new came forward, and in any case the police had their own problems. Smouldering resentment over pay rates flared into an industrial grievance. RIC men walked off the job in Limerick, Cork and Kerry.

The revolt spread in early August, plaguing the Dublin metropolitan force. In addition to pay, there was also disharmony over entitlements to married quarters, as well rostering, pensions and subsistence rates. Although not so regularly expressed, there was a suspicion that the authorities held their constabularies in low regard, even though they were the front line troops against simmering discontent.

One circular agitated: 'Should the state of things continue and men receive only empty compliments on one side and abuse and odium on the other, they [the government] may expect to see us in a short time leaving our positions'.

By the end of the month, some 250 Dublin constables were summarily dismissed for abandoning their duty to hold a meeting. That sparked an immediate strike by thousands of their colleagues. Blackleg 'special constables' were rushed to work, but the situation was deteriorating by the hour. Soldiers took possession of Store Street and the other abandoned city stations.

On Saturday 2 September, the police power vacuum left Dublin at the mercy of a mob, whose members were 'by no means slow to avail themselves of the opportunity'. Despite the presence of numerous special constables, chiefly Orangemen, disorder reigned supreme for several hours.

'Stone throwing, charges up and down the street, robbery, assaults upon women – all the usual diversions of the town roughs were freely engaged in,' the press asserted. 'At last however a dangerous spirit took possession of the soldiers, who charged the mob with fixed bayonets, pursuing them into the by-streets and wounding several'.

The following night Dublin was quiet and the agitation subsided. The DMP men presented an apologetic address to the lord lieutenant. Earl Spencer, in his turn, was moved to carry out what was nominally called an inspection tour of the RIC depot within a scant distance of his official residence. He surveyed the living quarters, the mess rooms and the riding school, until he at length addressed the assembled men.

Spencer spoke glowingly of the past irreproachable and loyal character of the force, its members' courage and their devotion to duty. He announced an immediate disbursement of £180,000 to those in the ranks in light of certain hardships, and promised the issues they raised would be 'promptly and carefully considered'.

His excellency added that the government was currently considering the issue of increased pay. 'The address produced a most favourable impression', and he was heartily cheered. It was enough – the police resumed their work with new heart and Spencer was able to write to another civic body that had sent in its loyal address that the 'most strenuous efforts' were once more being made to apprehend the Phoenix Park murders. He added, however, that it was to be hoped the 'highest power' would guide and aid their efforts.

One prominent nationalist leader had been handed over by Britain that summer. The bronze statue of Daniel O'Connell that adorns Dublin city centre arrived from its foundry by the steamer *Lady Olive*. It was brought by cart from the North Wall to Sackville Street and placed in a hoarding to await the official unveiling. That night some local added a green flag.

The statue ceremony in mid-August was an occasion of festivity that did much to lighten the mood. Official anxieties that it might spark renewed 'patriotic' fervour were heightened by the leaking in one newspaper of an official circular to all police divisions which had asked for estimates on the numbers from all country areas likely to descend on the capital, and whether any known malcontents would be among them.

It all passed off peacefully. Further conducive to the public calm was the opening of the Irish Industrial Exhibition, seen as a showcase of the achievements of Britannia's sister. Five hundred Irishmen left London for the exhibition's opening, as well as 2,000 on boats chartered for Dublin from Liverpool and Manchester, and it was finally estimated that on the opening day some 7–8,000 'persons from Great Britain' were present.

In September, James Carey and Daniel Curley were released from Kilmainham Jail. So too were many of the other persons held in the wake of the Kenny killing. There was simply insufficient evidence to charge them with anything. They would be watched and shadowed, but the terms of their detention under the 'Suspects Act' had simply run out.

The courts, meanwhile, continued to apply the law remorselessly. Mr Justice Lawson created a little bit of history by opening the first Special Commission created under the anti-terror legislation rushed through the Commons in the wake of the assassinations.

Four defendants in a piece of violence in Kerry found their case moved to Dublin, where Judge Lawson looked on as no fewer than nineteen potential jurors were challenged by the prosecution and asked to stand out.

The *Freeman's Journal* opined: 'We are unwilling to credit the rumour that the court has resolved that juries exclusively or almost exclusively Protestant shall determine, in some cases the liberty, in others the lives, of the prisoners on trial.

'Yesterday in the capital case, just as on the previous day in the Whiteboy case, Catholic gentlemen of admitted respectability and position were asked to stand aside when they took the book to be sworn. The inference therefore is that they were shoved aside from their duties as jurors simply because they are Catholic'.

Packing of juries was nothing new but this seemed far more systematic, as if a revival of 'an odious, and it was hoped, outdated practice'. The London *Daily Telegraph* took another view, as historian Tom Corfe points out, through an editorial: 'We must, to convict murderers, secure by hook or crook, by law or challenge, metropolitan, Protestant and loyal juries'.

A clash was looming, and it came with the publication of a letter in the *Freeman* from William O'Brien, who happened to be staying in the Imperial Hotel in Dublin when the jury in the murder case of *Regina v. Hynes* was sequestered for the night.

'I was awakened from sleep shortly after midnight by the sounds of a drunken chorus, succeeded after a time by scuffling, rushing, coarse laughter and horseplay. Along the corridor on which my bedroom opens, a number of men were falling about the passage in a maudlin state of drunkenness, playing ribald jokes'.

The door of his bedroom was burst in, and a man plainly under the influence of drink stood there unsteadily, hiccupping: 'Hello, old fellow, all alone?'

O'Brien rang the bell to summon help and duly 'ascertained that these disorderly persons were jurors, and that the servants of the hotel had been in vain endeavouring to bring them to a sense of their own misconduct'.

Francis Hynes was convicted 'on very thin evidence' by this bibulous panel and sentenced to death. But the consequences of the letter's publication, bringing the jury system into disrepute, were serious indeed for the editor of the *Freeman's Journal*. Edmund Gray, a former lord mayor of the city and the serving high sheriff, was also a nationalist MP. Yet he was dragged up before Judge Lawson for alleged contempt of court.

Lawson told him that he believed the claimed antics at the Imperial Hotel were 'totally devoid of truth', adding firmly that it was 'a most respectable jury … the foreman said all were perfectly sober, and I believe him'.

William O'Brien: 'As writer of the letter, I wish –'

His lordship: 'Sit down, Sir'.

O'Brien: 'Do justice to Mr Gray'.

His lordship: 'Remove that man'.

The unwelcome guest was ejected from the courthouse, and although Gray now made several efforts to address the court, all were similarly stifled. He was sentenced to three months in prison and ordered to a pay a fine of £500 to her majesty the queen.

Thus a national newspaper editor was sent off to jail, escorted by a troop of Hussars. The meting out of such a severe punishment by an already disliked magistrate outraged many, such that 'detestation of the judge was the prevailing sentiment in all circles in Dublin'.

And so the Invincibles tried to kill him:

[*The Times*] Dublin 12 November

The sense of security for life in which the country generally was beginning to indulge, and the growing belief that crime and outrage were not merely suspended, but were disappearing altogether, has received a rude shock by the startling news which spread rapidly through the city that an attempt had been made last evening to assassinate Mr Justice Lawson.

Happily it was foiled by the prompt action of his escort, who felled the man to the ground when he was about to carry out his design …

Judge Lawson had left his home in Fitzwilliam Square to walk to a legal dinner. He was attended as usual by four men in plain clothes, each one armed, being two detectives and two army pensioners from a force of twenty-five organised after the Phoenix Park murders to assist in the protection of important persons.

The escort did not cluster about Lawson, but walked two in advance and two behind, on either side of the street. The judge hated this accompaniment, having insisted on being left alone as far as possible, and had previously deliberately given his protectors the slip. On this evening, he was too tired to care.

Pensioner McDonnell noted a man appearing to shadow them.

He crossed the street, approached him from behind, and lightly touched him on the arm – as if to dissuade him from any half-formed plan to verbally abuse his lordship. The man looked around at this citizen, whom he thought in league with his purpose. 'It's all right, you know me,' he confided.

The man hurried off, getting ahead of Lawson, but then he crossed, turned and began walking down again towards the judge, reaching into his coat.

McDonnell burst through, grabbed the fellow, shouted for help. The would-be assailant was grounded under a press of bodies, and a revolver forced away from his clothes.

The attack occurred at the junction of Nassau Street and Kildare Street. The judge, seeing the mêlée, took the opportunity of passing into the Kildare Street Club for a bracing drink. A crowd meanwhile collected, further excited by a claim that the prisoner's confederate had got upon a tramcar and escaped.

Asked his name in College Street police station, the suspect said it was Corrigan, but refused to give any more information. Finally he admitted his name was Patrick Delaney and that he was a house carpenter living in Cork Street. It was swiftly learned that he had served five years' penal servitude for firing at a constable while fleeing from a purse-snatch in 1869.

The recovered gun was new and had evidently been supplied to Delaney. His home was speedily searched that night, but only photographs 'of a patriotic character' were found. Nonetheless, Delaney's arrest was 'the pinhole by which the British hoped to brighten their vision' of wider matters.

The attempted assassination was obviously entirely of a piece with the Phoenix Park killings. The London *Times* said as much the next day: 'It is not a matter of surprise that the same fell spirit of malice which shed the blood of Lord F. Cavendish and Mr Burke should seek another victim in the ranks of the faithful servants of the Crown'.

That same day the lord lieutenant and Lady Spencer visited Judge Lawson to express their sympathy with him and their joy at his escape. Droves of detectives at this stage were already busy trying to glean everything they could about Delaney's habits and associates, while the prisoner was brutally railed at, cajoled, and threatened in a subterranean cell.

Mallon already knew much about his prize prisoner. In particular, he knew that Delaney had worked for James Carey in the construction of a dispensary in Peter Street. Delaney was a carpenter, and he lived at 123 Cork Street – the very street in which the police believed the escape vehicle from the park murders had last been sighted.

The superintendent felt sure Delaney could cough up the entire conspiracy. He would deploy every device of interrogation to ensure that he did. Mallon even visited the miscreant, reminding him that he had seen Delaney recently on the quay near the Guinness brewery.

Mallon had been a bit early in going to work on the morning of the encounter and two of his children were with him, en route to school. They toddled on either side, the smallest holding his hand.

'Why didn't you shoot me that morning,' Mallon tested the gunman.

'What do you mean, Mr Mallon?'

'You had a loaded revolver in your pocket and you were out

there to waylay me,' the detective chief provoked. 'What stopped you?'

Delaney glowered, wary of a trumped-up charge. Then defiance overcame his reticence: 'Ah, sure as God, Mr Mallon, I was afraid I might hurt one of the children and I wouldn't like to have that on my conscience'.

The superintendent laughed, as if trumped in turn. He now had real hope of progress.

Undeterred by the failure of the Lawson attack, the men of violence now turned their attention to taking revenge on the jury system. Their next targets were two Dublin men who had served on a panel in the trial of Connemara man Michael Walsh for the murder of an RIC constable, the case being moved to the capital for 'security' purposes.

The foreman of the jury, William Barrett, and another member, Denis Field, had been seen passing messages to and from the crown solicitor from time to time before the trial ended in the inevitable conviction. These were said to be 'perfectly innocuous' notes, but the nationalist newspapers made a great fuss about the apparently biddable board of Michael Walsh's supposed peers.

These paper-passing jurors were marked to die, but panel foreman Barrett escaped his fate by being out of Dublin on the appointed day.

But that still left Denis Field, who finished work as usual in his premises in Westmoreland Street on 27 November, leaving at a few minutes to six o'clock in order to walk up Sackville Street to his home in North Frederick Street.

When coming up to his residence he bent his head to unfasten the buttons of his coat. Field felt a hand placed on his right shoulder – and a muttered accusation. He looked up and saw a couple of men in front of him, and two others behind. Instantly he received two heavy blows on the back with a sharp instrument.

He fell on his back, crying out 'Murder! Murder!' and saw the forms tower above. Frequent blows came down at him – he warded some away. 'When he was prostrate, a blow was aimed at his heart.

He put up his arm, and the knife or sword cane went right through it'.

He seized a weapon, parried it with his umbrella. He next took a severe impact which cut through his jaw and sliced through his tongue. Another dagger delved into his left cheek, ferreting for a quick end to his life.

Field closed his eyes, waiting for the death wound as if dead already. A moment or two passed, and dimly through slits he saw his assailants looking at him as he lay powerless. One by one, they departed. He was fearfully mutilated, his life in peril.

But he was able to rise with difficulty and he crawled to his own door. He remembered a boy running up to him and handing him his hat …

The attackers got clear away, but they had not finished the job. Despite several major wounds and many more of a lesser character, no blood vessels or major organs had ruptured. Field was saved by prompt medical attention, having hovered for a time between life and death. He eventually made a near complete recovery.

This savage incident further shocked the citizenry. Jurors began absenting themselves in droves from the calling-over of the lists. Those who were empanelled now demanded police protection even in the courtroom.

George Jenkinson, the assistant under secretary in charge of crime wrote to the lord lieutenant: 'Are we to wait for the commission of another murder before we proceed against any of these assassins? Knowing what is going on, and what valuable lives are in danger, are we to content ourselves with collecting information?'

The odium attaching to an informer prevented many people from aiding the police, while many witnesses were simply terrified to come forward. In the first few days, witnesses to the Field incident seemed non-existent.

Mallon became 'humiliated and despondent', according to his friend Frederick Bussy, writing nearly thirty years later. 'Outrage after outrage was taking place on the very threshold of his sphere of duty and he was utterly powerless. He confessed to me that he was "ashamed and vexed", and at last he was constrained to take his courage in both hands'.

Mallon protested to Samuel Lee Anderson, the crown solicitor, that he had lost all hope of securing a witness – let alone a conspirator who would turn queen's evidence – unless the government consented to put the Star Chamber clause of the existing act into operation.

This meant employing Section 16 of the bill enacted immediately after the murders. A magistrate could open an inquiry into any crime and compel any witness to give evidence before him – without benefit of legal representation. Anyone who refused could be summarily jailed until they agreed to co-operate.

He asked Anderson to bring the proposition to the notice of Earl Spencer. An inquiry should be launched at least in relation to the Denis Field attack. The former crown solicitor went to the lord lieutenant who at once approved, but only in regard to the latest bloodletting.

Mallon was asked whom he wanted as his grand inquisitor. He answered with the name of his friend John Adye Curran. The hunt for the Phoenix Park murders was about to take a quantum leap.

Star Chamber

A few days after the attack on Field, Curran received orders from the lord lieutenant to open an inquiry into the attendant circumstances. He sat for the purpose in a small chamber in the lower yard of Dublin Castle.

'On my first entry into the room,' Curran later wrote, 'I found there a man from the Board of Works nailing down a carpet for my use. On his departure, Mr Boulger, whom I had brought with me from the police courts, and whom I found to be a most efficient officer, asked me if I had remarked the wicked scowl which the man laying the carpet had given me. I replied that I did not.

'I found out afterwards that he was a member of the Invincibles and was the man who pointed out Mr Burke to his murderers'.

During the ten days following the opening of the inquiry on 4 December, Curran engaged in examining witnesses in the presence of Superintendent Mallon. There were just three persons in the room at any time, plus an occasional stenographer.

Some of the witnesses called saw the men and the car waiting for Mr Field's arrival, while others saw the attack itself, and a third set saw the car hurrying away. All seemed co-operative, and 'anxious only that the truth should come out'. Among the witnesses was W. J. Connellan, who watched the vicious knifing of Mr Field and gave an accurate description of two men

An early prime source was Mary Brophy, a of Mrs Cosgrave, who kept a lodging house at wicke Street and North Frederick Street. O November, she was out on a message for her would-be murderers' car opposite the house i

The Servant who saw the struggle

She spoke to the car man before re-entering the house, and after the attack saw the assailants drive away, her attention having been drawn by the cries of 'Murder!' outside. She told Curran 'very distinctly and positively' that she would know the car driver again.

Mary added that the car man closely resembled a man of her acquaintance named Richard Phoenix, who lived in Raheny. Her questioners immediately wanted to locate Phoenix, in order that detectives might see if he resembled any man already suspected. But it was a fruitless search. It was discovered Phoenix had left the country.

Another portion of Mary Brophy's evidence sent the police on a false scent for ten days. She informed Curran that she had looked at the number on the car and thought it was 147. She was certain the first two numbers were one and four.

The authorities were on watch all over Ireland for parties disposing of outside cars, and on Wednesday 6 December they arrested three men who were selling three such vehicles in Athy, Co. Kildare, one of which appeared to have been recently painted.

The men were brought before Curran the following Saturday, having been bailed by magistrates. One of them, Adam Brannigan, was found to be the owner of an outside car numbered 1477.

Brannigan had pawned the car on 2 December with a Mr Delaney, a few days after the Field murder attempt, instead taking out another car that was in pawn. This combination of circumstances excited the police, but it was eventually proven to be a wild goose chase, the servant girl having utterly imagined the number. The actual attack vehicle was later established to have been numbered 521 – nothing like what Mary Brophy imagined.

On the day after the opening of the new inquiry, Mallon re-
 a letter from someone who claimed to be an eyewitness. He
 ly ordered it to be investigated:

December 4th 1882,

Sirs,

The only information I can give yous [*sic*] concerning the attempted assassination of Mr Field in North Frederick Street is as follows:

On the night of the 27th November I was passing along North Frederick Street on an errand to the post office when I heard some men talking about shooting, and I stood to see what were they going to do, at the same time seeing a car on the opposite side, facing Hardwicke Street.

I stood at Mr Irwin's coal office and watched them. One of them said 'pull over to this side, and round the corner with you, quick, for heaven's sake,' and the other said 'here he is' at the same time, one of them coming over and asking me what I was looking at.

I said I was looking at a bloody lot of robbers, when he followed me with a stick and said he would leave it on my back, so I ran down as far as Frederick Lane, when I returned to see the thing out, and in a moment the three men were mounted on the car, flying round Hardwicke Street.

I saw no more until the wounded gentleman was brought into his own residence, so I said nothing until I was told to tell the truth of it. I can fully identify the attempted murderers if I see them brought before me. I enclose this, not to be made publick. Direct your answer to Michael Farrell, No. 3 Hardwicke Place, to tell me when to see you.

I am, yours truly,
An eyewitness to this.

The eyewitness appeared on 8 December in the shape of Michael Farrell himself, the supposed intermediary. Farrell delighted Mallon and Curran by picking out a photograph of the car man he had seen. It was of Michael Kavanagh, one suspect for the Phoenix Park driver whom Mallon had earlier discounted, citing the fact that he had been in America as the origin of underworld gossip.

This was a major breakthrough – because Mary Brophy had also picked out Michael Kavanagh a few days earlier, only to blot her copybook with a car number that had nothing to do with him.

Kavanagh, a twenty-three-year-old with an address in Town-send Street, was now very firmly in the frame. Background checks turned up that he was a friend of Peter Carey, brother of the familiar James Carey, who had by now become a nationalist town councillor for Dublin in the November local government elections.

Kavanagh had also associated with Patrick Delaney – the man caught red handed with a revolver in the attack on Judge Lawson.

A few days after the Field attack, Constable Joseph Tanner, 161-D, was talking in Dorset Street with a young girl. The latter, seeing a car pass, remarked blithely: 'That's like the car that had the men on it that went to beat Mr Field'.

'Oh, you know something about it', Tanner said and immediately reported the expression to his superior officers. The girl was brought before Curran on the 5 December and gave her name as Alice Carroll.

'I found her a most important witness in the case,' wrote Curran later. 'In the main she was most accurate and gave me very valuable information. She was most reluctant, and on more than one occasion she refused point-blank to come before me. In the end I had to issue a warrant for her arrest and only succeeded in making her amenable by threatening to lock her up'.

Carroll also identified Kavanagh as the car man, and then she produced a new name - Joseph Brady. He had been present on the same occasion, she affirmed.

Joseph Brady knew her parents, as she knew his, she said. Carroll went on to reveal that Brady had noticed that she had recognised him that evening. She told how he afterwards met her, and by means of threats, induced her never to divulge her having seen him attack Mr Field.

This was sensational stuff. Carroll eventually broke down and confessed to having witnessed Brady wielding a knife on Denis Field.

Joe Brady was a twenty-six-year-old stonecutter from North

Anne Street, one of twenty-five children. He was a low-level Fenian suspect, having been noted in police files as a member of a discussion group at York Street, believed to be a front for nationalist hotheads.

Brady and Kavanagh were thus coming in the net, while the old tenant, Fitzsimons, had also identified Peter Carey as the man who appeared to be searching for the knives in South Cumberland Street after the arrest of his older brother.

Meanwhile a slim and fresh-faced young man named Timothy Kelly was being flagged as a close associate of Joe Brady. He was a twenty-year-old coachbuilder, from the Redmond's Hill area of the city.

Brady and Kelly were both members of the choir with the Franciscans in Church Street. They had met there and formed a strong friendship. Now Kelly was identified as being on the scene of the Field attack. The witness W. J. Connellan picked him out as one of the knifemen.

Alice Carroll helpfully added that she knew of a Tim Kelly, and agreed when brought to observe him that the face was that of the man she had seen with Joe Brady, her family friend, at the time of the attack.

Joe Brady was dramatically arrested at his workplace on 14 December. He was taken to Dublin Castle and brought before Mallon and Curran. Here he put up a show of defiance. His detention was uncalled for, as he had nothing to hide and had done nothing. Brady replied 'I disremember' to every question about where he was on the night of the attempt on the juror's life.

A sense of unease was however beginning to percolate among extreme nationalists as the police now began to turn up more and more interesting associations, hauling many individuals off to answer questions on the spot at the Star Chamber.

A watchful and distrustful group of men gathered at Wrenn's pub, opposite the Lower Castle Yard, to observe who went in. They knew that the task Mallon and Britain's other minions had set themselves was to induce an informer to come forward and give evidence that could hang the rest.

Mallon, meanwhile, was working hard out of their view. His game was to suggest to every new interviewee through the subtlety of his questioning and detail at his command that he was completely advised as to the methods and movements of the group that he was learning had styled themselves the 'Invincibles' – just as claimed on the cards dropped at newspaper offices in the wake of the Phoenix Park assassinations.

By this means – throwing every straw he had at every interviewee – he hoped to impress upon someone of the more highly placed of the Invincibles that the game was up, wrote his biographer, Bussy. He wanted to implant the conviction on everyone questioned that there was somebody else 'peaching', or telling all they knew, and that the safest course for all newcomers to the inquisition would be to 'vomit the whole wicked business'.

Becoming a government pensioner under an assumed name would be infinitely preferable to dangling at the end of a rope or suffering prolonged imprisonment, he intended to convey.

With the assistance of a simple 'Yes' or 'No' here and there as the mistrusted figures passed through, Mallon was able to piece together elements of the jigsaw which he hoped would later confound some more important member of the conspiracy.

Some care was therefore required in marshalling the suspects. One stratagem adopted was sandwiching the witnesses, one between another, 'so as to create alarm by the very sequencing in which they were called, and to come hot upon one fellow when his intimate associate had only just gone out by the another door and they had had no time to confer'.

It was felt that an atmosphere of doubt would begin to corrode the inner workings of the evildoers, as each man became racked with misgivings as to the loyalty of his confrères.

But their opponents were scornful. P. J. Tynan, a dyed-in-the-wool Invincible who escaped retribution by fleeing to America, later wrote:

'Any man in possession of the key to the revolutionary situation could readily understand from the questions put by Curran that the British were completely at sea. Dickens' gentleman who got the head of Charles the First into everything had a counterpart in that black-whiskered, sallow-faced inquisitor, for a priest, or one who passed as a priest, got into every other question put by him ...

'Inquisitor Curran was mixing up different and distinct undertakings ... but instead of unravelling the threads of what he termed a terrible conspiracy, he was confusing himself and puzzling those he questioned as to what he was really driving at ...'

Undoubtedly the Star Chamber was making mistakes and being uselessly sidetracked; yet it was also stumbling doggedly towards the truth and gaining ever more knowledge. Its opponents, on the other hand, found their position incrementally more exposed.

But they still celebrated when Joe Brady was released having being detained in prison for two nights.

The victim of the attack, finally out of hospital, came before the inquiry to detail the terrible mutilation to which he had been subjected. In the course of his evidence, Denis Field informed Curran that the man who had stabbed him in the back had called out as he did so, 'Ah, you villain!'

Curran goggled. 'I at once remembered that I had seen these words not long before in connection with some criminal matter or other. The real question was where, and what was the matter?'

He searched his memory, and that evening sifted through some files. 'On inspecting Mallon's report of 30th August, I read in it that a cyclist named Meagle told Mallon that while passing the scene of the Phoenix Park murder, he had heard one of the men attacked in what he considered a scuffle call out, 'Ah, you villain!'

'I thought it probable that Meagle was mistaken in attributing the words to the party attacked rather than the party attacking. I at once came to the conclusion that the men engaged in the attack on Mr Field were the same as those engaged in the murders in the park'.

They had been guessing as much, and Mallon admitted that this was little more than a clue, 'but to me it was a certain conclusion that it was one and the same gang that was responsible'.

He had a problem, however. His warrant only empowered him to inquire into the attack on Mr Field.

Curran promptly reported his views to Lord Spencer and asked him to extend his brief to include the murders in the park. According to Curran's later account, his excellency replied: 'I should be only too pleased to do so,' adding as he began to arrange the matter that he had 'long since given up hope of discovering the perpetrators or bringing home guilt to them'.

Robert Farrell was known to be a member of the 'literary society' held at 41 York Street, and for a long time before the special inquiry he remained as closely shut up as an oyster. 'Who was the Secretary of the club?' asked Mallon.

'Joe was the only name I ever heard him called by,' was the answer.

'Shall I put down that his other name was Brady?' suggested Mallon. 'Yes, you may as well,' acquiesced the witness, 'but remember it was not I who told you'.

One morning Farrell went early to chapel and took communion. Mallon had his eye on him and as soon as mass was over, invited him to another *tête-à-tête* with Mr Curran.

Farrell took the oath readily enough, and then Mallon proceeded to hammer home the information he wanted confirmed. From time to time, he reminded the young Catholic of the place he had just come from, and the sacrament that had rested upon his tongue. 'Farrell was a better Catholic than he was a conspirator,' recorded Curran, from whose account this tale is taken. 'He found it very difficult to lie that morning'. Mallon pumped remorselessly for information …

On 14 December 1882 the London *Times* was still of the opinion the men implicated in the Phoenix Park assassinations and the attack on Mr Field were enjoying an immunity from detection.

This only drew attention to the 'widespread complicity of large sections of the Irish people' in what appeared to be an organised war upon the law and its officers.

Three days later there was a distraction as the Venezuela man, Michael O'Brien, alias William Westgate, was finally brought up under warrant in Dublin. The newspapers commented that he appeared to be a man of very limited mental capacity, and noted that the police did not attach any importance to his statement as to the Phoenix Park murders. For one thing, he spoke of a revolver having been in the hands of one of the assassins, a claim 'at variance with the facts'.

'The police do not know whether to look upon him as an imbecile or as a knave, who became tired of his visits to foreign parts, and managed by inventing a story to get back again at the expense of the Government'.

It was revealed that on the day of the assassinations the prisoner was on board the vessel *Ibex*, which sailed from Dublin for Swansea in the afternoon. A number of persons on board that vessel – the captain, mate and others – testified to his working throughout the whole day.

The case came before Curran as police magistrate, and he swiftly ordered a discharge.

The next day the newspapers, evidently having asked what progress was being made, had a little to report about the 'secret inquiry' which was being held in the Lower Castle Yard before the same Mr Curran.

'Public curiosity is stimulated keenly with respect to it on account of the scrupulous reserve which is maintained by all concerned', said the *Times*, evidently not getting much useful information themselves. 'They are impressed with the absolute necessity for keeping strictly private all the information which is communicated to them'.

But it insisted: 'The investigation shows, more clearly than any that has yet been held, the value of the 16th Section of the Crimes

Act. It has placed a power in the hands of the Executive, which, if discreetly and firmly used, may enable them to shatter to pieces the secret organisation which has spread such alarm in the city'.

Witnesses were being questioned by the heads of the detective police with a 'searching keenness, which indicates a thorough acquaintance with their character and habits', the paper said. The investigation was demonstrating 'an amount of knowledge respecting the workings of their societies which appears to have taken some of them aback'.

But while the *Thunderer* believed that many important admissions had been elicited, it also conceived that 'more would be obtained if it were not for the difficulty experienced in endeavouring to remove from the minds of witnesses the belief that, having taken an oath of secrecy when joining the IRB, they are morally bound to honour it'.

It could not resist the sniffy observation that 'the deficiency of moral training among the class from which this secret organisation is chiefly recruited, the artisans and labourers of the city, is painfully evident'.

That same night, as an example of the efficacy of the forces of law and order, Dublin police detachments and supporting forces of marines engaged in simultaneous raids on seventeen public houses in various parts of the city.

It was hoped to shake up the 'revolutionary party'. About 600 people were searched for documents and arms, but only a few were found. Praise for the raids ('admirably planned') soon gave way to 'considerable surprise' that they had been so unfruitful, even though many of the pubs targeted were 'well known to be resorted to by disorderly characters'.

In one pub alone, 105 persons were searched, yet no arms or treasonable papers found. The *Times* thought this would be reassuring, 'were it not open to suspicion that some of the scouts of the secret societies got a warning of the intended movement. It is certainly strange that only two old swords and a revolver, which was found in the possession of a sailor, fell into the hands of the police'.

The crossing of swords at the inquiry would continue after Christmas.

Dublin Castle, seat of the investigation

Harvesting Invincibles

Perhaps disappointed at the poor return on the festive raids, the newspapers became more dubious about the Curran inquiry, successive interviewees having walked free, with Irish publications in particular starting to take the view that it was all a gigantic trawling exercise.

All prisoners detained at the pleasure of the inquiry were released over the season, but the investigators were far from empty-handed. Gleanings had been privately obtained from Patrick Delaney, whose trial for the Lawson attack had concluded in conviction before the holiday, with sentence deferred to the New Year.

Men of a similar outlook as the defendant had filtered regularly into court and been glad to learn that Delaney was saying nothing in public to implicate others. His story was that he had sought to molest the judge on the spur of the moment, a tale everyone knew to be a concoction.

Yet Delaney's confederates knew that the real pressure would begin on him as soon as he was returned to jail with the realisation of his plight while everyone else began to put up holly. Daniel Delaney, the convicted man's brother, was subjected to 'searching interrogation'. Like his sibling and Daniel Curley, James Carey's close friend, this suspect was a carpenter.

It seemed that particular trade was woodwormed with anarchists. Dan Delaney suffered five hours of interrogation at the inquiry one day, and six the next. There was a fear among the drinkers in Wrenn's pub that this in itself might be a none too subtle message to Patrick as to the fate his brother might share. And yet they knew, as Mallon and Curran merely conjectured, that Dan Delaney was an active Invincible.

Also interrogated were the heavily implicated Timothy Kelly and the previously helpful publican James Mullett, even if police intelligence indicated that the latter had gone back to treasonable ways having gained release over the Bailey killing. Both now said little. Curran, nonetheless, now hardly doubted that he had before him members of the Invincibles. 'In plain words I was engaged in fixing the rope around their necks. I was able to extract a little of the truth from each of them.

'When it came to the point of calling before me those whom I suspected of being the actual murderers my position was indeed one of extreme danger,' he wrote. Guards were doubled at the Castle. Captain Talbot promised Curran ample police protection, and in late December 1882 his personal escort was more than doubled.

The next morning Curran's wife, on leaving their house in Terenure, was startled to see a number of police patrolling the grounds. They would continue to do so, day and night, for many months. For nearly eight years to come Curran would be under constant police protection wherever he went.

Threats had already come in against both he and Mallon, but most were nebulous and could be easily ignored. Yet there was one sinister suggestion. One of the men examined before Curran, 'who denied everything, but who had at the same time unwittingly given me a good deal of information', told the magistrate he should be very cautious going home on the tram.

Curran was slightly unnerved. His residence, named Riversdale, was three or four hundred yards from the end of the tramline. It was arranged that police from the local station would meet Curran and his escort at the terminus and walk with them to the garrisoned house.

Similar security, on a less grandiose scale, was put in place for Mallon, who had little time however for Curran's privately voiced fears about the lack of powers of search when a suspect was summoned before him at the Castle.

'For my own safety,' wrote Curran, 'when engaged in examining, I took the precaution of keeping my right hand in the side pocket of my coat, and in it I held a revolver at full cock with my finger on the trigger'.

The case could still go one way or the other. The *Times* hoped for the best, protesting that the 'police believe they have obtained sufficient evidence to sustain a charge of conspiracy to commit the murder', but regretting in the same sentence that 'if a similar inquiry to that now going on had been held after the assassinations, when the facts were fresh and the persons likely to know about the crime were accessible, it is probable that a clue to the mystery might have been obtained; but the difficulty becomes greater in proportion to the length of time, which every day increases'.

London newspapers, far more than the Irish, were anxious to convey the notion that the conspirators were finding that the government had received 'accurate information as to their plans and doings from some traitors in the camp'. They further predicted that 'the growing distrust and apprehension which they betray will be likely to lead many of them to make a clean breast of it in order to save themselves'.

But it had still not happened by the year's end. Instead, there was another useless confession. An Irishman named Quinn was charged in London with being concerned in the Phoenix Park murders, having been brought to Bishopsgate police station five days after Christmas by two drinkers from a nearby pub, the *Black Raven*.

The prisoner hotly denied he knew anything at all about it, although evidence was given that he had bowed his head to confide significantly to other patrons: 'I was one of the four that drove up Sackville Street to the Phoenix Park, and I should be glad to do the same again'.

Quinn said he made the remarks because one of the drinkers who later made the citizen's arrest had given him sixpence, bought him a pencil and given him some beer. He could at least be entertaining in return. It transpired that the bar-boasting Quinn had not been back to Ireland in twenty years.

Finally, on New Year's Eve, a letter issued on behalf of Lord Spencer to a resident magistrate appeared emblematic of long months of diversion, drift and frustration:

Viceregal Lodge, December 31st, 1882

Dear Mr Blake

His excellency having noticed that some man was brought up before the magistrates for having used disrespectful language when he was passing through Monasterevin, desires me to say that he would be glad if you would give directions at once to the police to withdraw the charges.

His excellency does not wish that a prosecution should take place for an act which was quite unnoticed by him, and which does not in his opinion deserve any attention.

I am, yours faithfully,
Courtenay Boyle

Investigations that withered on the vine had been a feature of 1882, but they were to end with the year itself.

Wednesday, 3 January 1883, was a highly significant day, both in public and in private. The open spectacle was that of Patrick Delaney's sentence to ten years of penal servitude for the attempted assassination of Judge Lawson. One plotter had been put away.

But the secret development that day, much more important in its ramifications, was the approach of the rattled Catholic, Robert Farrell, to Inspector Thomas Kavanagh to tell him that as a result of his previous appearance before the inquiry he was sure someone had turned traitor and given information that had led to such searching questions.

Farrell did not realise that Curran had put many of his questions 'assuming all my suspected facts to have been proven'. In other words, he had fallen for what was partly, if not mostly, a bluff.

The twenty-four-year-old van driver now told the inspector that he did not intend to be left behind to rot in jail when others were turning informer. He then proceeded to make a full statement, which he signed, giving details of the conspiracy and the names of those engaged from time to time in carrying out its objects.

Farrell's story was that he was sworn in as a member of the Fenian organisation in early 1876. A little later, a man called Daniel Curley became the 'head centre' of his circle, and in June of that year Curley told him that there should be 'an inner confidential circle formed', saying it would consist of the cream of the society. The Invincibles in shadow.

Mallon brought the police statement to Curran, but warned him that Farrell was afraid to come before him a second time in the Castle, as all members of the 'gang' were carefully watched going in. It was arranged that Mallon would bring Farrell to Curran's fortress home late at night to swear a formal deposition.

From Farrell came the positive assertion that he had known Joe Brady as a member of the Fenians for five or six years. Brady was in the circle commanded by Curley as 'centre'. Tim Kelly was also a member of the inner group, and Farrell named a series of others, including the Delaney brothers. He promised to testify against them all.

Farrell said Daniel Curley had brought him into Curley's Mount Street home and told him that he was to be his right hand. A man need only know his recruiter or 'right hand' in a circle. He could in turn recruit someone else, who would be his left hand. Curley told him that the organisation's purpose was to watch what was going on at the Castle.

Farrell now told how he was part of a group summoned to Pembroke Quay on 27 March 1882, not being told why. Brady, Curley and Kelly were among the others there. He learned that the plan was to stop a carriage on its way to the viceregal lodge. The attempt had fizzled out, but it had involved a 'low-sized man named Rankle or Rinkle'.

This was Larry Rinkell who had fled to America, previously named by Mullett and associated with the Winchester repeating rifle found in James Carey's loft.

There had been a conspiracy to murder the former chief secretary, 'Buckshot' Forster, Farrell continued. A large group met in Brunswick Street (Pearse Street) for the purpose – including the two Delaneys, Daniel Curley, Joe Brady, Tim Kelly, and the freshly-elected Dublin town councillor, James Carey.

Pages of foolscap were taken up in recording all this striking material. Finally, Farrell came to address the 6 May murders in the park. He had been brought down to Wrenn's pub in Dame Street at lunchtime that Saturday by a man named Laurence Hanlon, a fellow conspirator, he confessed.

There he met the chorister and stonecutter Joe Brady. He was asked what time he would get off that evening and ventured 7 o'clock or half-past. Brady replied: 'That's too late; there is something to be done …'

Farrell's statements were wholly different to those he had given to Curran in December. At his Dublin Castle interrogation, Holy Communion notwithstanding, Farrell had sworn that he was not a member of the Fenian brotherhood. He stated that the only society to which he belonged was the Liverpool Burial Society.

He had sworn that the meetings in York Street may have been nationalist in character, but all they did was play draughts, gamble and read books. Mallon had asked then with a disbelieving sneer if anything else had been carried on there except dice and cards.

'I never observed it. And if I did observe it, I would not be there. I would be at home with my mother'.

Farrell was now sheepishly admitting that his earlier sworn replies had been often untrue. 'I did not want Mr Curran to know that I was a member of the Fenians at all'. Today he was telling the police of every Fenian he could remember.

On 11 January, Mallon brought Farrell to Curran's house as arranged. Before they left Farrell had sworn a deposition that he was left in no doubt would be used in court. It was dated 12 January, a Friday, for midnight had come and gone by the time its composition was completed.

Later that same Friday, Curran sought arrest warrants for some two dozen suspects. In the afternoon Mallon informed him that 'a very hot exchange of words' had just taken place between the attorney general and Mr Jenkinson, the assistant under secretary for police and crime.

Curran had to hurriedly meet the two gentlemen. The attorney general was 'fairly irate' that he had not been informed of the evidence that Curran had acquired. Jenkinson, on the other hand, contended that it was very unfair to force his hand just when he might produce a witness who 'could prove the whole case'.

The magistrate asked why Jenkinson's witness had not been sent before his special inquiry. He may have suspected it was all jealous bluster, and indeed he later did examine the witness 'but did not believe a word he swore'. Curran wrote in his memoirs that the man was afterwards charged with arson, committed in various parts of the county Dublin.

But this was a crisis. The attorney general and Mr Jenkinson were in direct disagreement as to the necessity for the immediate issue of the arrest warrants. The attorney agreed with Curran after getting over the injury to his pride, but Jenkinson still thought a round-up would be premature and could jeopardise the possibility of future convictions.

At last, the two senior officeholders agreed that Lord Spencer should rule upon the matter. This compromise suited Curran, who believed he had a good relationship with the final arbiter. The attorney general and crime secretary adjourned that same night to consult his excellency at the viceregal lodge.

They returned, after a distressingly long interval, with the answer. Lord Spencer's orders were that if Curran and Mallon thought they had a good case they were to act on their own discretion.

Later that night, with the aid and consent of the attorney general, Curran signed warrants for the arrest of every man whom he believed to be an Invincible in Dublin. There were twenty-one.

Orders were issued quickly to divisional headquarters across the metropolitan area. Large forces of DMP officers were alerted and told to come to their stations in plain clothes. Detachments of marines were readied at barracks north and south of the river. Spotters were sent out to the homes of the targets.

At 11 o'clock came the order to go. Police cordoned off streets, sealed off the rear of houses and then banged on front doors, accompanied by rifle-wielding soldiers. In the next three hours, officers and their armed support took fifteen of the wanted persons into custody.

In one case, twenty police surrounded a house, entered and arrested the suspect, and also 'took the beds to pieces, broke open closets, took up carpets, and roused all the inmates from their beds', the *Boston Herald* later reported.

Joseph Mullett, a clerk described as 'well dressed, low-sized and a hunchback' was arrested at his home at a quarter past eleven while entertaining some friends. Beside his bed, the police found a six-chamber loaded revolver, a military belt and a dagger. A large quantity of books and papers were seized as Mullett, no relation to publican James Mullett, was taken in, the dinner party abandoned.

As the men were led away, howling their protests, special squads stayed behind, ransacking homes for documents and anything that might resemble a weapon. Wives screeched about the invasion, whole tenements were roused, and children cowered in their beds, all ignored in the relentless sifting of every possession.

Robert Farrell was among those arrested 'at his own suggestion, and for his own safety'. At 22 North Anne Street, five marines took Joe Brady from his bed to answer a charge of conspiracy to murder high persons of government. His multiple brothers and sisters stood rooted in amazement as he was led away.

James Carey, town councillor, was in bed in Denzille Street when surprised at midnight by the news that a deputation below awaited his appearance. He rose, dressed, and came down spluttering about his rights, that he was a councillor of the people and this was nothing less than an attack on his electorate. Nonetheless, he accompanied his captors to College Street police station.

The most given in the way of resistance was remonstrations. By breakfast time that Saturday it was all over, with the majority of the targets under lock and key in Kilmainham Jail. The *Freeman's Journal* did well to get a few scraps of news into its edition for that day:

'Persons were brought to Green Street and other stations about three o'clock. Up to the hour of going to press (four o'clock) everything was still surrounded by impenetrable mystery. But it is positively stated that amongst those arrested is one who occupies the position of a representative of one of the municipal wards of the city'.

The swoops were under the immediate command of Mr Mallon, the same paper noted.

The coup was satisfying for the authorities. Those arrested were on Saturday afternoon brought in a black caravan, escorted by a dozen mounted police, before two police magistrates, George Keys and William Woodlock. Each was formally charged that he, 'together with certain other evil-disposed persons, did conspire, confederate, and agree to murder certain public officials'.

The prosecution offered no evidence except the sworn identification of the prisoners by police officers. The importance of the case was indicated by the presence of treasury law officer George Bolton and Fenian investigator Samuel Lee Anderson as prosecuting solicitors.

Also present in court were Detective Superintendent Mallon, Under Secretary Hamilton, and police chief Commissioner David Harrel.

The prisoners, by contrast, included three carpenters, brothers Joseph and Laurence Hanlon, and Daniel Delaney; two coach builders, Timothy Kelly and Peter Doyle; two tailors, John Dwyer and Henry Rowles; and a clerk, compositor, van driver, shoemaker, builder, bricklayer, blacksmith and stonemason.

Publican James Mullett had somehow escaped the net, only to be seen in the precincts of the courts at 10 o'clock that morning for some business on a licensing matter. He was promptly arrested and added to the crowd.

It was an amazing assortment, but the bench was told that they would all be connected to a secret society. Crown solicitor Bolton cautioned the bench that pending further arrests 'it would be prejudicial to the interests of justice to go into evidence against the parties named'.

Mr J. J. Walsh, who appeared on behalf of Timothy Kelly, said that it seemed that anybody in the community was at the mercy of any persons who chose to swear an unspecified allegation. Bail in his case was opposed on behalf of Acting Inspector Joseph Warmington.

Applications for bail were in every instance refused. Town councillor James Carey could contain himself no longer: 'I'll take an action for false imprisonment', he snapped.

He was ignored as the formal business of remanding the prisoners in custody was carried out. 'It is monstrous that persons should be kept away from their homes without a particle of evidence against them,' Carey yelled again. 'It's even worse than the Coercion Act!'

The magistrates were wrapping things up, telling the men that they were all remanded for a week on a charge of conspiracy. As they rose to leave, Carey complained loudly and bitterly: 'I think the conspiracy is on the bench'.

The prisoners were removed under heavy escort to Richmond

Jail. Another four prisoners were picked up over the remainder of that weekend. At five o'clock on Saturday afternoon Dapper Daniel Curley, the fourth carpenter, was arrested.

At half past one on Sunday afternoon the police arrested George Smith, twenty-two, a bricklayer, and Pat Whelan, twenty-eight, a clerk. Both joined the conspiracy charge sheet. Whelan had been arrested some months previously in connection with the seizure of arms in Brabazon Street.

Shortly after three o'clock that day, four constables of the detective department brought into court the twentieth prisoner to be arrested. He was Edward O'Brien, aged forty, a shoemaker.

By his status and actions in court, James Carey had established himself as the leading figure of the band of detainees. The *Freeman's Journal* now had no difficulty in naming him, saying that 'much surprise has been expressed at this particular arrest', and adding that for some time past Mr Carey 'took a most active part in municipal affairs, applying himself with great zeal to measures for the improvement of the sanitary condition of the city'.

Carey's arrest in 1882 on suspicion of being concerned in the 'Amiens Street outrage' (the July killing of informer John Kenny) won him a seat on Dublin corporation in elections held in November. He defeated a liberal incumbent who had held the seat for twenty years, standing against Henry Rochford because he had once opposed the Freedom of the City for Charles Stewart Parnell.

Trinity ward generated only 272 votes because of property-owning requirements. Carey took 124 of these, to ninety-three for another liberal named Samuel Nalty, with fifty-one for Rochford and four spoiled. The result had been widely hailed, *United Ireland* calling it 'the highest water-mark of democracy yet touched in Ireland'.

Carey, on reaching the street after the electoral declaration, had been 'vociferously applauded by his supporters. He then got on an outside car and returned thanks for the generous support and confidence placed in him'. He had undoubted force of personality.

Not only had his previous arrest helped his nationalist credentials, but also the fact that while in jail he had been placed in solitary confinement for several days for discharging a rocket in the prison yard to celebrate the release of Michael Davitt.

An incendiary character indeed.

Kilmainham Jail

Treason and Treachery

'The city of Dublin has again been startled by alarming symptoms of social peril', editorialised the next London *Times*. 'On this occasion, it is not a crime, but a counter-stroke against crime, which has agitated the Irish capital.

'It is satisfactory to see that when the Dublin detectives have a serious piece of work in hand, they do not allow themselves to be seduced into showing their cards in moments of rash confidence to curious or interested enquirers. Local and professional traffickers in news may grumble, but their complaints against the police need no refutation.

'Moral proof that a conspiracy using murderous methods and instruments exists in Dublin has been for some time complete, though of course it does not follow that even now the Executive is in possession of legal proof'.

The *Freeman* reported apprehension the night after the arrests that outrages would be committed on the Sunday night 'by persons in sympathy with the prisoners'. It told how the streets 'swarmed with marines', but the city was perfectly tranquil.

It wasn't entirely so. A police raid was made on Sunday night on four public houses and 100 persons were searched, but no arms were found. At the Dorset Street pub of James Mullett (one of four he owned) a mob hooted and jeered the police, while at a premises in Grafton Street onlookers merely hissed.

The Irish newspapers speculated cautiously in the week of remand. There was reason to be careful with Castle manoeuvres, no evidence having yet been adduced, and there had been a long list of failures. Even the *Times* hoped that the sweep would prove to have been 'based on solid grounds', and furthermore that the stroke would meet with the success that its 'boldness and completeness' deserved. But there were no guarantees.

'The Executive say they have ample evidence and have secured the worst crowd in Dublin. The inner circle of the other side seems little concerned and think that nothing will come of the arrests', wrote an American paper. But the *Evening Standard* reported that it would soon be shown in court that there was a plot at one time to destroy the viceroy and his escort 'by means of bombs thrown from unoccupied dwellings or houses in the course of construction'.

The *Boston Herald* reported that 'evidence is growing that Delaney is the traitor who is giving information. He has just been sentenced to ten years penal servitude and it is thought he hopes for pardon, and to emerge with reward'.

Another claim was that the arrests were 'a bluff to influence the Mallow election next week', in which nationalist William O'Brien was to soundly defeat Solicitor General John Naish. Different publications, in sometimes subtle ways, pandered to the prejudices of their readers.

Robert Farrell had named Daniel Curley as the chairman of the Executive of Four of the Irish Invincibles. He had been arrested as a suspect in the early part of 1882, but was discharged. Now that he was back in prison, the authorities sought to question him again. But the 'soft-spoken gentleman' was not one to offer any information at such a critical juncture.

After blandly answering some questions put in the course of an examination that week, Curley abruptly asked magistrate Curran how he could suspect him of such an atrocious crime as the Phoenix Park killings. 'I am a married man with a wife and children', he said, conjuring the image of an unblemished character. Curran replied curtly that his respectability remained to be seen.

But things were moving adroitly along. All the prisoners were ordered to be kept in separate cells in Kilmainham Jail in order to increase the pressure and tension on each man. Vestigial records show the jail urgently had to request more warders to maintain this policy. Mallon did not want any strength to emerge from a sense of unity.

On Saturday 20 January, Robert Farrell spilled his story in public. 'The day will long be remembered by the bulk of those who were in court,' reported the *Freeman's Journal*, 'on account of the squeezing to which their sides were subjected, if for no other reason'.

An hour and a half before the start, the experienced hands were sitting in their places in Green Street courthouse, having been forewarned by the sight of crowds of a few hundred penned at one end of the street until the prisoners' wagons arrived.

At 12.20 p.m., two vans swept into the prison courtyard with an escort of fifteen or twenty mounted police, both preceded and followed by ten or twelve cars bearing scores of armed police.

The gates were swiftly locked behind them. The crowd surged in anticipation.

'Those who were fleet of limb and not deficient in courage climbed almost to the second story of a tumbledown house that is being rapidly converted into a pile of debris. From this exalted, if perilous, position, a clear view could be had of the occupants of the vans as they stepped out'.

Joe Brady came out smiling, and it was noticed that every prisoner offered a better appearance than they had in their previous outing before the bench, 'when many of them faced Mr Keys without a morning bath or breakfast'.

James Carey, TC, dressed in a very superior style, stepped out of a prison van smoking what was described as a mild Havana cigar. He was the very picture of splendid insouciance. Two young women, who had somehow gained the inner yard, emotionally embraced Pat Whelan.

At 12.40 p.m. the benches were thronged 'almost to agony' for their pent-up occupants. By jeopardising coat tails and breast buttons not a little, Mr Hamilton, the under secretary, succeeded in sharing a bench designed for two but now occupied by four.

Mr Jenkinson, the under secretary for police and crime, had 'a long and strong pull through the crowd' from the door to the clerk's bench before he secured an edge. Another Dublin Castle official found himself in a sea of special artists, 'who sketched everything from the clock to the tail of the roaring British lion on the Royal arms'.

The prisoners filed into court, their numbers having increased since the first day, because the G men – a phrase first associated with Dublin Castle detectives and later appropriated by American outlaws – had executed other warrants.

So large was the crowd of prisoners at the dock that spectator benches on one side of the court had to be cleared to accommodate the overspill. James Mullett, the publican, had something in his mouth, which he moved about from side to side. The reporters inferred that it was a wad of tobacco. James Carey stood at the back of the dock. They all affected an unconcerned air, such that 'from their cool bearing in the dock it would be hard to tell whether they were seriously apprehensive of danger from the position in which they are placed'.

Mr Murphy, QC, opened proceedings for the crown. He asked that the prisoners be returned for trial on the charges that would appear *prima facie* to be made out against them from the evidence he would offer. He called Robert Farrell.

Farrell would be two hours under examination. He had 'foxy hair, which stood straight up, and appeared not to have been tutored for some time with either comb or brush'. He stroked his moustache a lot, and was occasionally told to take down his hand so that he could be heard.

He began by saying that seven or eight years ago he had been sworn in as a member of the Fenian brotherhood. The oath was to obey implicitly all commands of his superior officers in the true spirit of a soldier.

Mr Killen, for Brady and Delaney, immediately objected. The matter had no connection to the Fenian brotherhood. 'The Crown might as well go back to the time of the Flood,' he said.

'Not at all,' Murphy coolly replied. 'There was a flood last week'. He nodded towards the deluge of defendants. Questioning resumed, and Farrell next told the name of the man who had sworn him into the Fenians. It was one Joseph Flood (laughter in court).

Farrell gave evidence of attending meetings at No. 10 Peter Street, and James Carey must have winced inwardly. Already associated with the street, having built a dispensary there, he realised the police must know that he had rented a room at that address from a man named Devlin in March 1877.

Still, what could they establish? Carey had wanted it as a reading or lecture room, and if certain persons conspired among the scholars, it hardly implicated him.

Farrell went on to describe other gatherings, in Cuffe Lane and York Street. There was money collected for the purchase of arms. Those in employment paid thruppence a week towards weapons, such as revolvers, with which they were often issued.

Mr Carey attended meetings in Peter Street, where military drilling was repeatedly carried out, he said, and Farrell altogether identified fifteen of the prisoners as having been present at such meetings. There had even been an inspection by the American Fenian John Devoy at one point.

He next told of his recruitment by Dan Curley to join an inner circle. He asked Curley what was its purpose, to be told that it was 'chiefly intended to assassinate Government officials'. Hearing this assertion, the defendants snorted contemptuously

Farrell then drew in other defendants in an account of an attempt to ambush chief secretary Forster's carriage. The press scribbled furiously. He recounted the attempt of 27 March, when 'the instructions that Curley gave me were to stop the carriage on the bridge. Of course I understood that others were to stop it as well'.

He had been issued with a revolver that day. Curley told him that 'King' Kelly and Joe Brady would 'do the remainder'.

This statement naturally aroused hot legal objections. The charge was one of conspiracy, and the approver could make claims as to his conversations with Curley, but he was not entitled to drag in hearsay about others, such as Brady, who could have been 'a hundred miles away'. [Was 'King' simply 'Tim' misheard?]

The official carriage, Farrell continued, went past them and Curley seemed vexed. The plan had been for Larry Rinkell to get his cab in front of it, with his white horse a signal that Forster was immediately following. But the official carriage had been too quick for Rinkell, who now drew up late. Rinkell said, somewhat superfluously, that the carriage had gone. Brady and Kelly also heard this remark, said the witness.

Brady hissed from the dock: 'You are a liar'.

Farrell, Brady and Kelly got on Rinkell's cab and followed the carriage along the quays and into the park. They stopped when it turned down the road to the lord lieutenant's residence.

Back on the quays, there was an inquest on what had gone wrong before the group broke up. Ironically, the only victim of the ambush was an Invincible named Joseph McMahon, who died in a most bizarre way.

Farrell learned about it a day or two later. He had a conversation with the defendant William Moroney, shoemaker and plotter, who said the fatal accident occurred when McMahon was returning from the aborted mission on the quays.

McMahon was with Tom Martin, the compositor, when they met a friend Joseph Brennan in Dorset Street. They entered Dunlop's public house for a drink, ordered two bottles of porter and a pint of stout, and repaired to the snug. Soon afterwards, Joe McMahon's revolver went off accidentally, the bullet tearing into the base of his heart.

Brennan ran into the street, but Martin remained. The shopkeeper alerted two passing policemen and they apprehended Brennan, who initially gave a false name. McMahon meanwhile was barely alive, but was pronounced dead on arrival at the Mater hospital.

The press initially reported the death as a murder, and Brennan was charged with it. He subsequently pleaded guilty to manslaughter, and Judge Lawson declared that he would deal lightly with the prisoner, giving him twelve months.

'He [Moroney] told me that the revolver went off accidentally', said Farrell, who rapidly passed on from this episode to bring home some evidence against Joe Mullett, the dinner-party hunchback, who now 'sneered contemptuously at some of Farrell's statements and seemed much amused at them'.

Farrell connected Mullett with the attack on Denis Field. The witness said he himself had mustered for the attack, meeting the car man Michael Kavanagh and others in Westmoreland Street on the night. But Dan Curley had then given Farrell a loaded revolver and took him and a separate party to meet the other juror, Barrett, at Westland Row train station. The other section remained behind to take care of Field.

Joe Mullett had said it would be 'a great job if the two things (jurors Barrett and Field) could be done on the one night'. The plan at Westland Row was for Joseph Hanlon to give Barrett a letter on his arrival and for him then to be killed while distracted. But Barrett never turned up.

Farrell said his role had been to shoot the expected policeman at Westland Row if he tried to intervene. Meanwhile the other party had largely managed to carry out their mission, even if Mr Field had not quite been despatched to the next world.

The witness said one of the defendants, Joseph Hanlon, had told him later all about the Field attempt. Brady and Kelly carried it out, Hanlon said, and then jumped on the escape car, Kelly losing his hat in the process.

The driver of the car was Michael Kavanagh, of Townsend Street, whom he had met himself before the parties divided, Farrell insisted. Kavanagh had lately been arrested by the authorities but was not yet in the dock.

Hanlon told Farrell how he had shadowed the target as Field made his way home, and waved a handkerchief as a signal for Brady when he turned into North Frederick Street. Hanlon allegedly recounted: 'Brady had Mr Field on the ground, and stabbed him several times'.

This evidence was highly damaging, even though Farrell's information was second-hand and little more than hearsay. Cross-examination began, with the witness admitting that he had been thinking of leaving the organisation for four years. He had in fact resigned on occasion, but had been threatened by Joe Mullett, and so had resumed his soldiery.

He still wanted to leave. 'I saw the nonsense of it. There are persons who live by it, but they decoy the people'. He was pressed further, and at one point talked of 'the Assassination Club', a phrase that caused the prisoners to a man to burst into laughter, but which was a boon to the press.

'I repeatedly tendered my resignation,' offered Farrell weakly. 'Plenty of the members of the dock will tell you that. I wanted to get out of them altogether'. Four or five of the prisoners now turned their backs on Farrell, 'and ceased to give the evidence even a careless hearing in order to chat among themselves'.

Farrell finished: 'Joe Mullett is the man who has put me here today, by his threats'.

His evidence over, the day concluded, and the men were remanded for a further week. Bail was refused. Farrell had failed to throw much light on the Phoenix Park murders, but his evidence 'went far enough to cause many a breath to quicken'.

The caravan of vehicles moved out of the courthouse pound to return the accused to Kilmainham. The large crowd beyond the walls cheered the prisoners in the vans, but the police, in the leading and following cars, were hooted and booed.

That night, which Farrell spent in a police station, there were reports that the home he shared with a brother and sister in Kennedy's Lane had been attacked by a mob and the windows and furniture smashed.

'In the Police court yesterday it was a curious study to observe the efforts of the prisoners to hide their excitement and concern under a show of indifference or bravado as they saw Farrell get into the witness box', crowed the next issue of the *Times*.

'They talked together, nodded to friends they recognised, and at certain points tittered or laughed outright to show it was all a good joke, but at some of the most telling and startling parts in his evidence their anxiety could be seen to prevail over a defiant demeanour.

'Brady, who is alleged to have been the man who stabbed Mr Field, and who had been selected to murder Mr Forster, is a large, portly-looking man who, in another place, would be regarded as a jovial fellow …'

'Never has an informer told a tale as strange, as astounding, as blood-curdling, as that deposed by Robert Farrell', wrote the *Freeman's Journal*, which devoted blanket coverage to the proceedings.

'Upon his story, whether it is a revelation or a fabrication, it would be premature and improper to pass an opinion or criticism at this early stage. Suffice it to say that a feeling much stronger and more anxious than mere curiosity or expectancy is aroused in city and country'.

Such restraint was hardly exhibited in the British papers, whose appetite had been whetted. They saw a clear link between the described attempts on the life of Forster and the subsequent taking of that of his successor. Earl Spencer briefed the queen on developments, but warned that a conviction for the Phoenix Park killings would still need to meet a high standard of legal proof.

The *Freeman's Journal* thought the evidence thus far produced established only the guilt of the government. 'The truth is that the existence of an assassination committee is the most terrible condemnation of the Castle system which could be conceived. The assassinations did not commence until after the regime of Coercion had been well inaugurated, the public agitation suppressed, and its leaders imprisoned'.

Later that week the same newspaper protested that the prisoners on remand were 'as cut off from home and friends as if they were in Siberian exile. No letters, no visits. This is the sum total of the bitter complaints of their much to be pitied wives and little children'.

It claimed the wife of van driver Edward McCaffrey had been denied the privilege of sending her husband a strong pair of boots. Another who brought a warm coat for a brother was told they could bring the prisoner some underclothing, but nothing else.

'Some of the accused men are wretchedly poor, yet the wives manage somehow. Jail regulations have become exceptionally rigid.'

The *Times* gloried that 'the revelations in the Dublin Police Court on last Saturday will probably have one useful result. Unless they are completely refuted and overthrown, they will close the mouths, for very shame, of those who only a few days ago were assailing Lord Spencer's vigorous administration of the law in Ireland.

'We desire to abstain from prejudging the case of the accused, but we are at liberty to say that it will require an extraordinary amount of rebutting evidence to prove that the organisation described by Farrell was a mere fable'.

Turning Informer

There was good news for the patriot class in the long wait for the next appearance. Nationalist William O'Brien became MP for Mallow, defeating the solicitor general, John Naish, in what had been a government safe seat.

O'Brien was the man whose hotel room had been burst in by drunken jurors, and he himself was awaiting trial for 'seditious libel' over articles denouncing organised jury-packing by the authorities.

The *Freeman's Journal* exulted that his triumph, by a margin of nearly two to one, was 'the registration by Mallow of a general feeling against a system of government which imprisons the press and subjects its writers to punishment and the company of public malefactors, and which has hung over the people the threat of suspension of even the shreds of a semblance of trial by jury'.

A less sanguine development, for more radical elements, was the release of a letter from Pope Leo XIII to Cardinal McCabe of Dublin, praising him for encouraging his flock in 'bearing the ills of an unhappy lot in a Christian spirit, and not allowing their aims to overstep the bounds of duty and religion'.

Evil societies, the pope warned, sought remedies worse than the disease. They adopted a course 'calculated to lead their fellow countrymen not to safety, but to destruction'. The cardinal was enjoined to keep his faithful people 'entirely apart from those who were led away blindly by their own passions, who think they serve their country by steeping themselves in crime, by drawing others into the same depraved courses, and by imprinting a foul stain on their country's cause'.

The letter had been written on New Year's Day, before the arrests, and its disclosure now smacked of calculation. It could not have aided the work of the Fair Trial Fund begun in London to collect money for the prisoners on remand.

The collectors had a manifesto claiming that 'once more British gold has done its work and the spy and informer are let loose in order that British power might be upheld'. Its assertion that 'these wretches can only survive by concocting imaginary crimes', seemed further fetched.

Things were undoubtedly going the Castle's way, despite the electoral defeat.

There had been no serious outrage in Dublin in the two months since the Field attack, and the lord lieutenant evidently felt he could celebrate, holding the first levée of his second term in office on 30 January, eight months after the assassinations.

The splendid ball 'relieved Dublin Castle from the melancholy of past months', the press commented, when the citadel had been a lonely place where a car would dash in or out with some official, 'followed by the inevitable outside car carrying his protection party on the lookout for assassins'.

The *Times* glowed with satisfaction over the resumption of gala occasions: 'The Castle is a centre of loyal light, and sheds a genial harmonising influence throughout at least the higher circles of the social system'.

Michael Kavanagh, the car man, had not been among the early arrests, even though he had been fingered for both the Field crime and the Phoenix Park slayings. He did not try to flee, not knowing his predicament, and the police delay in apprehending him at his Townsend Street address may only be guessed at. He was finally picked up however and brought to Kilmainham Jail.

By 27 January, there had been a change of venue. It was thought expedient to have the next court hearing in Kilmainham courthouse, adjoining the prison, rather than mount the inconvenience and risk of bringing a large amount of prisoners a long distance 'through some of the lowest quarters of the city' to Green Street.

A hole was knocked in the side of the prison wall by the authorities and a new gate built to allow a speedy transfer. It is still there, known as the 'Invincibles' gate.

On appearance day, a large crowd of sympathisers and the curious were kept at bay by a substantial force of police. Admission was granted by ticket only, to none but those properly authorised, and 'still the courthouse was inconveniently crowded'.

It was yet widely expected that Patrick Delaney, the convicted would-be killer of Judge Lawson, would be put into the box as a witness for the crown, the newspapers having predicted as much, but instead of the twenty persons who appeared in Green Street, only five were now put forward.

They were Joseph Brady, Timothy Kelly, an uninvolved tailor named John Dywer, Robert Farrell's talkative friend Joseph Hanlon, and Michael Kavanagh for the first time. Farrell had always spoken of this man as 'Myles' Kavanagh, but such inaccuracy could not have played a part in his delayed arrest.

These five men, arraigned on conspiracy, were further charged with attempting to murder Denis Field. Kavanagh was described as of dark complexion and 'decently dressed for his station in life'.

The first witness to appear was the seventeen-year-old servant Alice Carroll, who wore a turban hat trimmed with brown velveteen, and a red muffler. Not in the least awed by her surroundings, she did not get on the witness chair, but stood near the counsels' table. Carroll 'surprised all by the quick precision of her answers and the sharp combativeness with which she met her cross-examiners'.

The defence directed its efforts to the impeachment of her general character, 'it being insinuated that she stopped out late at night and frequented public houses'. Significantly, perhaps, Carroll admitted that for days after witnessing the attack she did not say a word about it to her parents, even though her father was reading about it nightly in the *Evening Telegraph*.

She nonetheless publicly identified Brady and Kelly. She said

she saw 'something glittering in the light' as Brady attacked Field. She also identified Kavanagh as the driver of the getaway car.

The next local witness was Michael Farrell, who identified the same trio. William James Connellan then entered the box and identified Tim Kelly as the man he saw holding a 'bright instrument' which he threw up onto cushions on the car after turning the corner, where other occupants promptly covered it. Kelly then jumped up on the car, losing his hat in the process, and the gang made its escape. A man in the street named James Egan picked up the hat, asked people was it theirs, and ultimately took it home to Phibsborough.

Informer William Lamie, who had first given private information about James Mullett, now publicly supported Farrell about meetings. The other defendants had by this point been led into the dock, and Lamie identified Brady, Curley, the hunchback Joseph Mullett, and others. They had been administering oaths and talking treason and murder at a premises in Aungier Street, known as the

'Regular Carpenters', a little ironic in light of that trade's apparent outlook.

Lamie also described a plot formulated in Hanlon's pub in Capel Street to kill Superintendent Mallon. The chief of detectives would have to be 'dealt with', the men decided, with Lamie construing it as an assassination plot. This was all useful material, but it did not advance the prosecution's grand strategy very far – although some defendants were clearly in a great deal of trouble on the Denis Field attempted murder charge.

The greatest sensation came in the last remark of the day. Crown counsel James Murphy, applying for another week's remand, told the magistrates that the prosecution would then be 'able to throw light on the mystery of the Phoenix Park murders'.

This cliffhanging reference was momentous indeed. It may have played further tricks with the confidence of the prisoners, who were still housed separately in Kilmainham under suspension of many usual rights and entitlements.

The prisoners may or may not have learned of a strange, even bizarre, advertisement that now appeared in the national press at the behest of the authorities:

> The gentleman who was invited to skate on the Viceregal Lodge pond some winters ago, and who related that incident to some parties at the polo ground, Phoenix Park, on the evening of May 6 last, is requested to communicate with the Assistant Under Secretary for Police and Crime, Dublin Castle.
>
> Any of the gentleman's friends who know of the fact of his having been so invited to skate will please draw his attention to this advertisement, lest it escape his notice.

At the same time, Detective Superintendent Mallon was continuing his intrigues. He made sure to put together at a crucial moment the car man Michael Kavanagh and Peter Carey, brother to the town councillor. These two men were taken out of their cells one day and sent down to Dr William Carte, the prison doctor, being told it was for 'the usual medical examination'. The pair went happily, glad of companionship.

Mallon had already taken the precaution of telling the medical officer what he had in mind. The result was that when the younger Carey and Kavanagh were brought down to the doctor's room, the warders were temporarily dismissed and the two prisoners directed to wait outside.

Meanwhile Mallon had been busy. A small section of oak panelling in the passage outside Dr Carte's door had been removed on his instructions. It was replaced by a grille of perforated zinc, which had 'all the appearance of an ordinary scheme of ventilation'.

Mallon took up a position on the hidden side of the panelling and metaphorically glued his ear to the metal. What happened was exactly as he had dreamed. The two young men came out of the surgery and immediately planted their backs against the panelling.

Kavanagh commented on the fact that he had heard that Mallon had been 'very good to the little mare', referring to his horse, since he had been locked up. There was a pause, and the same voice suddenly confided in his companion that he had been thinking the best course was 'to tell Mallon all about it'.

The other man might well have been expected to scotch all such thoughts – but instead he sympathised with the sentiment. Peter Carey went further: 'But for goodness sake, don't say my brother James was in the park'.

Kavanagh assured him that he would not.

Now Peter Carey, never involved in the actual killing, could not contain his curiosity. He ventured a question that was music to the ears of the man listening behind the panel like a pantomime villain. 'Who was on the car with you?' he asked.

'There was Joe Brady, Tim Kelly, that fellow Caffrey, and the wee fellow who was up for the attempt to shoot Judge Lawson', answered Kavanagh.

That was enough for Mallon to be going on with. Within a

few minutes, Peter Carey had been seen by the doctor and taken back to his cell. Kavanagh, next in, confided to Dr Carte that he thought he would 'like to see John Mallon'. Mallon was there on the spot, it was later recalled, 'to catch him when he was red hot, before he had time to change his mind'.

Then commenced another fencing match behind closed doors, for the car man wanted to deliver an assorted parcel and to keep back many of what Mallon knew to be the choicest plums. Yet Kavanagh was heavily handicapped, without his knowledge, because of what the detective had overheard.

When he denied all knowledge of where James Carey was that day, Mallon declared with great emphasis: 'I *know* James Carey was there!'

'Ah, begob!' exclaimed Kavanagh in agitation. 'You know as much as I do myself. I will tell you the whole truth'. And he did precisely that. Mallon, exultant, had his second informer.

A day or two later, Mallon secretly had Kavanagh brought out of the jail. It was the eve of the prisoners' next appearance. He put the car man in a trap and drove over the whole route taken by the killers on the day of the murders. He wanted to piece everything together and to get the sequencing right, as well as to pick up 'whatever tiny threads of corroboration might be available'.

Having journeyed through the Phoenix Park and along the escape route the party stopped at Chapelizod to give the prisoner some breakfast. Kavanagh, enjoying his importance, ordered a steak. When he was well into it, Mallon reminded him that it was a Friday and that he was eating meat on a fast day. Kavanagh threw down his knife and fork in sudden realisation.

'What's that,' Mallon snapped, as his friend Frederick Bussy recounted years later. 'You'd be participating in the brutal murder of two innocent men and then you'd pretend to be sticking at eating meat on a Friday? You blackguard!'

Kavanagh resumed his meal.

The next day at Kilmainham the prosecution had to make good on its promise. Eight prisoners were placed in the dock – the Carey brothers, carpenter Laurence Hanlon, Joe Brady, Tim Kelly, coach-builder Peter Doyle, the lately arrested Edward O'Brien, who lived in Kilmainham, and Edward McCaffrey, a mineral water van-driver unlucky enough to live in Peter Street, about which so much had been heard. McCaffrey was the man who had been denied a new pair of boots.

The clerk read out a momentous charge against them: 'That you did, on the 6th day of May, 1882, feloniously, wilfully, and of malice aforethought, kill and murder Lord Frederick Cavendish and Thomas Henry Burke'. When he had finished, the prisoners laughed. Brady in particular guffawed his contempt.

John Fitzsimons was the first witness produced, putting on glasses and peering closely at the dock to identify his landlord, James Carey, and that man's brother. He told of finding the knives in the loft. Inspector James Smith then produced the knives and an appalled thrill ran through the packed court.

It was pointed out that they corresponded with the type of weapons employed in the assassinations, and surgeon George Porter was next into the witness box to say as much. He called the weapons 'surgical amputating knives', and the court learned that one blade was exactly eleven inches long and the other a quarter-inch shorter.

Stephen Hands was produced, and journalists learned that he was the first material witness, having been out with his wife Sarah on 6 May when they noticed two groups of men lying about on opposite sides of the road. Both he and his wife had been struck by the fierce appearance of a particular man in one group.

A hush descended as he was asked whether he saw the ter-rible figure in court. Hands said he did – and he pointed out the defendant in the centre of the front row, Edward O'Brien.

A ripple of excitement mixed with surprise animated the gal-leries. O'Brien, admittedly fierce in aspect, was not one of the prin-cipals in the public mind. But now Hands stated that there was another man he recognised, whom he had seen standing beside an empty horse and car in the park. That man was in the corner of the dock, on the right. Joe Brady smiled slightly.

Sarah Hands followed her husband into evidence. She had been frightened when walking past a group of four men lying on the grass, and had stepped aside on the path to prevent her dress touching the face of one of them. It was O'Brien, the wild-looking one, and she had turned and looked at him when she passed. Like her husband, she also picked out Brady, who had by now changed his place in the dock.

Next sworn was the park ranger, George Godden, whose descriptions had been hopeless in Mallon's view, but who today managed to identify Brady as the man he saw sitting next to the horse and driver, facing the witness, as the murder car fled the assassinations.

Dr Charles Cameron, the city analyst, had examined the knives and pronounced that two tiny spots of blood remained, on opposite sides, near the handle. Near the tip was a minute trace, like rust, the nature of which he could not ascertain.

Farmer Francis Joseph Powell spoke of seeing four men together under a bunch of trees in the Phoenix Park. Having seen their faces, he now specified two of the quartet as having been the prisoners Brady and McCaffrey. The latter, referred to by Powell as the man in the back row with the sandy beard, smiled and nodded.

Brady was momentarily impassive, as if he began to feel the noose of justice fixing itself around his neck. It was by then four o'clock, and the case was further adjourned into February. The prisoners filed out – and reporters rushed to file their copy.

'The two prisoners who are most positively identified, Brady and O'Brien, are men of such marked individuality that their faces would probably be indelibly imprinted on the mind of any intelligent person who once saw them', claimed the *Times* in partisan language.

'Brady is a man of above the average size, of strong Celtic features, the lower jaw being wide and sensual, and his eyes also large, and with a reckless expression alternating between humour and mischief. O'Brien, on the other hand, is a cadaverous-looking creature, with sunken eyes and attenuated visage, whose pallor seems more ghastly in contrast with his black bushy hair and beard'.

There was a little less certainty about the knives: 'The case for the Crown depends very much on their identity, for when the defence is opened an effort will be made to show that they could not have been used in the murders … It may well excite surprise, however, that if they are the instruments used in the murder, such highly tempered blades are not hacked and dented, but seem uninjured and so little stained by their terrible work.

'The natural supposition at the time was that they were thrown away or destroyed, but it may be that the conspirators, having other work of the kind to do, and finding them so effective, did not wish to incur the cost and possible risk of procuring other implements'.

Instead it was the police who were now doing all the procuring, whether some witnesses had been encouraged to improve their evidence or not. And there must be that suspicion, at least in the case of the park ranger.

The next few days saw the arrest of a coachbuilder named Thomas Doyle, of Cross Kevin Street (a workmate of Tim Kelly), and a man named by Michael Kavanagh as the driver of the other ambush vehicle. His name was James Fitzharris, but he was better known as 'Skin the Goat'.

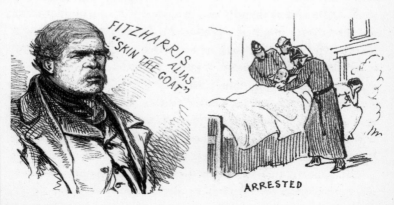

FITZHARRIS ALIAS "SKIN THE GOAT"

ARRESTED

The Net Closes

The advert seeking the 'skater on the pond' in the Phoenix Park may have seemed like a form of code to some, but it was actually in earnest. A man named Ladley had been in the park on the day of the assassinations, and had struck up chat with a stranger.

When Earl Spencer passed up, the other fellow remarked: 'That's a good man. I remember one winter paying five shillings to skate on the pond in the Zoo, and leaving it disgusted as the ice was rotten. I then took a walk in the park and met a gentleman who asked me where I had been skating.

'He brought me into some private grounds containing a grand sheet of ice. The gentleman stood on the bank while I was skating, and I asked a man nearby who he was. The answer was 'Lord Spencer'.'

After telling this story, said Ladley, the man crossed to the main road and spoke to two men who were sitting on a seat, seeming to recognise one of them. The physical location suggested to the Curran inquiry that the two men were part of a murder team.

The adverts eventually produced a letter. It came from Co. Carlow, and an elderly man named Michael Glynn. He remembered the circumstances stated in the advertisement, and received a wire asking him to Dublin Castle.

Glynn told Mallon and Curran that the man he had recognised and spoken to in the park was James Carey! Glynn was himself a master builder, and Carey had been a former employee, and before that had apprenticed as a bricklayer with him. Glynn helpfully pointed out the very seat in the park, opposite the polo grounds, where the conversation had taken place.

Mallon, meanwhile, tied up another loose end. Attempted murder convict Patrick Delaney had been a lot less co-operative than the press had imagined, with all their speculation about him becoming a crown witness. Instead, Mallon ordered him produced from Kilmainham in order for him to be formally charged with the Phoenix Park murders in line with aspects of Kavanagh's confession.

Patrick Delaney was held overnight at the Castle in a last attempt the break him down completely. Mallon had to give a receipt to a warder who didn't want to return without his prisoner. It said that the convict, giving his number, 'has been identified with complicity in the Phoenix Park murders and has accordingly been charged and is detained in custody by the superintendent of G Division of the Dublin Metropolitan Police'.

Delaney 'nearly died of fright' after the charge was levelled, 'and cried and shrieked and prayed', according to one version. 'I saved your life more than once Mr Mallon', declared Delaney. 'Good God, are you going to hang me now?'

It was progress on all fronts. They had tracked down a rumour that a woman, coming to see a servant in the chief secretary's household, had witnessed what she thought was a scuffle and turned back in fear. A constable had heard the tale from a park ranger.

The ranger was questioned and at first denied all knowledge, but then admitted he had heard the tale from his daughter, a servant in the lodge. A cab was sent there at once, and the frightened poor woman arrived wringing her hands in her apron. She said she knew the story because the would-be visitor, whose name she did not know, was going to see her former friend in the kitchen, Charlotte Noakes.

Where was Charlotte? She had left the service and returned to England. The woman did not know where. 'She must have written to you announcing her safe return,' probed Curran, knowing that Charlotte's visitor could provide vital visual evidence.

The housekeeper returned to the lodge and rifled through her belongings. In a few hours, she returned triumphant. The letter she brandished proved Lottie had gone back to her father in Devizes, Wiltshire.

Curran immediately wired the local constabulary. The next morning he received a replying wire saying Charlotte Noakes had been found and that the name of the visitor who never came was Emma Jones – then in service of a lady in Carlisle. Two officers were despatched there immediately.

'I told them not to come back without her. At the same time I wrote to her mistress that there was no charge of any kind against the girl, and that she was required only as a witness'. A few mornings later, Emma Jones was in Dublin.

She admitted that she saw the scuffle, which very much frightened her, and that while it was going on two men walked back from it, towards her. This echoed the account of Samuel Jacob, who saw the pair hurrying towards town within a moment of the murders.

And so to the moment of truth. Emma Jones was shown the album of photographs of the detained men. She had not the slightest hesitation in picking out the face of one who was 'indelibly printed' on her memory. It was dapper Dan Curley.

Michael Fagan, a blacksmith from artisan dwellings in Buckingham Street was one of the prisoners who had been arrested on Robert Farrell's evidence. Now came information from Dr Carte, the Kilmainham doctor, that one of the detained men had mentioned Fagan encountering a friend as he lay in the grass of the Phoenix Park while awaiting the arrival of Burke.

The account was that the unknown man had actually nodded in friendly recognition at the recumbent Fagan as he walked by in the company of a sapper [Royal Engineer].

It was a useful tip. Finding the person who recognised Fagan meant finding first another, as in the Emma Jones case. Finding the sapper would likely lead to the name of his walking companion – the man who greeted the prisoner Fagan and who could provide material testimony to Fagan's presence in the park immediately before the assassinations.

Crown investigators wrote to the general in command of the

Royal Engineers regiment at Mountjoy barracks in the Phoenix Park in an effort to identify the sapper. The general, in turn, paraded his men and explained what was required – who had walked out with a friend that terrible evening?

A private then fell out of the ranks and said he remembered the incident. But he said he had been walking with two friends, not one, and provided their names. Both were Fenian sympathisers. The men were hauled in and denied being anywhere near the park on 6 May. They were then separately confronted with Private Sandford, the informant, and threatened with jail for withholding information. The pair broke down and duly admitted that the man that one of them had greeted was indeed Michael Fagan.

Kilmainham prison was meanwhile a hothouse. The prisoners were being systematically 'sweated' for information in a nexus of both the investigation and detention apparatus. Every warder was made aware of 'the stake for which justice is playing in this affair'. Every scrap of intelligence was needed.

'Not a ruse known to detective science was neglected,' wrote chronicler Tighe Hopkins. 'The object was to bring the prisoners to implicate one another, and their fears and suspicions of treachery were most cunningly played upon'. They were allowed exercise individually only, but 'chance' meetings were allowed between particular comrades – through repeats of the doctor visitation device and other schemes – that allowed their talk to be overheard.

'By word and suggestion they were made to feel that they had been betrayed on every side, and above all, that the chief traitors were of their own number'.

Governor J. R. Gildea was meanwhile making subtle bargains with families pleading for access to their loved ones. He was always sure that, whomsoever he was talking about, they were not the worst offender and had been led into it by others ... a crumb of comfort seized on by many relatives with alacrity. Further empathy from him claimed greater insights from them, often inadvertently given. And when finally allowed to visit, a mother or wife seeking to save a husband or son could unconsciously do the governor's bidding. The pressure and promptings could only yield a seam of small but useful details, with greater prizes still to pitch for.

Mallon was even making sure that Michael Kavanagh did not change his mind about the full confession. The latter was walking the exercise yard alone one day, when Mallon walked in with Fitzharris, the cab man he had just arrested on Kavanagh's information.

Thinking he was wanted to verify the man's identity, Kavanagh began walking over, but Mallon brusquely bade him to continue walking. He engaged Fitzharris, or 'Skin the Goat' in conversation. The superintendent purposely assumed an air of great mystery and earnestness while talking and listening to the replies from 'Skin', as if he had a new best friend.

They spoke of ordinary matters, but the playground trick produced the same jealousy as it might among six-year-olds. The scowling Kavanagh feared Fitzharris was competing to give information, and much of it must be about Kavanagh himself. Mallon then began jotting private notes in a pad, which mystified the second car man, but further alarmed Kavanagh.

Eventually Kavanagh was called over and sent back to his cell in the company of a warder, while Mallon ordered Fitzharris to take his turn at exercise. The latter thought nothing of the discussion while awaiting his walk, but it preyed on Kavanagh's mind as intended.

An hour later, Mallon entered Kavanagh's cell. He told him that all the men detained with him had volunteered to become approvers for the crown in order to save their lives, and that Skin had made a clean breast of it that day.

Kavanagh, enraged, insisted that he wanted to give evidence first. It drove him demented that a man he had provided as a prize might gazump him in providing information to the police. At first Mallon appeared to hesitate – he had so much information already – but soon he relented.

Kavanagh could still be a crown witness, but Mallon made it clear he would no longer tolerate any holding back, as Kavanagh had tried before. He would call him as witness first thing on the morrow, and if Kavanagh played games, he would not have the slightest hesitation in withdrawing his testimony, treating him as hostile, and returning him to the dock. The rope would beckon thereafter.

On Saturday, 10 February, the prisoners began to fill the dock again, most not having seen each other since the last occasion, and they greeted one another warmly. Fitzharris, the new accession to their number, was recognised by several who shook hands with him as an acquaintance.

The newspapers loved this new arrival, with his strange moniker. 'Fitzharris is a coarse, ruffianly-looking fellow', said one. 'He is long beyond the middle age and his hair and beard are turning grey'. Another description had his face 'of vermilion hue', and the rest of him 'gnarled as an oak, and grizzly as a bear'.

One of the English newspaper correspondents, describing his countenance, said it presented the appearance of having been, at some remote period, 'badly battered by contact with a traction engine'.

Less attention was paid to Pat Delaney, who sat in front of the dock with two policemen specially guarding him, finding himself implicated in a charge which could end his life before he was long embarked on penal servitude. 'I'm on the same charge', he told the prisoners, in case there was any doubt to his being witness or accused.

Probably the defendants still expected to see their co-prisoner Kavanagh ushered into the dock when they heard the order 'Bring up Michael Kavanagh'. They knew precisely nothing of his turning traitor. There was a general stir as Kavanagh suddenly walked past the dock and his friends – and shock as he climbed onto a witness chair on a long table before the bench.

'A murmur of sensation rose in the court, and the prisoners shared in the excitement. The utterance of the unexpected name changed their whole demeanour', said one account. Another said that 'when he appeared on the table every face became livid. From that moment, the occupants of the dock, faces etched with concern, paid the deepest attention to the proceedings.

'There was not the slightest levity displayed by any of them as on previous days. They felt the strength of the net which is gradually being drawn around them'.

Kavanagh was nervous and very pale. He as much as possible kept his face turned from his former companions. Prosecutor Peter 'the Packer' O'Brien examined him: 'On the 6th May last, were you the owner of a car?'

'I was'.

There was no beating around the bush. Kavanagh told how he was in Dame Street when the lord lieutenant's arrival procession passed. He had earlier picked up both Tim Kelly and Joe Brady and brought them into town. Along the way he stopped and picked up two more – Patrick Delaney and a twenty-six-year-old labourer named Tom Caffrey, who stood with the others in the dock.

They went to a favourite haunt, Wrenn's pub, opposite the Castle yard. Later he drove the four men 'all along the quays to the park'. The audience grew all ears – Kavanagh led them with the car up to the Phoenix monument, where they could see the chief secretary's lodge; they turned around and came back down the road to the Gough statue.

One of his passengers then remarked: 'There is no sign of Skin ...'

Fitzharris exploded in the dock: 'You swab! Don't call me nicknames!'

Kavanagh, undeterred, said Fitzharris soon arrived with another car of Invincibles. Skin passed by and stopped further up the road, on the left hand side. Kavanagh's people got off his car and began walking towards the Phoenix. James Carey now came over to him with a man named Joseph Smith.

Kavanagh didn't know Smith, but he managed to pose a self-excusing question at this point.

The crown witness claimed he asked: 'What mission are yez on?' and got the reply 'Watching the Secretary'.

Carey and Smith then went to a bench to watch the polo, and soon a strange gentleman [Glynn] came up and spoke with Carey for a time. Meanwhile Fitzharris had dropped off his party further up the road, rounded the Phoenix, and was on his way back.

Kavanagh moved his car to the other side of the road, turned it about, and put a nosebag on his mare. The other two men crossed also and sat at a bench looking towards the city. After a time Smith suddenly exclaimed: 'He's coming!' Kavanagh looked in the direction indicated and saw two gentlemen walking up. One was taller than the other and dressed in grey. Someone told him to 'look sharp', and Kavanagh took the nosebag off the horse. All three jumped aboard.

He drove Carey and Smith up to where a number of men were waiting under the trees. One of his passengers was waving a white handkerchief, and 'gave it a shake in the act of wiping his nose'. When they reached the larger group, the pair got down, and one declared: 'Mind, it is the big man'.

Kavanagh could see Brady, Kelly and Caffrey there, among others he did not know. He was momentarily distracted by another cab as it passed, taking a fare down to the city. He recognised the car man, William Noud, who would later confirm seeing Kavanagh and the pair exchanging a professional salute.

The moment was approaching. Kavanagh noticed two men on bicycles passing. The group of men suddenly moved down the path, behind his vehicle, which was facing toward the Phoenix column. The witness presently heard an exclamation – 'Oh!' – and looked around.

The grey gentleman was down. The other man, sprawled in the road, was also down. He had an umbrella with him. Kavanagh turned his face. He was frightened and claimed not to have seen any more of what occurred.

The 'same four men' who had been engaged in the attack – Brady, Kelly, Delaney and Caffrey – quickly climbed up on his car. Kavanagh drove off, 'as hard as ever I could go', up to the Phoenix column, down to the Fifteen Acres, and out the Chapelizod Gate.

The killers went across the bridge over the Liffey, turned left, and out by Crumlin and Roundtown (Terenure). At that point, the car turned left again, towards the city. At Palmerstown, Tim Kelly got off. Brady also got off at some stage – 'He wanted to wash his hands before he went into town' – but then remounted. Kavanagh finally drove his vehicle and passengers to Davy's pub in Leeson Street, where Joe Brady gave him a pound. The passengers entered the pub, and the witness went home.

Kavanagh's lips had been 'quivering with emotion' as he described seeing the two gentlemen on the ground. The prisoners did what they could to intimidate him – Brady 'uttered a growl of hate and fury, like that of a wild beast', when Kavanagh turned to point to him, but the press noted that Brady later buried his face in his arms.

He rested on the bar of the dock, 'while the nervous working of his face indicated the agitation and excitement under which he laboured'. The general silence was only occasionally broken by such exclamations as 'You scorpion!' and 'You're a liar' from the freshly accused Fitzharris, who, with arms folded and face as red as his muffler, scowled upon the witness from the dock. Much of the defiance had gone out of the others.

After the park account, Kavanagh was led into describing the Field attack. He identified Kelly in the dock and looked for Joseph Hanlon, who refused to turn around in the dock to allow his face to be seen. It hardly mattered – Kavanagh had done enormous damage.

The day ended with evidence from the bird-nester Jacob – 'connected, consistent and bearing the stamp of veracity' – which supplied strong corroboration of the approver's tale.

'Such a story of ferocious and deliberate crime as revealed when the informer Kavanagh entered the witness box has rarely been heard in a court of justice', wrote the *Illustrated London News*.

It 'places vividly before the mind's eye the chief incidents of the ghastly Phoenix Park tragedy ... we now know, what was only before surmised, that the intention of the assassins was to take the life of Mr Burke only, but that the accidental meeting of that gentleman with Lord Frederick involved in the same fate the chief secretary, who during the deadly strife nobly defended his colleague.

'The security of the Murder League that planned and carried out the slaughter ... has been completely shattered by the skill and silent perseverance of the Dublin detective force'.

Carey Cracks

A diver had been at work for several days in the Ringsend Basin, trying to find the sword cane and other weapons used in the attack on Mr Field and afterwards thrown in by Kavanagh on behalf of the organisation.

The elaborate hunt was carried out from the Royal Navy vessel *Ophelia*, supervised by senior police officers on the dockside, and watched with curiosity by sometimes hundreds of spectators.

Kavanagh had no idea what became of the knives used in the park assassinations, but said the ones discovered in Carey's loft were of the same type he had disposed of. For the prosecution, securing an identical second set of Weiss & Co. knives from the basin would tie up the case against town councillor James Carey in particular. It was reported that 'if necessary the basin can be drained for the purposes of facilitating the search'.

Kavanagh's car had been examined by the police soon after the killings, but the panelling was slate-coloured, and not the red or brown described by witnesses – which rather called into question the ability of witnesses to suddenly identify perpetrators in the park after nine months, particularly since the original descriptions had been so inaccurate.

No witness, for instance, mentioned the distinctive white hat Kavanagh said he had been wearing on 6 May, and which he swapped with Tom Caffrey for a brown one after the killings. Yet in a further short hearing, four days after Kavanagh's informer evidence, a farmer named Patrick Cahill swore faithfully that he recognised Caffrey from the crime scene.

Michael Glynn, of the skating story, publically identified his

one-time apprentice James Carey the same day, and he also claimed to recognise little-known Caffrey, who was fast becoming as
heavily implicated as the others. Yet Glynn had only been speaking to Carey.

Meanwhile Thomas Huxley, Mr Guinness' gardener at Farmleigh, whose original statement had been 'of a general character
and only related to time', according to an internal police document
prepared by Superintendent Mallon, now felt somehow qualified
to recognise Timothy Kelly as having been on the getaway car.

And Patrick Murray, dismissed by Mallon in the same breath
as Huxley, managed to have taken particular notice of a cabman
towards the town end of the park. That man, he said, was James
'Skin the Goat' Fitzharris …

On the day before Kavanagh's court testimony, the police had
arrested Joseph Smith, a twenty-four-year-old handyman named in
passing as having been in the park. Smith, from South King Street,
cracked at once. He worked in Dublin Castle, and had been the one
who had glowered at John Adye Curran having nailed down the
grand inquisitor's carpet.

Smith confessed he had met James Carey within a week of starting work at the Castle. He had been introduced to him by Fitzharris, who ironically often worked as car driver for Detective Superintendent Mallon.

In fact, Mallon had arrested Fitzharris after taking a trip with him about the city and returning to the Castle yard. It may be that Kavanagh already knew that 'Skin the Goat' was friendly with Mallon – which was even more reason for him to avoid being upstaged.

Joseph Smith said he had seen Fitzharris frequently at the Castle, and quickly got to know him. 'Skin' took him to Wrenn's public house in Dame Street to meet Carey, after learning that Smith was familiar with the appearance of both the chief secretary, Buckshot Forster, and the under secretary, Mr Burke.

This was about three weeks before the assassinations, although Smith had already been a member of the Fenians for three or four years. Carey brought him to his house one April evening, and administered the oath of the Invincibles by swearing him in on a penknife.

Smith couldn't remember a word of the oath, except that his life was forfeit if he failed to obey orders. He got to know Daniel Curley and Joe Brady thereafter. On the morning before the murders, Friday 5 May, he had been brought to the Phoenix Park to spot Mr Burke.

The four of them were there, but they missed Burke's carriage going in to his work in Dublin Castle. At 11 o'clock Joe Brady walked over to the lodge to ask if Mr Burke was in, and was told he was not. The would-be assassin thanked the servant and meekly retreated.

The disappointed quartet got up on the car of 'Skin the Goat' Fitzharris and left. They stopped for a drink at the Royal Oak pub, just outside the park gate. They decided to meet at the pub again that evening. When Smith returned after work he found Brady, Curley, Joe Hanlon and several others whom he did not know.

They arranged to congregate in town again the next day. Smith was working at the Castle because of the new viceroy's procession, but finished work at four o'clock and was paid his wages. As he crossed to Wrenn's, he was met at the door by James Carey who took him around the corner into Parliament Street. They got into Fitzharris' car. Joseph Hanlon was already there.

They went along the quays to the Phoenix Park, up past the Gough monument, and eventually stopped on the right hand side, opposite the Polo ground. They climbed off, went across the road, and Smith watched a little of the cricket. He knew he was there to identify Burke, but claimed to have no idea of what else was involved because he was 'not told'.

He saw Burke coming on an outside car. He saw it stop, and Burke get off to join another gentleman. 'I went a couple of yards from Carey, and he stood up and said, 'Who's this?' I said, 'It's very like Mr Burke – it is Mr Burke'.

'Well, up with you,' said he, 'on the car at once'.

'Kavanagh got very nervous and white, and I got actually as bad'.

They drove up to the others, Carey taking out a white hand-kerchief and putting it to his mouth. 'He asked me had I one, and I said I had, but it was rather dirty'. Carey had no time to consider the ridiculousness of this remark – he ordered Smith to take it out and signal anyway.

They arrived, Carey dismounted, and Curley came over to him. They spoke, and Smith heard the phrase 'mind, the man in grey'. Carey then ordered him off the car, and to go away. Smith left the main road, heading south to join what is now the Khyber Pass road.

The two gentlemen were coming up, but still a long way away. 'Just before I got out of sight I looked back and I saw the men walking four deep, and at that time Mr Burke and the other gentle-man were 20 or 30 yards behind, and I saw no more', Smith said.

A short while later, Carey caught up with him at the Island-bridge Gate, somewhat out of breath. They crossed the bridge to Kilmainham and had a drink together. Later they caught the tram to College Green, but sat apart from each other on the top deck.

A week after the murder, Carey appeared and paid him three pounds. Smith did not ask what it was for. Carey had paid him a similar sum after being released from 'suspect' detention after the murder of police informer Kenny. Smith may not have wanted it, he told detectives, but 'do you think I was going to throw it away?'

Smith's capitulation, along with that of Farrell and Kavanagh, gave the prosecution virtually clinching evidence. James Carey, in particular, could feel the rope at his throat, with the evidence of three approvers against him, plus the corroboration of his presence in the park by Glynn, his former employer.

The town councillor had been unnerved by Kavanagh's testimony, and it was later said to have 'forced his lips to save his neck'. But Mallon had been working him assiduously in prison, creating trust by ferrying letters between Carey and his wife Maggie, with the councillor gratified to see that Mrs Carey's replies had not been opened.

Mallon subtly worked the guilt angle, telling Carey his brother Peter's fate was inescapably entwined with his own. In carrying the letters to Mrs Carey, he also let her know that some of James' confederates in Kilmainham were singing like songbirds to their captors. Mallon badly wanted the satisfaction of cracking Carey or one of the leaders – who knew where it might lead? – even if the prosecution may not have needed it so much after Smith's confession.

P. J. Tynan, a self-styled leader of the Invincibles, later wrote in his rabid book, penned in American exile: 'It is possible that Carey was weakening. What some people in Dublin feared came true; Carey's wife was the first to move. She went to Mallon, as she expressed it, to save her husband'. Husband James she urged with personal and imploring appeals to think of his children.

Mallon's biographer, Bussy, recounts a tale of how the psychological warfare finally bore fruit. He transports us to the past in the present tense – 'One day, between the lights', before the sun has completely set and a tiny while prior to the actual necessity for artificial illumination, there is the heavy tread of several pairs of feet and the clanging and jingling of keys along the corridor onto which Carey's cell opens.

It is late for the governor to make a round of the jail, and although the doctor and the priest may be on his way to visit a sufferer or penitent, a single warder only would accompany either of them.

Yet here is the tramping of at least three persons. Obviously something unusual is happening. James Carey instinctively moves to the door of his solitary den. Nor is it merely idle curiosity that prompts him. These are terrible times, when every unusual incident is pregnant with meaning to the guilty conscience; when even the unexpected sight of one's own shadow has a momentary terror in it.

The recent campaign of 'history-making' has miserably fizzled out … the blood to be gambled for is no longer that of others, and consequently every cast of the die is fraught with dire significance.

By some lucky accident, or maybe the merest chance – few will ever be able to appreciate the luck of that accident or chance as Carey did – the little shutter before the grille, through which the warders inspect prisoners from time to time, has been left slightly open.

A small chink remains, through which Carey can command a view, by pressing his cheek tightly against the cell door and almost forcing one eye into the niche of the passage beyond, covering a range of barely four feet.

Just sufficient to whet the appetite. No more! Nothing to satisfy the all-consuming thirst for information, nothing to seriously alarm, and so put one on one's guard …

The party passes the door behind which Carey strains his eye and every nerve and every muscle to catch a glimpse of them. One man is tall and straight, wearing outdoor attire; another is much shorter and similarly clad; and the third is a prison warder.

It dawns upon him that his eye is of no use to him. His ear he must rely upon, and he is successful in hearing the order: 'Bring me a small table, a chair, some pens, ink and foolscap paper. Oh! And bring some blotting paper too, and be smart about it'.

The table, the chair, and the writing paraphernalia arrive, and at last the gas is lit. That is something gained. The mental agony of the next hour needs no description; it is indescribable. He lives a year and ages ten within the period of those sixty minutes. Something portentous is taking place – but what?

He dare not even try to think, for the suggestions which present themselves to his fevered brain are either too terrifying and horrible, or they are absurdly inadequate to account for all the ceremonial of the visit to the cell next door.

But the racking ordeal ends at last. The attendant is again summoned; the table and other things are removed; the cell is securely locked, and the party return from whence they came. The tall, straight man carries a number of sheets of foolscap, which have evidently been written upon, and as he passes the four feet limit of his vision in the full light, Carey recognises – merciful God! – John Mallon, the relentless, unerring policeman'.

As Tynan wrote: 'The belief implanted in his weak mind that it was a race between Curley and himself decided the issue – for this foul lie was purred out with proper emphasis by the feline Mallon. So Carey fell, and the machinery of British rule in Ireland dreamed they had found a saviour'.

The empty-cell trick played on Carey, a father of seven, must have been hard to bear. Bussy says they played it again the next night, encouraged by the intelligence that Carey had asked a warder who it was in the cell next door. The warder refused to answer.

Again they brought the writing materials and the foolscap, and this time the crown solicitor, George Bolton, accompanied Mallon into the vacant room for a while – all for Carey's benefit. The mental horrors of that night must have been extreme for the prisoner, but his anguish was as nothing compared to the following morning, when the same warder, now part of the game, suddenly appeared to take pity on him and confided in a whisper that the prisoner next door was an old friend – Daniel Curley!

172

Mallon now visited his prime cells in Kilmainham, and to Carey hinted that his comrades had betrayed him. Carey said he would not listen. Mallon next assured Dan Curley that Carey had given way, and saw sterner resistance: 'You would say that, Mr Mallon,' was the reply. The detective shrugged, as he shrugged again when bringing another letter to Carey from his wife, 'probably your last, James, for Dan intends to see that your neck is snapped like a twig'.

Carey collapsed. 'I want to tell you everything, Mr Mallon. I will do it for my children, for my poor wife, and my brother, whom you will also have to protect'. Mallon, disguising his glee, instead expressed reserve. He would have to see how good the confession was, and whether or not it trumped that of Dan Curley. Exasperated, the protest came: 'Give me the paper and I will write it down!'

The man was now 'sold over to his wretched destiny', wrote Tynan. 'He, who the previous day had before him a patriot's death, was now steeped in the slime of poisonous treachery, and his name stained for all generations, not only of Irishmen, but of all patriotic liberty-loving mankind. By one fell stroke he had precipitated himself from virtue to infamy'.

The first statement Carey drew up in his cell was torn up and returned to him. 'This is ancient history', said a cursory Mallon. The abject creature before him promised to do better. 'I don't want your evidence, Carey', came the same dispassionate voice as before. 'I've got the rope about your precious neck, James Carey, and I mean to hang you'.

Carey moaned in hopelessness. He began a flood of protestations and appeals. He was a ringleader, and he knew the real powers in the organisation. He could tell it all. He knew it was his last chance, he said. He would hold nothing back. His blue eyes implored the grey-bearded policeman. Mallon appeared to relent.

For a long while Carey wrote. John Mallon passed out of the prison possessed of a swathe of hand-inscribed foolscap pages. He went to the Castle to get them copied.

The reaction of his colleagues differed. Curran of the Star Chamber strongly opposed his being taken as a witness, 'as I considered we had ample evidence without having to rely on his testimony'. Carey was one of the leaders and paymasters of the gang, he argued, and deserved his fate. He reasoned that, as they were identified in the dock, less prominent members would offer themselves as further approvers.

Crown counsel George Bolton disagreed, as did lead prosecutor James Murphy. They were of the opinion that a man of Carey's position turning queen's evidence would be a warning to all who might in future be tempted to engage in similar conspiracies.

Lord Spencer regarded Carey's breakdown as 'the greatest event since the landing of Henry II', and congratulated all concerned. He telegraphed the news to London and sent a special messenger – but the word came back that government opposed the acceptance of the town councillor's testimony.

Spencer, although surprised, did not brook this resistance for a moment. He insisted that if Carey's evidence was not taken, it was likely neither his comrades nor himself could be convicted. If it was a ruse, it worked. London promptly capitulated the point. The hesitations of Downing Street were out of the way.

Thus James Murphy, QC, visited Carey in his cell in Kilmainham, and got him to verify his signature and statement. Carey, no longer a wretch, but a man of regained confidence, did so. He was told the charges against both he and his brother would be withdrawn, and their families taken into protective custody. The crown would provide them with a new life in the colonies after the trials were over. All Carey had to do was go into court and make good on his promise.

Home Secretary William Harcourt informed Queen Victoria of the breakthrough. Securing a leader's evidence against his fellows, he told her, would 'strike the deepest terror into all the secret societies' and break them for generations.

The Betrayal

On 17 February, the prisoners once more made the short journey from prison to courthouse. Carey, kept in a separate cell, had to be primed with brandy because of his nerves. The other defendants were used to different groups being shuttled in and out of the dock as evidence to various charges was heard.

There had been cases of prisoners feigning sickness in prison, or actually sick, as in the case of nineteen-year-old tailor John Dwyer, who was discharged because he was so obviously near death from consumption. A particular absence did not necessarily amount to much …

The door of the court at the left side of the bench was opened and the prisoners entered in single file between a guard of policemen. The scout Dwyer was dying in hospital, but here was the fullest detachment yet, the men looking 'miserable in the extreme', according to one report.

'A more wretched or repulsive-looking group than they could hardly be collected in Madame Tussaud's Chamber of Horrors', wrote the *Penny Illustrated*, little realising that James Carey's effigy would soon join the exhibits in that emporium.

Edward O'Brien, absent for two days, placed his gaunt and haggard form to the front, with Joe Brady, formerly a central figure in every sense, now standing in the second row. His vocal harmony from Church Street choir, Tim Kelly, 'the alleged powerful assistant of Brady in his bloody work', seemed as unconcerned as ever.

'His boyish face betrayed only in its reckless expression the slightest indication of the ferocity which was shown in the perpetration of the murders. Brady appeared to have greatly changed,

his face having lost its fullness and colour. The prisoners, however, seemed to be in good spirits.

'Their general aspect has much deteriorated since they were first charged, their hair hanging in tangled masses over their foreheads, their faces apparently unwashed, and with an air of slovenliness about those who were remarkable for the assumption of respectability in their dress'.

If some prisoners noticed James Carey's absence, they saw that his brother Peter was still ranked amongst them. Their hearts had not assumed even the possibility of what was about to break upon them.

The magistrates came in; all stood up, and were seated again. Preliminary paper-shuffling passed by, Mr Murphy rose to his feet, and without looking at the dock, declared: 'Mr Carey, please'.

The stupendous moment at first is ordinary. A medium-sized man with slouching gait, shoulders rather inclined to be rounded, a blotchy face, 'beer-seasoned nose', moustache, whiskers and beard, enters court.

A yell of execration and despair! Wild and simultaneous, 'a loud wail of terror at the eclipse of a last ray of hope'. Distinct, and yet inseparable from 'a howl of rage and hate'. Reports agree on the shock and shrieks – 'Surprise was swallowed up in rage. Brady made an effort to seize him by the neck as he passed, and maledictions went up from the pen where the betrayed men were imprisoned'.

Another account: 'The prisoners appeared astounded. James Mullett forced his way to the front of the dock and beckoned to his solicitor, who went up to consult with him'. Still another: 'When James Carey ascended the table (to the witness chair) a wave of excitement seemed to pass over the whole assembly and break with full force upon the faces of the prisoners in the dock.

'They seemed paralysed with amazement and alarm, and their pent-up passion found expression in a general hiss'. It was, wrote P. J. Tynan, the British government in Ireland's greatest thunderbolt – James Carey as a public informer. 'Dublin city was astounded, all Ireland horrified'.

The commotion was suppressed, but not the glaring, the waving of fists and furious gestures. And then Carey fixed his eyes on the dock. 'Ah, I was before ye after all, Dan', he loudly commented to Curley. Reporters noted the remark – cruel, self-satisfied, and victorious.

As Carey was sworn, he appeared to be nervous, but well under control. He settled in the chair, dressed in a tweed suit 'which has suffered from hard wear', and a long brown overcoat, from the pocket of which there hung the end of a yellow and light green handkerchief.

'Were you ever a member of a society or body of men having the name of Invincibles?'

'I was'.

There was a committee of four at the head of the group when it was first formed in December 1881, Carey testified. The initial quartet included himself, publican James Mullett, Dan Curley and Edward McCaffrey. When Mullett was arrested over the Bailey murder, Curley replaced him as chairman. Joe Brady filled the vacant place.

The object of the society, said Carey, was 'in the first place to make history, and in the next to remove the principal tyrants of the country'.

'What do you mean by removing?'

'Of course, put them to death'.

Indignation and disgust swept over the prisoners' faces as they eyed with scorn the man who had once been their guide and leader, now telling all he knew. 'Burning blushes of shame overspread the cheeks of the informer's brother as he turned away his face to avoid the reproachful glances of his fellow prisoners'. The press noted that throughout the day not one of his companions in the dock exchanged a word with Peter Carey.

James said he had been a member of the Fenian organisation since 1861, when he had as a comrade Thomas Brennan, subsequently secretary of the Land League. This involvement of a prominent political figure, in an organisation supposedly dedicated to non-violence, made the scribes of the press work harder and listen more closely.

Carey said he had personally subscribed nearly the entire amount for a monument to be erected to the memory of the rebel Stephen O'Donoghue, shot dead in a Fenian attack upon the constabulary in 1867.

A man named John Walsh had come to Dublin from London to establish the society, said Carey. They were to act on instructions which would come from overseas. Walsh had sworn him in, along with the few other leaders.

Carey said he could quote the oath he took on a penknife: 'With my own free will, without any mental reservation whatever, I will obey all the orders transmitted to me by the Irish Invincibles, nor to seek more than what is necessary to care for carrying out of such orders, the violation of which shall be death. There were more words than that, but I forget them'.

The men in the dock laughed. Carey said the Dublin branch was to consist of only fifty members and these were to be all 'picked men'. Again the defendants laughed, this time derisively.

The lord lieutenant, Earl Cowper, and chief secretary Forster were the first victims marked out by London for removal, said Carey. After these tyrants had been got rid of, the Irish branch would be left to choose its own targets. Walsh stayed in the city for a time. He introduced the four inner council members to a man disguised as a priest, known as Rev. Father Murphy.

Another laugh, but Carey was solemnity itself. He afterwards discovered this man to be Mr P. J. Sheridan of Tubbercurry, Co. Sligo, a prominent Land League organiser and orator.

The court heard that a Captain John McCafferty, a Fenian leader sentenced to twenty years penal servitude in 1867 but afterwards released, was next on the scene. He brought funds, often up to £50. To McCafferty Carey suggested that knives were the best weapons for their purpose. They were soon forthcoming.

One morning a woman, whom he was afterwards told was Mrs Frank Egan, wife to the secretary of the British branch of the Land League, arrived at his house, Carey said. She delivered to him a Winchester repeating rifle, a couple of revolvers, six knives and a supply of ammunition. The woman came over a second time with an almost identical consignment, save for two fewer knives.

Carey was now asked to examine a photograph. Did he recognise that man? He did indeed, said Carey, but he never knew his name. The photograph was asked to be marked 'Exhibit No. 1' – giving rise to the newspaper labelling the mystery individual 'No. 1'.

Carey said the bearded, bespectacled 'No. 1' had all the bearing and language of someone who had seen military service. He supplied all the funds, superintended the arrangements, and on occasion chided them for their lack of industry. He told the witness that money would be forthcoming, to the extent of £1,000 if necessary. He paid for all work done promptly, even liberally.

Mr Murphy said that the witness might soon have the opportunity of identifying the man if police work went satisfactorily. He then asked the witness to turn to the group's efforts at assassination.

For months they had watched the movements of the chief secretary, 'Buckshot' Forster, said Carey. They dogged his footsteps, familiarised themselves with his movements, and awaited the opportunity for an ambush, even in daylight and in the most public thoroughfares of Dublin.

Quite coolly Carey mentioned the methods to be adopted for an attempt on Forster's life in Brunswick (Pearse) Street. The horses were to be shot, and the occupants of the carriage and any bystanders who interfered were to be disabled.

The court heard of an elaborate plan to intercept Forster in the Phoenix Park. A series of lookouts developed sudden sniffles as his carriage came out of the Castle, with handkerchiefs held to faces as it reached the quays and moved further along, as if a cold was quickly spreading. As the carriage turned onto Kingsbridge, another handkerchief went up.

Then there was an outbreak of health. Henry Rowles, a fifty-year-old tailor, related to Daniel Curley and the two Hanlons, carpenter brothers alongside him in the dock, unaccountably failed to give the signal. Forster's carriage rounded the corner, made the park, and shuttled safely home.

On another occasion, Mr Forster had slept on board the mail steamer at Kingstown instead of coming up to Dublin where the Invincibles were lying in wait for him. On no fewer that three separate occasions the chief secretary was saved by the accident of a military escort passing along the quays with an ammunition wagon at the very moment his carriage was being driven to or from the Castle.

On the evening when the hated Forster, now the ex-secretary, had left Ireland, members of the Invincibles had walked up and down the platform at Westland Row and searched a train's compartments for their intended victim. By the merest chance, Forster had gone to the port for his departure much earlier than expected.

'He wasn't in the carriage,' said Carey. 'If he was, he wouldn't be alive today'.

The Invincibles then switched their attentions to the permanent under secretary, Thomas Henry Burke. Carey confirmed that on Friday 5 May the gang had been watching for him in the park, and again sought an opportunity the following morning, the infamous sixth. That afternoon they gathered again.

Carey said he was not familiar with Mr Burke and brought Joseph Smith along as a spotter. This man was an innocent tool and did not know the purpose for which he was required, Carey maintained. There was 'some movement among the prisoners' at this unexpected assertion, and the witness declared, in answer to some remark: 'I will save every innocent man I can'.

Carey said that his car, driven by Fitzharris, pulled up opposite the polo ground, a little above the Gough statue.

'After a few moments I went over to look at the polo match,' while the others remained where they were. 'I stopped at the polo ground until Curley came to me. Curley said, "What are you doing here?" I replied: 'I am looking at this game. I never saw it before". He said: "It's not here you should be; you should be over [the road]; you can't tell the moment he might be coming up".'

Carey did as he was bade and sat with Smith on a bench at right angles to the main thoroughfare, with a good view down to the park entrance. The builder Glynn then came up, spoke with him, and went away at a few minutes past seven.

At ten minutes past seven Smith suddenly started from his seat and advanced a few paces, exclaiming: 'Who's this? Here he is!'

Carey continued: 'Smith said, "Come on", and he made for the car, I being twelve or fifteen feet behind. Smith told Kavanagh – of course, I did not know his name – to be quick. "Hurry up! Hurry up!" and Kavanagh took off the nosebag, and Smith and I got on the car'. Smith now seemed the leader, as Carey told it.

The court fell to a 'painful excitement', the silence broken only by the voices of counsel and the witness, Carey graphically describing the hurrying away to warn the gang and the signalling with handkerchiefs.

In a voice barely audible, he named the men who were waiting to perform the deed on the opposite side to the viceregal lodge. They were Joe Brady, Tim Kelly, Pat Delaney, Thomas Caffrey, Michael Fagan, Joe Hanlon and Dan Curley.

'With an obvious effort he raised his voice to describe the fatal scene, the departure of Smith, and the last consultation between Curley, Brady and Carey'. The witness was dismissed by Joe Brady as the moment for action neared, and Carey thus followed Smith cross-country, making the Khyber pass road for exiting the park.

The unsuspecting targets were now only about 250 yards from the assassins, who had meanwhile split up into three groups to take their places on the path. Carey, amid dead silence, recited the final scene: 'When I was about 250 yards away from the place where I left those men – I looked around occasionally before that, but at that distance I looked – I saw the seven men meet the two. The first three were abreast – Curley, Fagan and Hanlon, twelve feet after them Kelly and Brady, and six feet behind Delaney and Caffrey.

'I saw the two meeting the seven, and the two passed through the ranks. They let them pass through. I said, "it is another failure"'.

Mr Murphy: 'Don't mind what you said. What did you see done?'

'I went on a few steps further, and I looked around. I saw a right-about movement made by the last four. I went on a few steps further and I looked again, and I saw the two men in the rear getting to the front, and closing on the first two men'.

'The two gentlemen?'

'The two gentlemen. What I saw then I will describe. I saw one figure coming in collision with the two gentlemen. The man in grey was on the inside. I did not know the other. I saw this man, Joseph Brady, raising his left hand and striking with the left hand the man in the grey suit. That is all I saw'.

Carey then said he made his way to the Islandbridge Gate. 'It was seventeen minutes past seven o'clock when I left the pathway. About twenty minutes past seven it was all over. I looked at my watch; I timed my own movements accurately that day'.

He overtook Smith, and then went into Coady's pub, telling Smith to meet him at the tram. After a drink, he and Smith took the tram to town, and went to a pub in Grafton Street. Later that evening, Carey said, he met Daniel Curley.

'What did Daniel Curley tell you?'

'I asked him, 'Is it true what I hear, that Lord Frederick Cavendish and Mr Burke were both killed?' 'Yes, I believe so,' said he. 'Of course, I don't know whether they are killed or not.

'I was close upon the two gentlemen,' added Curley, 'and I saw Joe Brady tackle one of them and follow him into the road. I saw him then come back from him. I saw him wipe the knife on the grass to take the blood off it, and then he started. I saw them all on the car, and I saw them going away'.

'And what did Curley say then?'

'Then he came away with Fagan and Hanlon. Their cab went down towards the Park gate'.

Curley told Carey that his party saw the two men on velocipedes following them, and they covered them with revolvers. Curley, Fagan and Hanlon were all armed in this way. The cab, driven by Skin the Goat, flew off in the direction of Phibsborough.

That same night, Carey said, he also met Brady.

'I asked him why he let them pass, and he said a car passed just at that time [Noud] and it caused them to hesitate, and Brady told me then that they turned about face and attacked them. He said that he put his hand on Mr Burke's shoulder and struck him, and that when doing so the other gentleman turned round and struck him with an umbrella in the face.

'He said he got excited and struck him on the arm. He said, "The gentleman then ran down the slope and into the road, and I followed him and settled him there." He said, "I looked round and saw Timothy Kelly at Mr Burke, who was lying on the ground."

'He also said, "I saw him coming away from Mr Burke, and I put the knife into Mr Burke's throat."

The whole court recoiled at the re-lived slaughter. Brady seemed 'overcome with emotion', and leaned his head against Edward McCaffrey's shoulder in the dock, unable to maintain his careless demeanour.

Carey described a meeting held a night or two afterwards in McCaffrey's house in Peter Street.

He, Brady, Curley, McCaffrey and the mysterious No. 1 were present. Brady gave the whole account of what had occurred. The knives were produced, and the superior officer said they were to be destroyed.

Carey said he joked at the meeting that they were 'national relics'. He suggested that the knives should be kept for the Irish Exhibition to be held later that summer. The atmosphere in court became even colder at this callous cheerfulness. But Carey's proposal was overruled.

Dr Charles Cameron, the city analyst who found 'blood' on the knives found in Carey's loft would undoubtedly have felt uncomfortable, had he been in court, at the next revelation: 'They were broken into little bits and the handles were burned'.

(Cameron often appeared as an expert witness in the police courts and was invariably asked thereafter, when he supported a charge of excess water in butter or shortage of fats in milk: 'Did you testify that the rust on the knives in the Park case was a bloodstain?' He squirmed in embarrassment each time.)

The intact knives produced in court had different handles to the ones actually used, said Carey. Those had been improved with cord wrapped around the handles, at McCaffrey's suggestion, to give a better grip. This version of events, replete with the ring of truth, was heard 'with an eager attention which nothing could have intensified'.

The witness spoke of speculating with Dan Curley as to where the money was coming from, whether from the Land League or from America. Prosecutor Murphy asked if the prisoners Curley and McCaffrey received any money while they were in prison, and if he knew from whence it came. Carey said it came from the Land League, Parnell's engine of agitation, and McCaffrey had sent back his first cheque because it was not sufficient.

The last sight of No. 1 was in October 1882 at Blackrock railway station, when Carey told his controller of the disposal of the murder knives.

Carey's evidence closed and the prisoners were put forth in batches of five for identification. As Carey turned uneasily around, he was greeted with angry cries and menacing looks and gestures.

Fitzharris – 'You hired assassin. I don't belong to you at all'.

Caffrey – 'You are a double-backed informer'.

Joe Hanlon – 'A ruffianly one too'.

Martin – 'He has seen me in prison but could not have known me before'.

Patrick Delaney, pale and emaciated, came forward, seeming to be 'almost in the grip of death', by one account. He held up a quivering finger, shaking it at Carey 'more in sorrow than in anger', and said in a hollow voice: 'Mr Murphy, there is the man I may thank for my whole misfortune in life, from my childhood up'.

Carey's personal carriage

Trial

The prisoners were committed for trial after Carey's apparently conclusive evidence. In the meantime, John Dwyer had died of consumption, and in late March 1883, the number indicted was reduced further by the death of fifty-year-old tailor Henry Rowles. He was the man who had failed to 'catch cold' when Forster's carriage was passing. Now he was dead of suspected heart disease.

A report circulated that Rowles had been poisoned in prison, a story that had no foundation but which worried the authorities amid growing signs of public disgust at Carey and a resultant upswing in sympathy for the men he accused. Every effort was made to induce Rowles' wife and friends to allow a post mortem examination so that the cause of death might be put beyond all possible question, but they would not agree.

Rowles' funeral was described as a very poor affair. 'Had Rowles not failed to give the signal on the day when Mr Forster was supposed to have been murdered, it is probable more honour would have been paid to his memory,' said the *Times*.

But while the funeral cortege 'consisted chiefly of his personal friends' when it left his home in Fishamble Street, it did prove the focus of nationalist sentiment – despite what London newspapers reported. Fresh successions of mourners to the procession were received as it went along, said Irish reports.

'At Emmet's house, in Thomas Street, a crowd had collected which fell into ranks when it [the cortege] passed. About 400 young men of the artisan class marched in the procession in military order, six deep'. Rowles was borne shoulder high to the grave in Glasnevin, where his coffin was deposited amid the wailing of the widow and the silent weeping of others as three uniformed constables stood by watching, with many other police in plain clothes.

The uneasiness of the authorities came amid newspaper revulsion at Carey's self-serving conduct, and in some cases at his very deployment. 'There are Governments who would rather let 99 guilty men go than convict one innocent man on Carey's evidence', wrote *United Ireland*.

The *Irish World*, published in New York, dubbed it 'the most unblushing perjury ever witnessed in any court of justice' and claimed it had 'unmasked the most diabolical conspiracy between Crown lawyers and hired informers'.

Many dubbed it tainted evidence, pointing out the danger of a witness over-egging the pudding to make sure of saving his own life. There were already many inconsistencies in the crown case, apart from the sharp point of the 'blood' that was actually rust on a knife, with some glaring doubts about third-party identifications. And yet independent witness evidence to the men's presence in the Park was obviously needed to corroborate informer evidence.

Even the *Times* had written: 'No prisoners are likely to be convicted on the uncorroborated evidence or in the teeth of contradictions and inconsistencies detected on cross-examination'. It believed a 'network of testimony' would be put in place, but the nationalist papers instead feared jury-packing and witness bribery.

The trial of Joseph Brady, the first of many for the double assassination opened in Green Street courthouse on Wednesday, 11 April 1883, before Judge William O'Brien. Feverish excitement attended on the case, the prisoner being conveyed from Kilmainham prison under mounted military escort, with armed police and marines following on cars.

The judge, known as 'hatchet-face', according to reporter J. B. Hall, was of a singularly cadaverous appearance. Brady was dressed in a long frieze coat, his black hair carefully brushed, and his spirits did not appear to have suffered in any way since his confinement.

He rested his left hand on the rail in front of the dock while

187

the jury was sworn. His right was behind his back, playing with a short stump of pencil. At length the twelve men who would decide his fate were empanelled, all but three or four being men of mature age, with grey hair and whiskers. Not a good start.

The case for the prosecution was opened by the attorney general, A. M. Porter, and he sketched the evidence to be submitted in the trial. Brady listened with apparent unconcern, occupying himself at one moment in picking his teeth with the pencil.

With careful, plodding steps, the attorney general brought his audience to the moment of the assassinations. Brady, 'a man of Herculean strength', had driven the amputating knife through Mr Burke's body at one blow and then turned on Lord Cavendish, fracturing his arm in two places as he ran him through, following him into the road and remorselessly finishing him, then returning to coldly cut Mr Burke's throat.

He was not there as an apologist for the approver James Carey, the attorney added. The evidence would not merely rest on him or Michael Kavanagh, but sufficient evidence would be produced from the field of the murders to show that Brady was there and took the escape car.

Concluding, he said it was a melancholy and painful thing to have anything to do with a trial on a capital charge, but he and the jury must do their duty, and this case would result in a severe lesson being taught to persons who entered these conspiracies and involved themselves and their families in disaster.

It would show how little assurance could be placed by assassins in those who urged them forward. If further illustration was required, they had it in the melancholy fact that Brady, who was ready to do their business in this conspiracy, was now in his time of danger deserted, and obliged to appeal to the crown and government, whose officials he was employed to assassinate, for mercy and clemency to provide him with counsel for his defence.

The closing of the speech brought 'symptoms of applause', which were immediately checked.

The calling of Carey as a witness created a sensation far exceeding even the earlier scene at Kilmainham. Knowing him, as nearly everyone in court had done as a town councillor and a citizen of repute, and one with a reputation for ostentatious piety, his impending presence produced a striking effect. Every head stretched forward, and every breath was held.

Carey coolly approached, his hair and beard carefully trimmed, dressed in tweed with a gold watch chain, presenting a 'dandified appearance'. He held a hat in his right hand, and his left was casually in his pocket – and still there when he ascended a few steps to be sworn.

'Here he was, bending his neck over the Holy Book preparatory to roping necks,' wrote Bussy, Superintendent Mallon's confidant, in 1910. Bussy claimed there had been a plot formed by the prisoners after Carey's first betrayal, 'for the powerful Joe Brady to clutch the renegade as he came into court, drag him into the midst of the sufferers from his falsity, and trample him to death before police or prison assistance could reach him'.

There had been just one more remand appearance after that, when a line of policemen was drawn up in front of the dock as a guard. At the close of his evidence, Carey had walked away from the dock, in the direction of the bench, and leapt a barrier to go out another door. The prisoners then had cried such things as 'leave us a lock of your hair!' and 'Oh, come this way!' Carey answering with the modest words, 'There is no necessity'.

Now there was no one in the dock but Brady. Carey sat down, crossed his legs, and settled himself into a comfortable position.

He spoke slowly, in a low voice, often being urged to raise it. During his evidence he had occasion to look straight at Brady, who 'cast a look that spoke volumes' when their eyes met. Carey shifted his position, and looked at him no more.

He told of Brady telling him to send the spotter Joe Smith 'to hell out of it', when Carey and Smith arrived to alert the killers of their targets' approach, of Brady telling Carey directly 'You can go away, we do not want you'.

Then, as Brady took copious notes of the evidence, Carey told what he had seen of the murders, and of asking Brady later if it was true that Cavendish was also dead. Brady had replied, 'I don't know who it is [killed with Burke], but only for himself he would not be the way he is now'. The other man [Cavendish] had struck him with an umbrella and called him a ruffian, but for that he would have escaped, Brady asserted.

Carey said he had asked Brady was it true that he had been so cool as to wipe the knife on the grass, before leaping onto the escape car, and the prisoner replied that it was so.

'The hideous incident of the flashing knives, the brief struggle of the victims, and the final fatal blows was dreadful to listen to,' wrote reporter Hall. 'It is but a mild statement to record that Carey left the witness chair amidst the undisguised disgust of those who had listened to him'.

On leaving the table at the end of that first day the approver was brought close to Brady and 'received the same appalling and loathing look'. He was hurried away by his guards.

Carey's cross-examination came the next day, under questions from Dr Thomas Webb, regius professor of criminal law and Brady's lead defence counsel. His first question was unusual: 'Are you a man that makes any profession of religion?'

'No, not *profession* of it'.

'Pray Sir, don't attempt to bandy or chop logic with me. Do you make any profession of religion?'

'I am a professed Roman Catholic'.

'Were you ever a member of any religious sodality?'

'I was'.

'Had you any rule as to the periods on which you were to receive Holy Communion?'

'Yes, once a month'.

'While you were a member of that sodality, did you receive Holy Communion once a month?'

'I had the honour'.

'Did you in March 1882?'

'I did'.

'In April 1882?

'I did'.

'In May 1882?

'No'.

'Is it your testimony here that you assisted in the Holy Mystery of your religion when you were steeped to the lips in blood?

'I was not'.

'You were not?'

'No, I was not'.

'Were you not the prime mover and director in the murder of Mr Burke?'

'No, I was not'.

'What?' cried Dr Webb, repeating the question.

Carey answered: 'Not that portion of it'.

'I ask you again, were you not a prime mover and director in the murder of that unfortunate gentleman?'

'Well, yes I was. (After a pause.) I did it on compulsion'.

'Were you not a paymaster of assassins?'

'On compulsion'.

'Was it under compulsion that you took the Communion?'

'No'.

'Was it under compulsion that you joined the Invincibles?'

'No'.

Webb moved on to Carey's sitting on a Fenian court martial against those suspected of giving information to the authorities. The witness did not appear to notice the irony as he agreed that he had helped to pass capital sentences on 'traitors'.

He sat on them while he was a member of the religious sodality, Webb pressed. But Carey argued that the men had condemned themselves by breaking their oath. He admitted that he knew the same rule applied to himself, with a similar penalty involved when joining the 'inner circle' whose object was to remove tyrants.

'And still you joined it?'

'Still I joined it'.

Turning to the assassinations, Carey agreed that it was his job to see that Burke was identified. He was one of two men who held up white handkerchiefs as a signal that he was coming.

'And do you think your guilt is diminished because you were one of two?'

'No, I am only explaining it to you'.

Were your last words before you parted from the men who you say were the murderers, 'Mind, it's the man in grey?'

'Exactly. Those were the last words I said'.

He added: 'The way there may be no mistake'.

'The way there may be no mistake; and was that under compulsion?

'No'.

As Webb probed Carey's evidence, the witness made a sudden declaration; 'Oh, I could swear a lot more things. I am only telling half the things that happened, just according as they were asked me. I am more friendly to you than you think, Mr Webb. Bear that in mind'.

Webb: 'Don't address me except in answer to my questions. I don't want to have any communication with you'.

If Carey had hoped to relieve the pressure, it was a futile expectation. Webb asked him who first suggested knives as an instrument of murder. Carey replied: 'My depositions state that I did. Not knives, daggers'.

'Did you at any time suggest that the daggers used in this abominable murder should be sent to the National Exhibition?'

'I did'.

Carey admitted that he had wanted them preserved as relics. He was still a member of the sodality at the time.

'Have you received the Royal pardon?'

Carey smiled. 'I don't know. I have got no official intimation of such'.

'Do you know whether your pardon depends upon whether

Conspirator, councillor and approver, James Carey

Queen Victoria [top left] doubted Gladstone's liberal policies and found a kindred spirit in 'Buckshot' Forster [top right]. Government informer William Lamie [above left]. Publican and sometime rebel, James Mullet [above right].

Robert Farrell [top left] was first to tell all. Patrick Delaney [top right] was sent to assassinate Judge Lawson. Phoenix Park getaway driver Michael Kavanagh [above left]. Co-conspirators Edward McCaffrey [above right] and William Moroney [inset].

James Murphy   George Bolton   Thomas Webb

Where would-be assassins
met after a failed mission

'Healthy' Henry Rowles failed to catch cold, but still died before trial [top left]
Carpet laying conspirator Joseph Smith was an Invincible inside the Castle [top right]
[Centre] Lead prosecution counsel and crown solicitor; Brady's defence counsel
[Below] Dublin Castle inquiry room. Kilmainham prison doctor William Carte [inset]

Daniel Delaney [top left] with Thomas Doyle [inset].
The 'prime minister of the Invincibles' Daniel Curley who said he would rather die
with honour than live by informing [top right]
James 'Skin the Goat' Fitzharris [left] and the 'fierce-looking' Edward O'Brien [right]

Joe Brady [top left] and Timothy Kelly [top right] who both died in the execution yard at the hands of William Marwood [below left]. Governor J. R. Gildea of Kilmainham [below] where a black flag signalled a prisoner's successful despatch.

Marwood,
Executioner.

Thomas Caffrey [top left].
Thomas Martin [top right]
with Peter Doyle [inset].
Michael Fagan [middle left]
and the approver Peter Carey
[middle right]

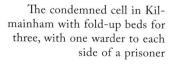

The condemned cell in Kilmainham with fold-up beds for
three, with one warder to each
side of a prisoner

Brothers Joseph and Laurence Hanlon [top]

[Centre] Mrs Maggie Carey and her son Thomas. Patrick O'Donnell [extreme right, centre] who shot husband and father James Carey aboard the *Melrose* [above] off the coast of South Africa.

Carey the accursed outcast in a contemporary drawing [left]

your evidence is regarded as satisfactory by the crown or not?'

'Certainly not. There were no terms of that kind'.

'Are you certain of your pardon?'

'Well, I believe so'.

'When had you first reason to believe you were pardoned?'

'On the day I gave the first information. (*With emphasis*:) I confirmed the information already given'.

On the night before his evidence being accepted he was informed that he would be pardoned, Carey said.

'By whom were you informed?'

'By Mr Mallon and some others'.

'Where did this interview between you and Mr Mallon take place?'

'In Kilmainham, my country residence' (laughter).

And your brother Peter?'

'He was included in it'.

After Carey came the evidence of the approvers Robert Farrell, Michael Kavanagh and Joseph Smith against Brady. Kavanagh told of Brady's role in the killings and said the knifeman had come the next morning to the house in Townsend Street where Kavanagh was lodging. 'He took me down under an arch and gave me two pounds there'. This was in addition to the pound Brady had given him the previous evening after the escape from the Park, and Brady later also brought him a harness.

Then came the independent corroborative witness, park ranger George Godden. He saw Brady on the getaway car leaving the scene. He was sitting close to the driver (Kavanagh), behind his left shoulder. The left side of the car was presented to Godden's view.

A crucial point here for the defence was Kavanagh's evidence that Brady had been seated behind his right shoulder during the flight from the scene. The defendant would therefore have been on the right hand side of the car, facing away, when it passed Godden, who could only have seen the two men who faced him on the left hand side.

'What side do you say Brady was on when you were driving off?'

Kavanagh – 'He was on the right hand side'.

'That is where you put him?'

'That is where he got himself'.

The park ranger however claimed to have seen all five men on the car, and had provided detailed descriptions. Mallon regarded him as 'very sensible and steady', and he was later paid a 'considerable' reward for his information.

Dr Webb opened for Joseph Brady. He told the jury that they would in future look back on this moment as the most memorable of their lives. One of the effects of a crime like this was that it awakened in the mind of the whole community a sense of the 'wild justice of revenge'.

There was a cry for punishment, an impulse for immediate vengeance. Society itself turned savage; the law was in danger of becoming lawless, and Justice threw away her scales, tore the bandages from her eyes, and struck out wildly with her sword.

He warned the jurymen that if any trace of this feeling existed in their minds, they must make every effort to purge it. He did not appear as the advocate of the guilty; he was assisting in the administration of the law as much as the crown counsel and the jurors themselves.

The evidence by which the charge was supported was as portentous as the crime. No man who listened to the evidence of Farrell, Kavanagh or Carey would to the day of his death forget the perjury, the disregard of every law, human and divine, the shamelessness …

Farrell was obliged to admit that all he swore before was false. It was almost idle to speak of Carey. No words of his could increase the feelings of indignation that must agitate the jurors when they remembered what he swore.

He reminded them that Carey was the prime mover of the conspiracy, its concoctor, one of its directors, the man who first

suggested the knife as the instrument of murder, the paymaster of
the assassins, the man who marked his victim and gave the signal,
the man whose last words were, 'Mind, it is the man with the grey
suit'.

Yet, great as was the horror which passed through the world
when the crime was committed, Web lamented, there was a greater
thrill of surprise and outraged conscience when they heard that
the arch-fiend of the pandemonium he had created was selected
by the crown and granted a pardon!

What would be the sentiment of the civilised world tomorrow
when they read what had occurred that day? This man, steeped to
the lips in blood, was all the time a member of a religious sodality,
desecrating the holiest sacraments of the religion of Christ.

It was such a man who was selected for grace and pardon, by

what moral arithmetic he failed to comprehend. Even admitting that the unfortunate prisoner at the bar was guilty, there was no honourable mind which would not sooner taken the position of Joe Brady than occupy the place of James Carey.

Did the jury think that the men who sacrificed two innocent victims would hesitate to sacrifice a thousand Joe Bradys by perjury while their own necks were in a halter? It was on the knife, and not on the Four Evangelists, that Carey should have been sworn. The evidence on which the jury was asked to act was unreliable and preposterous.

Evidence would be given to show that Joe Brady was innocent.

Conviction

Bluster aside, Joe Brady had no real answer to the charge, but the defence went through the motions. Their first witness was a girl named Annie Meagher who swore she saw him on the day of the murder at the Dorset Street home of her uncle, Christopher Flynn. She also went for a walk with him at such a time that he could not have been in the park, engaged in assassination.

The attorney general, in cross examination, confined himself to bringing out that she was a personal friend of the prisoner and that her uncle was a stonecutter at the same works at which Brady was employed. On leaving the witness chair, Annie flashed a smile at the dock, which Brady returned.

Then came a publican, Thomas Little of 180 North King Street, who swore to Brady being at his house on the night of the murders from before nine o'clock until eleven. His evidence was turned into knots at the expert hands of prosecutor Murphy, such that the judge had to warn the witness to refrain from raising his voice in a threatening manner to his cross examiner.

Annie's uncle and his wife were next to back up the alibi evidence. Brady's fellow stonecutter held up reasonably well, but Mrs Ann Flynn confessed that she, Annie and Joe Brady's mother had talked over the looming trial. Her husband had said to her: 'You remember Joe Brady being here on the night of the 6th, and you will be able to prove it'.

'Both she and her husband gave no good reason for remembering with such accuracy all that happened on May 6th', remembered one scribe, 'whereas they could tell nothing whatever about the 4th or 5th'.

JUDGE WILLIAM O'BRIEN

Cross-examined, Christopher Flynn admitted he had gone to jail for a week rather than give a deposition to the Curran Inquiry about what he knew of Joe Brady. The prosecution would later make much of that – why would Flynn give alibi evidence for his friend now, but refuse to be put on oath about the same man a few months earlier, if he was indeed innocent?

The day's sitting was brought to a close a few minutes after six o'clock. 'Immense crowds of people had gathered in the streets near the courthouse. As the cavalcade passed down Capel Street there were hisses for Carey and cheers for Brady, and so marked were the demonstrations that the police arrested two men and hauled them off for the night.

Decision day for Joe Brady was Friday the thirteenth. The prisoner was seen to be more lifeless than at any time since his arrest. His faced was pallid. Leaning forward on the railing, he listened to a last piece of evidence in his favour. A young man named James Edward Kennedy claimed to have seen Annie Meagher walking with her beau shortly after seven o'clock.

Richard Adams rose to sum up for the defence. He began with a protest against the 'modern practice of trial before the bar of public opinion'. He asked the jury to put out of their mind statements as to Brady's guilt which had appeared with indecent haste in the newspapers.

He asked them to compare the evidence of Annie Meagher – unstained, and without a breath of suspicion – to that of Carey – liar, hypocrite and murderer by profession. Let them weigh Judas James Carey against innocent Annie Meagher, the latter's evidence corroborated by Kennedy the clerk, and he would await their verdict without fear.

Judge O'Brien summed up with the most solemn gravity. The

jury had defence evidence before them that seemed to bestow an alibi on the prisoner. An alibi was usually challenged on various grounds, one of which was that it rested on an innocent mistake, and another that it was a wilful falsehood.

Annie Meagher, niece of the defendant's work colleague, said that she met Brady between four and five o'clock and that they went to Burgess' public house in Britain Street (Parnell Street), keeping company until ten minutes past eight o'clock.

His lordship pointed out that she had been in his company since the day of the murders, and there was nothing which could have tended to fix in her mind the circumstances of the particular evening. This ignored the obvious event – but the judge next proceeded to emit a highly-coloured comment: 'That kind of defence is frequently resorted to, and invented, especially by women, in cases where its production would assist one of their own friends'.

He then reviewed the other defence testimony, which he suggested was open to the interpretation that a witness was assigning to one day that which belonged to another. And then his lordship went through the evidence for the prosecution …

At thirteen minutes past three o'clock, the jury filed out to begin their deliberations.

They were back forty minutes later.

Every face of the twelve wore a grave and solemn expression. Brady ascended to the dock and 'strove to assume a smile, but it was a very sorry effort, and the pathos of his face told a tale of uneasy working within'.

It was a moment of intense excitement and no one was more ill at ease than the prisoner.

Mr Geale (clerk of the court): 'Mr Foreman, have you reached a verdict on which all of you are agreed?'

'We have', replied Richard King, insurance agent and spokesman for the twelve.

How say you, is the defendant guilty or not guilty of the charge on the indictment?

'Guilty, my Lord'.

As quick as lightning, all eyes were swept from the jury box to the dock. A sudden start, an increased pallor, and Brady had recovered himself. By 'a wonderful effort' he placed his hands without tremor on the bars in front.

Geale, addressing the prisoner, declared: 'Joseph Brady, you have been found guilty that you did, on the 6th of May, 1882, feloniously, wilfully, and of malice aforethought, did kill Thomas Henry Burke. What have you to say now why judgment and execution of death shall not be awarded against you, in accordance with the law?

'I am not guilty of the charge,' replied Brady. 'It has been all paid informers that swore against me here. They would swear against His Lordship, or any man in the whole court, as well as me, to clear the guilt of themselves, any of them. I am not guilty of the charge'.

Mr Justice O'Brien: 'Joseph Brady, you have been found guilty upon cumulative and overwhelming evidence such as to preclude any intelligent person from entertaining a doubt of your guilt of this most dreadful crime.

'Considering that other persons still remain to be tried on the same charge, I desire to abstain, to forbear from dwelling upon the atrocity, the cruelty, and the injustice of that most heinous crime. I certainly will not say a single word to aggravate the pain of the dreadful situation in which you now stand.

'For the life which you have taken, your own life must be forfeited. You have now, after the lapse of so long a period of time, having all the advantage of a deliberate and fair trial, and of the highest and most zealous advocacy that the profession of the law could furnish, been found guilty, and have to follow your victims to eternity'.

Brady: 'I am not the first that has been sworn against innocently. That is one thing'.

Mr Justice O'Brien: 'I think it my duty to declare that I entirely concur in the justice and the propriety and the necessity of the verdict which has been pronounced by the jury against you, and I entirely believe the evidence on which that verdict was pronounced'.

His lordship now assumed the black cap. A silence fell.

'The sentence of this court upon you, Joseph Brady, is that you be taken from this court to the prison in which you were last confined, and on Monday, the 14th day of May in this present year, you be taken to the common place of execution within the walls of that jail, and there be hanged by the neck until you are dead, and that your body be buried within the precincts of the prison, and may God have mercy upon your soul'.

Joe Brady bowed to his counsel: 'Thank you, Mr Adams. Thank you, Dr Webb'. He was led away. Many of the persons present remained so gripped at the scene they were watching that there was little commotion.

Annie Meagher, the girl with whom Brady had been walking out, fled from the court. She ran the few hundred yards from Green Street to Brady's home in North Anne Street, where his mother had decided to wait for news. The two women collapsed in tears together.

Joe Brady's father had been unable to get into court. He walked about the nearby streets to ease his troubled mind. Turning a corner, he met a running newsboy from the *Evening Telegraph*. Throwing him a question, the boy yelled 'Guilty!' and scurried on.

The trial of dapper Dan Curley followed immediately on the next day available to the court, Monday 16 April, with the same *dramatis personae*. Peter Carey, brother of James, had now been taken into protective custody, having similarly turned informer.

Newspaper reporters were being privately briefed that Peter Carey would swear that Dan Curley had suggested that one of the Invincibles' own members be killed in order to protect the group. The claim was that Curley had advocated the 'removal' of Michael Kavanagh, the getaway car driver, as a precautionary measure because he was 'addicted to drink' and 'liable to peach'.

Daniel Curley was put into the dock after the empanelling of a new jury, and looked quite collected and self-possessed. 'He is a remarkably fine looking man', enthused the *Freeman's Journal*, 'about five and thirty, of splendid physique, with features of almost perfect mould.

'He wears a brown moustache and beard, and his hair is carefully brushed back from his forehead, which is large, well-constructed and indicative of much intelligence'.

James Carey was the first witness and again told the story of the assassinations, relating a new detail. Brady had told him, he said, that when the murder gang initially walked past Burke and Cavendish 'the former was speaking to the latter about the attempt on Mr Forster'. They had but seconds left to live themselves.

Carey, whose empty house was now under police guard and many of whose tenants had either abandoned his properties or entered into a rent strike, was cross examined by Dr Webb, who immediately accused him of being a murderer.

The witness reddened, and answered after some hesitation: 'I was not. I shed no blood'. He said he thought the attempted assassinations were only 'playing at soldiers'.

Dr Webb, taking up this statement, forced Carey to admit that he had been concerned in no less than twenty attempts on Forster, 'and you call that playing at soldiers!'

Carey, in a moment of apparent recklessness, now said he would not cry much if Mr Forster were assassinated, 'and I would not like to see him in heaven'.

Webb exclaimed: 'What? Would you pursue your vengeance beyond the confines of this world?'

The witness remarked: 'I would not like to meet him there', and the court laughed.

Robert Farrell gave evidence of Curley swearing him into the Invincibles and about various manoeuvres, and the next day Peter Carey followed his brother, his 'beloved brother' as he called him in his depositions, into the witness box.

Peter, who had been friendly with the car driver Michael Kavanagh in Kilmainham jail, said distrust had grown up after the killings, with Kavanagh at one point remarking that his car was 'as good as gold', a phrase with a double meaning.

He swore that this comment had come to the ears of Curley,

who declared less ambiguously that Kavanagh 'should be wiped out'. Dan Curley bent his head in the dock, and was seen to take copious notes.

Kavanagh himself gave evidence as to Curley's involvement in the plot and in the park, and as he identified the defendant, Curley cast upon him 'a look of haughty contempt which made Kavanagh look rather sheepish'.

James Carey had said it was Curley who dropped in cards to the newspaper offices boasting of the bloody deed, and Henry Robinson of the *Daily Express* gave evidence that he had found in the office an envelope with the words: *Executed by order of the Irish Invincibles*. Inside was a card of the same nature.

Carey said it had been intended to place one of the cards on the corpses.

Emma Jones, the servant girl produced from Carlisle, was next to give evidence. She had seen Curley close to the scene of the murder, when she had seen 'something glittering', followed by one man falling to the ground. She identified Curley in the dock as the man whose face was 'burned into her mind' from eleven months earlier.

Jones was the only independent corroboration, and when the prosecution's case closed, the defence lost no time in emphasising that the prisoner must be acquitted if the independent testimony failed to point to the participation of the prisoner in the crime charged against him.

Dr Webb compared the case to the Popish plot of 1678, and instituted a forcible parallel between James Carey and Titus Oates, who had also 'masqueraded in the garb of religion'. Carey was a traitor, a corrupter of the innocent, murderer in heart, and murderer in effect – and it was on his evidence that the jury was called upon to consign an honest, industrious working man, who had led a blameless life, to an early grave.

All the water of the sea could not wash out James Carey's guilt, yet he was endeavouring to slip the noose from his own neck onto that of Dan Curley. He called on the jury to discredit the evidence of all the informers as not only tainted, but contradictory, incoherent, and impossible to credit, even if it had been sworn by men before whose eyes great rewards had not been dangled.

He concluded 'in language of great solemnity and impressiveness', warning that the Almighty had delegated a portion of his prerogative to the jury and stating positively that he would call evidence to show that Daniel Curley had not been in the Phoenix Park that evening.

Peter Hanlon, the prisoner's father in law and the uncle of the two separate accused, Joseph and Laurence Hanlon, swore that Curley was in his company in Burke's public house in Mount Street at about seven o'clock on the night of the murders.

Hanlon never sounded like a credible witness, and in cross-examination first denied and then admitted that he had given an alibi for Joseph Hanlon on the night of the attempt to kill Denis Field. That alibi conflicted with the version of his movements given by the nephew himself, which further diluted the uncle's evidence.

A gas fitter named Pat Hopkins said he spoke to Curley for a few minutes outside Burke's pub at a time estimated at a quarter past seven. The publican's assistant, Joe Manning, then produced an order book from the pub showing that a 'D. Curley' had bought a pint bottle of whiskey for 2s. 6d. that evening.

The next day saw closing speeches. Richard Adams, for the defence, mentioned that the informer Carey need not be troubling himself about the possibility of meeting Buckshot Forster in heaven. 'This felicitous touch was received with considerable merriment,' one implication being that neither would get there.

The attorney general, replying, asked what motive Carey could have in implicating Curley unless he were guilty? 'There has been a suggestion that in order to save himself the informer was concocting a false charge against an innocent man.

'But if it were found out by those representing the Crown that instead of giving a true statement or a true confession, Carey was implicating innocent persons, nothing that had passed could then save him from the consequences of his own crime'.

Of Emma Jones, the sole independent witness, he said: 'There are times when the impending perpetration of a great crime, when a fixed determination of a terrible result, would give expression to a face that would never be forgotten, and so Curley's face might have become embedded in her memory'.

The judge, summing up, hit some key points. Why, if Curley had been sold a bottle of whiskey, did he not take it home with him instead of remaining at the pub to have more liquor? Why was his absence from work on both the Friday and Saturday not explained? Evidence had been given of Curley being in Carey's company on the Saturday, yet the alibi evidence only dealt with the time from six o'clock onwards.

Judge O'Brien commented that Carey seemed to be blamed much more for having given information than for his actual participation in the crime. He exhorted the jurors to 'do their duty' with the independence, courage and firmness of men to whom the highest function under law was assigned. The jury retired.

After an absence of nearly three-quarters of an hour, they returned. There was a deep and awful pause; and as that fatal word 'guilty' was uttered, Curley suddenly grew pale, but almost immediately afterwards appeared to regain his composure.

He was asked if he had anything to say, and he made 'several attempts to summon the courage to speak' before declaring distinctly that he was not guilty of the charge. The summing up by the judge had been biased and unreasonable, he declared.

When Emma Jones had picked him out at an identification parade in Kilmainham, Curley said he had been standing to the left of the twelve or fourteen men who were there, but was 'pointedly ordered to come and stand in the centre'.

He said he asked no mercy, but denied the charge between God and his conscience. 'I do not pray for pardon. I expect none from the British government. They are my avowed enemies. I may tell you that, my lord'.

Curley paused and launched himself anew. The judge had pointed out the defects and contradictions in his alibi evidence, but had presented the evidence of informers without challenge.

He admitted that he was sworn in as a member of the Fenian organisation eleven years ago when he was in his early twenties. 'That was the first oath I ever took, and I will bring that to my grave, faithfully and truthfully.

'I know the position in which I am standing here. I am standing on the brink of the grave. I will speak the truth. I never spoke to Peter Carey about Kavanagh, or anyone else.

'As to my own life, if I had a thousand lives to lose I would lose them sooner than go to my grave under the name of an informer, that I should save my life by betraying my fellow man'.

Curley said he did not drink at home and neither he nor his wife were ever addicted to alcohol, adding: 'take my life if you will, but do not touch my character'.

Then he fixed his eye on the twelve. 'Gentlemen of the jury, there is one thing certain, although you have found a verdict of guilty on the evidence of perjured men. I pray may the Lord make you suffer in this world for acting contrary to your conscience in giving this verdict.

'May you suffer in this world for it, but may you expect heaven in the next; heaven to you in the next, I say. It is far better to die than live, when foul dishonour only life would give'.

The judge waited until Curley had 'conveyed with the fervour of a genuine feeling' all the points which exercised him. He then expressed his agreement with the verdict, whose justice and necessity had been confirmed by Curley's own statements.

'I only express the hope that none of the youths of this country will be tempted to follow the deplorable example which you have set, nor to engage in those dark and mysterious conspiracies that have culminated in a crime which must be satisfied with your death and that of those engaged with you'.

He put on the black cap. The day when Dan was to die was fixed for 18 May. He ordered him taken down. Curley, as he left, thanked his counsel, and then looking up toward the gallery declared: 'Goodbye to all. God save Ireland'.

A voice from the gallery was heard to echo the aspiration: 'God save Ireland!'

The contemporary chronicler, Tighe Hopkins, wrote: 'There were considerations which made it hard to sentence him, and his wife and children were in court. He clung to the rail of the dock as he stood up to receive him doom. He was the only man who melted the court into tears.

'There were tears at the reporters' table and tears in the eyes of the judge when, at the third essay, he put on the black cap'. This latter aspect seems harder to credit, and it may be that the reporters could not see through their tears, but the next day's press coverage was undoubtedly sympathetic to 'the handsomest of the band'.

The *Freeman's Journal* that 19 April editorialised:

Treason doth never prosper; what's the reason?
For if it prosper, none dare call it treason.

It added of Carey: 'It is impossible for human power to add one hideous feature to the foul thing he is. He sinks into an abyss of infamy, in comparison to which the pit into which other conspirators are buried is a pinnacle'.

Condemnings

That same day the trial of Timothy Kelly opened. He must surely have known his fate, for the architect had already been into Kilmainham with a view to erecting the scaffold. But Tim Kelly would end up being tried three times on the same charge.

Kelly was extremely youthful, simple-looking to some, and had an air of 'bewildered anxiety'. Others referred to his pendulous upper lip and 'cold blue shifty eye'. But to many he was, literally, a choirboy, and 'the extreme youth of the prisoner made his appearance to stand trial for murder an extremely distressing one'.

The defendant himself appeared unconcerned. He followed proceedings with the 'unaffectedness of a studious schoolboy', and within two hours of his trial opening, while the attorney general was busy framing a terrible indictment against him, he turned to the chief warder of Kilmainham, who was seated beside him.

The officer produced a pencil and paper, and Kelly scribbled something. He handed it back to the warder, and then gestured to Fred Gallaher, the editor of *Sport*, who was standing in court. The note was passed to the pressman, who unfolded it, scanned its contents and nodded solemnly to the prisoner.

At the lunch adjournment, it was discovered that Kelly had asked Gallaher to put a shilling for him on some horse running that day. Owing to the strangeness of the request, Gallaher, some policemen and others had all chosen to take a plunge on the same nag. The horse was beaten.

The next day, at twelve minutes before six o'clock, the jury retired to consider its verdict. After an hour and ten minutes, they returned with the news that they could not agree. One juror apparently would not consent to send the youth to the scaffold, although the same battery of informers had gone into evidence.

The following Monday, 23 April, Kelly was arraigned before a fresh panel. The trial this time lasted barely a day and a half, with the jury retiring at lunchtime. At seventeen minutes past two, the foreman returned to say that they could not agree. The judge sent them back for further deliberations, but in half an hour came the same answer.

Sent out again, they remained deadlocked. Once again, the suspicion grew that independent evidence to Kelly's presence in the park was lacking, while it was said that two jurors could now not bring themselves to send a young man to his death. In the empty court the prosecution ruefully reflected on the juror Richard Green of Burgh Quay, who at Brady's trial had indicated that he could not serve because he had a conscientious objection to capital punishment. If only they would tell them in advance.

At half past five, the second trial of Tim Kelly was aborted and the jury discharged. Kelly was returned to Kilmainham.

While private debate was underway about the wisdom of attempting to put Kelly in jeopardy of his life for an unprecedented third time, the fourth prisoner, Michael Fagan was put into the dock. Fagan 'advanced unconcernedly', perhaps because he had not been one of those who escaped on the actual killers' getaway car, and therefore might only expect a long period of incarceration. The twenty-four-year-old blacksmith was 'of a heavy cast of countenance', and declared himself 'not guilty' of conspiracy to murder.

James Carey again gave evidence. A compositor from the *Irish Times*, who was called and initially refused to give evidence, corroborated the approver's account of Fagan's involvement. Told he would go to jail if he persisted in his uncooperative attitude, the man finally relented, was sworn, and testified crucially to seeing Fagan in the park that evening.

This man and another printer from the same workplace had been the men walking with Private Sandford – who had come forward after it was learned from an Invincible's leak in Kilmainham that one of their number had been greeted by a man in the company of a sapper.

The second compositor initially also refused to be sworn, theatrically throwing down the testament, but the threat of a year in jail, to begin with, soon concentrated his mind. He gave similar evidence. Meanwhile counsel for the crown suggested pointedly that the two men had been intimidated.

The informers Kavanagh, Smith, Farrell and Peter Carey added their evidence, and the prisoner's employer proved Fagan's absence from work on the day of the deed and the day before it. Finally, there were documents seized from his home at the time of the swoop on the suspects, which showed he had been collecting money for a secret organisation.

The records showed an acknowledgment of over £25 received in June 1881. As if the case against Fagan needed anything further, there was a large cartridge pouch and belt found in his home at Artisan Dwellings in Buckingham Street.

The defence was forced to admit that Fagan had indeed been in the park. But it maintained he had left the area soon after being saluted by his acquaintances, and was not there when the murders were committed. He was merely an accessory before the fact.

Kavanagh had given his evidence, as usual, that the men who climbed up on his car after the killings were Brady, Kelly, Tom Caffrey and Patrick Delaney.

But the crown, in its closing speech, said the limited admission made on Fagan's behalf had 'riveted home' the guilt of the prisoner in associating with a murder gang. If an explanation had been produced for Fagan's absence from work, it would have been better than 'twenty thousand alibis of pints of porter and looking at the clock at twenty minutes to seven'.

The jury went out, and a look at the clock when they returned showed they had been gone for only thirty-five minutes. The unanimous verdict was that he was guilty of conspiracy to murder.

Fagan again denied any part in the actual slayings, but Judge O'Brien was not to be denied. He again donned the black cap, surprising many. Fagan, who had left the Park with Curley on Skin the Goat's car, was sentenced to hang on 28 May. He cried out: 'I am a Fenian, and I will die one'.

On Monday, 30 April, the cabman James Fitzharris, alias 'Skin the Goat', was put on trial for murder. He presented a most remarkable appearance. Although plain to the point of ugliness, there was 'something almost comical in the expression of his rugged face', and he had a habit of winking to friends whom he recognised in the gallery, or even to strangers who happened to catch his eye.

He had the reputation of being an 'honest, decent type of cabman', and seemed quite incapable of being a bloodthirsty conspirator, especially since he had been driving so long for the Dublin Metropolitan Police themselves.

The newspapers wanted to know how he came by his extraordinary nickname. One story told was that it arose from the fact that he once killed a goat with his clasp knife after he discovered the animal eating the straw out of his horse's collar.

A more colourful, and less likely, version was that he had been 'the possessor of a very fine goat' which he kept in his back yard. Once, when extremely hard up and at his wit's end to procure the means of satisfying an 'unquenchable thirst', a friend told him that the hide of the beast would fetch a tidy sum when it died.

The obvious problem with this story is that the car man could simply have sold the creature *intacto* to obtain money for drink, but an English readership was led to believe that 'Fitz ruminated on this remark, and in a rash moment sacrificed the poor goat, sold his sleek and silvery skin, and thus gratified the inner man at the expense of those finer feelings which it may be supposed he possibly possessed'.

Skin the Goat was from Sliabh Buí, near Ferns, Co. Wexford,

but had been living in Lime Street, Dublin, for many years. Many police officers attended the trial of a man they had trusted as a friend for almost the whole of their careers, and there was said to be a genuine sympathy for the prisoner.

His trial lasted only a day and a half, and there was no independent sighting. Skin made no admissions, and the informers themselves were vague about his connection to the gang. Carey in particular managed to convey the impression that Fitzharris was little more than a permanently available cabbie.

Nevertheless, the crown pointed to one plot for Skin's white horse to get in front of Buckshot Forster's carriage as a signal for the would-be assassins. It argued that the original plot for the killing of Burke envisaged Fitzharris' cab running the under secretary's conveyance off the road in the Phoenix Park so that a second load of killers could do the rest.

The fact that Burke was on foot made two vehicles ultimately unnecessary, but did not invalidate the cold, callous intention to murder, the crown maintained.

There was genuine relief and pleasure among many in court when the jury returned after half an hour and acquitted the grizzled defendant of the murder of Thomas Henry Burke. Private smiles may have flashed between some police officers, but the crown speedily applied for the defendant's remand, saying that it was anticipated that he would be charged at some future day with being an accessory.

The sitting of the court on Wednesday 2 May lasted less than an hour. But on that day, two of the Invincibles admitted their guilt. They were Thomas Caffrey and Patrick Delaney, the latter already serving penal servitude, and both aboard Kavanagh's car as it left with the actual bladesmen, Brady and Kelly.

'Slowly and wearily, Delaney advanced to the bar. His features, wan and pale, bore marks of mental anguish, while the settled air of melancholy which hung on him drew from many looks of pity'.

He spoke in a sad tone of voice when making his statement of admission to the judge, saying: 'I am guilty of being in the park, but I did not commit the murder'.

Judge O'Brien: 'What is that? Does he plead guilty?'

'I plead guilty, my lord'.

The bench directly addressed the prisoner, telling him that the punishment for the crime of murdering Thomas Henry Burke, 'whether you plead guilty or not guilty, is the same – death'. He was asked again how he pleaded. 'I plead guilty, my lord'.

Delaney was asked why sentence of death should not be pronounced on him. Here he seemed to have calculated that his best hope lay not in avoiding conviction, but in making a plea that might ultimately lead to clemency and the commutation of a death sentence by the government.

Delaney declared: 'My lord, I was betrayed into this without knowing what it was at the commencement. I had to obey their orders or take the consequences of death by not going. I saw the murder taking place, but I took no hand, act or part in it. It was Brady and Kelly committed the murders, and no other persons.

'And my lord, about the Judge Lawson affair. It was me that saved Judge Lawson's life. I was put on to shoot Judge Lawson, and the only way I had to get out of it was to draw [a detective's] attention to me. I preferred to go to prison sooner than commit it'. He spread his hands in appeal.

The judge, who had presided over Delaney's trial for the Lawson attempt, said he knew something about the prisoner. 'It is a melancholy thing to see a man like you – a tradesman of great skill [Delaney was a carpenter], capable of earning large wages, now arraigned and doomed to death, as you must be doomed, the consequence of your plotting against members of society.

'You showed on the occasion of your arrest for the attack upon Judge Lawson some trait of feeling and consideration for your unhappy wife and family that led me to entertain some pity for you. See what you have brought yourself to, and see the misery and ruin you have brought upon your wife and children by this system of conspiracy in which you were engaged.

'I have but one duty to perform, and that is to pronounce the sentence that the law commands and requires upon your plea of guilty'. He assumed the black cap, and Delaney was given 2 June as his day to die.

'I thank you, my lord', said Delaney hoarsely and he was removed.

Patrick Delaney, who had given information in custody, was indeed reprieved. A term of penal servitude was substituted for the capital sentence, and he was later released on grounds of ill health.

Superintendent Mallon's biographer later declared such preferential treatment farcical. Delaney had always been a 'snivelling and contemptible ruffian', he maintained, but one who had safeguarded his life by 'whimpering, sneaking and babbling'.

Thomas Caffrey could have no such hope of pardon because he offered nothing to the authorities. They reportedly regarded him as 'a fairly average specimen of the Irish *amadán* – a fellow who would pull a car out of a ditch and could be trusted to keep a pipe alight or mind the coats at a fight, kick an objectionable stranger or run a mile with a message, so long as there was drink at the end of the task'.

Caffrey was determined to plead guilty, telling worried counsel that he 'did not want to give anybody any trouble'. Caffrey was on the killers' escape car, but Mallon was of the view that it would be a pity to carry the law to the ultimate finality in his case.

But here he was, confirming to the judge that he knew what he was doing in making his plea, and that he had conferred with his solicitor and told him of his intention.

O'Brien was satisfied, and the defendant was asked why sentence of death should not be passed. Caffrey replied: 'My lord, I have got to say, standing here on the brink of my grave that I did not know what was going to happen twenty minutes before. I was ordered to go there, and if I did not go there my life would have been taken. That is all I have to say, my lord'.

The judge: 'I have no means, Thomas Caffrey, of judging the truth of the statement you have now made. I do not desire to be understood as necessarily conveying that the statement is untrue'.

He quickly added, however: 'You are a terrible example of the awful consequences of your crime. I know nothing whatsoever of you, except that I assume I am right in concluding that you have been drawn into this crime, and that you have brought yourself to this friendless and deplorable condition by having been a member of a secret society whose purpose was assassination.

'Your fate is an additional reason for all persons of your class and station to at once come out of this wicked conspiracy that has carried ruin and desolation into many a home in the country'. He assumed the black cap. Caffrey was to be hung on 2 June.

Mallon's friend, Frederick Bussy, wrote later wrote: 'Caffrey would never have been hanged for the crime to which he pleaded guilty, had it not been for other offences of which he was never openly accused.

'There had been two very dark agrarian murders – one at Loughrea and the other at Barbaville (Co. Westmeath). In the former case, Mr Blake, a land agent, and his escort had been waylaid and riddled with lead. At Barbaville, Mrs Smith, a small landowner, as cruelly done to death by similar methods'.

Mallon traced the weapons used, claimed Bussy. 'They found their way [to the other crime scenes] via Dublin, through Dan Curley. They were consigned as "stair rods", and some were transferred to Loughrea by Thomas Caffrey while others were taken down to Barbaville by Michael Fagan'.

Bussy said these were 'facts asserted by John Mallon' and that the suspected involvement of Fagan and Caffrey in other killings – while untested in court – 'motivated the law officers and Castle officials in their selection of those who should be subjected to the extreme penalty'.

The rest of the shattered Invincibles were dealt with on charges of conspiracy to murder. James Mullett, the publican, the secret informer who had gone back to plotting, looked abashed as he declared: 'I am guilty of conspiracy'.

Iullett had been in Dundalk jail on 6 May, and for some time ;iously, and it was impossible for him to have played any direct rt in the assassinations or their planning. But he was identified with a background role in the attack on Denis Field and the planned killing of his fellow juror, Barrett.

O'Brien told him: 'You have been mixed up in many crimes, but the worst of your crimes is this – by your influence and superior position you have led others into an abyss of crime'. His sentence would be ten years penal servitude.

William Moroney, his hair unkempt, his dress slovenly, pleaded guilty. His solicitor, Mr McCune, rose to make a speech in mitigation, emphasising that his shoemaker client was of excellent character.

Judge O'Brien now offered surprising words of praise for the Invincibles: 'I take it that he is a man of excellent character. All these persons appear to have been of singular personal probity'. Perhaps the judge was being sarcastic, but the transcript would suggest not.

Addressing the prisoner, O'Brien told him that he was 'extremely desirous to make some exception in your favour', but devastated the prisoner by adding that he had brought into the plot the man who had just left the dock under sentence of ten years penal servitude. Accordingly, he would serve the same.

And so they would all fall like ninepins – the 'fierce' man Edward O'Brien pleaded guilty to conspiracy and had his sentencing deferred; the same with Thomas Doyle, Peter Doyle, Daniel Delaney and Thomas Martin. All admitted guilt. Laurence Hanlon, aged twenty-four, denied the attempted murder of Field, but was found criminally liable in any case.

'I will not be the last', Hanlon shouted as he was being removed from the dock, sentenced to penal servitude for life. Prisoner officers quickly pinned him arms to his sides and thrust him downstairs to the netherworld. As he was entering the cells below, Hanlon bellowed distantly: 'God save Ireland from informers!'

Executions

Joe Brady preserved a 'placid demeanour' as the banging and saw-
ing sounded the scaffold's completion in the small exercise yard,
the drop tested by weighted sacks with a stretching yaw and creak
of rope. He couldn't quite see it from his condemned cell, but he
could hear enough.

There were two warders with him at all times, watching his every
move. While he slept, they slept on either side of him, the three beds
folding up to the wall when not in use. An anonymous donor sent
over books from London for the prisoner, but the constant scrutiny
must have been unsettling.

Fr Kennedy visited him daily, but even here the warders were
within a few feet, if trying to look as inconspicuous as possible.
Brady had always been scrupulous in the practice of his religion,
and asked to be attended by a nun from the Sisters of Mercy.

Only in matters of diet and letters were the prison rules suddenly relaxed, Brady's food got better and he could receive as much
correspondence as was sent him, it having first been subject to the
usual scrutiny. Letters came in from one brother, a tailor, another
a clerk, and from a Brady sibling overseas who was a first mate in
the merchant marine.

A reporter from the *Freeman's Journal* who visited the family
home in North Anne Street, found sixty-year-old Brady's father
to be 'half-dazed' with what was about to befall his son. 'There is
no use in looking back, and we must try to do for Joe what religion
leaves to console him and me', said the bearded artisan, his face
described as leathery and like a 'sunburnt Italian' from years of outdoor work.

Mrs Brady was bereft, already mourning her 'best boy'. She pointed out that Joe had for nine years held a collection plate at the door of the Church Street chapel. 'For years, Sir,' she told the reporter, 'that boy did not taste food until he had first heard Mass'.

The mother stared into the fire amid copious tears. 'His would be a heart of stone who remained unmoved as this old woman cried for her darling boy', the pressman wrote. She got up and paced about the narrow house, an apron held to her damp face. 'Ah, Sir, Joe was never the scoundrel at home they say he was abroad, and to his poor mother he never once said an unkind or harsh word'.

Joseph Brady was hanged on the public holiday of Whit Monday, 14 May 1883. The morning dawned fine and grew brighter, 'making the circumstances more impressive by contrast with the freshness and beauty of the scene without the gloomy jail'.

A 'very large' contingent of the third battalion of the Grenadier guards from Richmond barracks were deployed against a crowd of early-morning onlookers estimated as at least 5,000 persons. Force was to be used if the holiday crowd turned ugly.

The place where Brady died is about a mile from the scene of the assassinations. This is a contemporary account by an eyewitness:

'At seven o'clock, the military and police took the circuit of the prison wall. The Grenadier guards were stationed at short intervals. Cavalry and infantry moved to and fro, the parade of armed men being intended to overawe any attempt at holding a rumoured mock funeral.

'Towards eight o'clock, orders were given to the police to clear the thoroughfare before the prison, which they did.

'The people gathered in knots here and there, and an immense concourse massed on the road opposite the eastern end of the gaol within sight of the flagstaff. The convict's mother was in the centre of a group of women weeping bitterly, a picture of misery.

'On Saturday afternoon, the doomed man said farewell to his father, mother and two sisters. The scene was a touching one: the females gave vent to their anguish, but the father controlled his feelings, while the malefactor was calm, cool, resolute, his fortitude

Crowd outside the jail for Brady's execution

never deserting him. Since sentencing, Dr Carte ordered him every comfort he desired, but the only solace he cared for was a cigar, which he smoked every day.'

On Monday morning, at twenty-five minutes to seven, Canon Kennedy and Fr O'Reilly repaired to the condemned man's cell and administered extreme unction [the last rites]. Brady slept well during the night and rose at six. Two warders were in the cell with him. His first impulse was his devotions. Asked would he take any breakfast after the sacrament was administered, he declined.

He asked permission to write a letter to his mother, which was granted, and the letter handed to the governor. At a quarter to eight, the executioner William Marwood entered the cell and pinioned him. Brady offered no resistance as his arms were strapped, preventing his moving them in any direction.

Brady's last words before being pinioned were 'take the book', as he handed a Roman Catholic prayer book called *The Key of Heaven* to a warder.

As the procession solemnly moved towards the scaffold, the priests reciting the litany for the dying and the convict answering the responses, the spectacle was awe-inspiring in the extreme. Brady walked firmly, with a smile on his face.

Canon Kennedy presented the crucifix, and he kissed it fervently, uttering not a word. He did not even say 'Farewell'. He mounted the steps of the scaffold with assurance, bearing himself firmly. When Marwood proceeded to pinion his legs, he did not offer resistance but stood firm as a rock.

Having pinioned the convict's legs, Marwood adjusted the rope. He placed the knot under the chin to the right. It was a relief to hide his face with the cap.

Joe Brady, his face covered in a white cotton sack, stood on the edge of eternity. The hangman's preparations over, Marwood nimbly stepped to one side and looked over in readiness towards the governor for the signal.

Mr Gildea checked his watch. They all waited for what seemed a very long time, the prisoner standing erect on the trap, until the governor finally nodded with grim deliberation. Marwood instantly whisked away a bolt, the trap fell, Brady's huge frame hurtled down the 'long drop' and in a matter of seconds it seized suddenly – to sway stiff and lifeless.

'Except to comply with the law, there was no need that the body should hang for an hour'. Brady was hanged in the same tweed suit he wore during the trial. Directly the drop fell Dr Carte went to the pit, and raising the white cap, looked at the convict's face and neck.

'The face was tranquil, almost as in life. The moment the drop fell, a black flag fluttered at the head of the mast erected over the roof at the eastern side of the gaol. Its appearance excited deep emotion amidst the spectators outside, many of whom knelt uncovered to offer a prayer, while others, with hats off, exclaimed "May God have mercy on him".

'The women in the crowd were the first to kneel, and their example was followed by a number of men. A large proportion of the crowd shortly afterwards dispersed, but numbers awaited the inquest, at which the verdict returned was – "We find that the said Joe Brady, on the 14th inst., died from rupture of the spinal cord in the neck from hanging, according to the sentence passed upon him on the 13th April, 1883".'

Journalist Frederick Bussy, covering the trial and inquest, later saw Superintendent Mallon come out of the jail and go towards a waiting car. He approached, hoping for a comment from his old friend, but was startled to hear Mallon shout from twenty yards away: 'Don't speak to me!'

The policeman climbed into the car and was away in a moment. Bussy however described a confession by Mallon 'as nearly as possible a quarter of a century after that event', which would be the year 1907. They were at a dinner party and Mallon asked if his friend had noticed that he had a parcel, tied up in something white, as he entered the car.

'Well it was Joseph Brady's head I had in a table napkin, and I was taking it over to the Royal College of Surgeons to be left for Dr Carte, and this is the reason I did not want you to speak to me or to detain me'.

Bussy wrote shortly after to the chief secretary, George Wyndham, to enquire about this surgical examination, but received a reply that nothing was known about the alleged incident. 'Thinking that there was possibly some doubt as to the precise propriety in removing the head of an executed convict from the prison in which he had paid the last penalty, I decided to let the matter drop'.

Tim Kelly had meanwhile been fighting hard to avoid Brady's fate. A week before the latter's execution, Kelly's third trial opened in Green Street. There had been a good deal of comment as to the wisdom of putting a man thrice in peril of his life after two 'very carefully selected' juries had disagreed.

There were many consultations between the highest authorities. A number of lawyers opined that a lower charge could be proffered, others that the honourable course in defence of the judicial system was to offer a *nolle prosequi*, or withdrawal of the prosecution. The pillars of the system would hardly fall, and it could help to fortify public confidence in the administration of justice.

Others took an opposite view, suggesting that one victory would encourage a new wave of intimidation of witnesses and jurors. The law could not be swayed from its course. Lord Spencer was said to have approached the matter with solicitude, with Bussy being of the opinion that 'his very strong leanings were on the side of leniency'.

In the end, Spencer sent for Mallon. Had he any reason to put this young man on trial for a third time? The detective superintendent replied that his duty ended with making persons amenable to justice, whereupon matters passed from his hands.

He was asked if he had any reason to think Kelly guilty.

'I have, my lord,' answered Mallon.

As to what the reason was, Mallon answered: 'He told me so himself'. That settled matters.

The third trial opened with new determination on the part of the crown. The attorney general used more vigorous and forceful language in his opening address, describing the prisoner and his conduct in stronger terms than ever before, and ended with the announcement that Joseph Hanlon would be a witness.

The prisoner was 'startled visibly', for here was another approver to put him in the park. Hanlon, a twenty-three-year-old carpenter, brother of the implacable Laurence, followed the usual informers into the box. Bearded and of good features, he climbed easily into the witness chair and Kelly's spirits promptly drooped.

Hanlon gave evidence of being told to leave the impending murder scene by Brady, and of joining Curley and Fagan in walking away. They left Tim Kelly behind, he said. He looked back and saw the government gentlemen encounter four assassins, including the defendant.

'When we got to the cab door we looked round again, and saw the two bodies lying on the ground. Kelly, Delaney and Caffrey were then on the car, but Brady had not yet mounted'. Hanlon said he left on Skin the Goat's car, at a good pace along the North Circular Road.

They went down Aughrim Street, had a drink on the quays, and then walked down Parliament Street, where Curley said he had a letter to put into the *Daily Express* office. Cross-examined, Hanlon claimed not to be an informer because 'I have told the Government nothing except what they knew before. I am sorry to be compelled to be in this position'.

'Who compelled you?'

'Those that sold me. It was to save my own life'.

'Was it to save your own life that you came here to swear against Tim Kelly's life?'

'Yes'.

The next day saw Thomas Huxley, the gardener on the Guinness estate at Farmleigh, give evidence. Mallon had previously dismissed his account as relating only to timings, but now he was able to identify the prisoner as one of a group of men he had seen in the park that evening.

Charles Stewart Parnell commented privately: 'On the Crown case alone, putting aside the alibi, I fail to see how the jury could convict the boy at the bar. Huxley, the Englishman, is the only independent witness. On that alone an honest conviction is not possible'.

The defence supplied alibi evidence, but after the rough treatment of some witnesses and the court room exposure of one as an ex-prisoner who had lied about his circumstances, it was never going to be enough. All then hinged on the final address on the defendant's behalf.

It fell to Dennis B. Sullivan, QC. He told the jurors that everything that could prejudice the prisoner's case had been crowded into the last week as if by way of fatal preparation. He had to ask them to judge the case on the facts alone.

He asked them to consider whom the instigators of the murders would select as their instrument. Would it be Kelly, a lad of nineteen, an epileptic, suffering from St Vitus' dance, whose health necessitated frequent attendance at hospital? Would they not rather select those like Carey, who could come and boast of a score of attempts on the life of a person, and whose nature knew no remorse?

He reviewed the evidence at length and again asked the jury to cast all prejudice from their minds. The British empire would still exist if this poor youth did not die, but terrible would be the meeting between Kelly and a juror 'in a future state' if that man should suppress a doubt in order to bring in a verdict of guilty.

Judge O'Brien summed up, telling the jury that the old maxim of the law was that they should not convict on the evidence of informers unless that testimony was corroborated in some way by an independent witness. But it was no *rule* of the law, he said, and they were not bound by it. They would be right to bring in a verdict based on one informer alone if they thought that evidence worthy of belief.

Fortunately, there was independent evidence in this case, which they could accept or reject, the judge said, referring to the dubious Huxley. If they considered the evidence pointed to the prisoner's presence in the park, they should bring in a verdict of guilty, no matter what the consequence might be.

The jury filed out. When they had gone, Kelly spotted a friend in the gallery and waved in greeting. Then, in less time than it takes to think of the weird act, he raised his arm to its full extent, and bending his wrist so that his extended forefinger pointed downwards, he made a sweeping motion so as to indicate a circle round his neck, and finished by tossing his fist upwards as though tightening a cord.

'He accompanied this action with a cluck of the tongue, and followed it by a jerk of the thumb over his shoulder towards the jury-box. His meaning was fully apparent'.

Some of the reporters present were amazed. Only a short while before they had noticed some of the jurors actually moved to tears by the 'masterful oration' of Mr Sullivan, which the judge later commented had placed the defence counsel at the front rank of the Irish bar. Yet it took the twelve just twenty-seven minutes to complete their deliberations. Kelly read his fate in their grave countenances as they filed back into court. He leaned over to a warder and said very audibly, 'I'll bet you a bob this lot hangs me'. A gambler to the last.

The foreman handed down the issue paper and the clerk of

the crown read out the verdict – guilty of murder. Kelly had a few words before sentence, mainly in thanks to his counsel, hoping that they might live long to defend the innocent.

The black cap appeared, but the defendant was no longer interested. As the date for him to be hung by the neck was declared, 9 June, he was already stooping to pick up his hat, and turning around to take a last farewell of friends in the gallery. He smiled, kissed his hand, and threw a loving valediction towards them.

As he vanished to the cells, several women were sobbing piteously in the attendance while others looked to be much affected. The court was cleared, and Kelly's brother was seen outside, leaning against the courthouse wall, weeping.

Daniel Curley, described as the 'Prime Minister of the Invincibles', wrote a last letter to his darling Jane and their five children:

My dear and most ever-beloved wife and children,
I take this opportunity, the last on this deceitful earth, of saying a few words to you, hoping that you will forgive me for the step that I took with regard to my trial – I mean for not trying to save myself as others did; but I could not stoop so low or bring myself to do so.

My dear wife, I will die as I have lived, faithful to my principles and to my country's cause. I will do as all honest men do, bring my secrets to the grave with me and leave them that is at freedom to enjoy it.

Dear wife, I will say no more on this subject, as I have domestic business to speak upon. I request you to keep a vigilant watch over our dear children. Keep them to their school and religion and off the street, as you yourself know that I dread to see children getting the run of the street.

Dear Jane, do not think that because I say this I have not confidence in you. Yes, dear wife, I will die at rest; I know that you will do what is just to them. I will also request of you not to let them out of your sight or care to anyone as long as you can help it, my dear and faithful wife.

Now about yourself. As I have told you before, I will not ask to restrict you in any manner. If you think it well to change your widowed life, you can do so with all my wish and blessing. I never like to see anyone tied I love. I love liberty.

But, my dear wife, if you ever change your life, be very careful in your choice in a companion. Deceitful men! My dear and faithful wife, I love you. Excuse me, I cannot speak of this matter, as it was very hard to tear my trustful heart from you and offer it to God – and what a trial!

[That] the base and brutal deceiver should be the cause of separating two loving and trustful hearts ... but God's will be done. That is my only consolation. My dear wife, I will ask you to be attentive to your religious duties. No matter how much you are engaged in the business of the world, never neglect that.

My reason for saying so is that I shall die with the hope that we shall meet in the Kingdom of Heaven, never to be parted by the power of man. Dear wife, I am sure you will be glad to hear that I die in peace with all men, forgiving enemies. May God forgive them the injury they have done me.

I am happy and at peace with God. Oh, may God protect you and the children in this deceitful world. Remember me to Frank, Peter and Nelly, Mr and Mrs Hyland, Granny Misey, and all friends. Believe me to be your faithful and loving husband,

Daniel Curley.

To his affectionate and faithful wife and dear children, Mary, Jane, Michael, Peter and Daniel. Pray for the soul of your dear husband. May the Lord have mercy on my soul.

The afternoon before his execution, Curley said goodbye to his family in the condemned cell. His wife clipped a lock of his luxuriant hair to take away. Thereafter he remained closeted with his religious consolers, warders watching.

He slept badly, rose at six, attended Mass. Returned to his cell, Marwood entered and pinioned his arms. Some other prisoners could see Curley walk into the large exercise yard, making audible responses to the litany for the dying.

They entered the small yard. The governor had evidently made it clear it was not for him to give any future signal, so Marwood shot the bolt as soon as he was ready. Daniel Curley 'descended heavily, and it appeared that death was instantaneous'.

The black flag ran up to the masthead, and the crowd outside, smaller than during Brady's despatch at 2,000 persons, groaned in horror. 'Curley's father uttered a piercing cry and fell upon his knees. The incident sent a thrill of pain through the hearts of all who witnessed it'.

The inquest was conducted with Curley's body lying on a table. Journalists could see a little blood beneath the nostrils, and skin of a purple shade beneath the eyes. The dead man looked as though he were sleeping. On his breast was pinned a cross.

The same verdict was returned, and then the remains of Curley, like those of Brady, were interred below the scaffold, the funeral service performed by the two clergymen who had attended the deceased.

During that day, a crowd gathered outside the shop in Thomas Street where Jane Curley had worked as a confectioner since her husband's arrest, but it was closed and guarded by police. On the door was a card with the inscription 'Daniel Curley. Died 18th May 1883, aged 35 years. Rest in Peace'.

In the case of the condemned man Michael Fagan, a plea by the prisoner's mother for commutation of sentence had been addressed to Queen Victoria, only to be referred back to the lord lieutenant for his consideration. On the Friday before the due date, Spencer let it be known that there was nothing in the circumstances of the case to induce him to change the sentence, and that the law must take its course.

Fagan's execution 'attracted very little popular interest', the *Times* reported, neglecting to mention that the morning was cold and threatening. The crowd was estimated to number from 200–500 persons. The doomed man's mother, who had travelled from Mullingar with her blacksmith son's brother and sister, wandered up and down the roadway outside.

The illiterate prisoner bore up well, but obviously left no letter or testament, although some newspapers reported a doubtful alleged remark as he left the chapel with minutes to live to the effect that he hoped all Irishmen would keep away from secret societies.

Marwood met him in the yard, unbuttoned Fagan's shirt collar and tossed it aside, and surveyed the judicial victim from head to foot. Led to the scaffold, Fagan ascended without delay, clutching a low crucifix in a pinioned limb. Marwood placed him in the centre of the drop, arranging the noose roughly around his neck, with the brass ring, through which the rope ran, positioned hard against his epiglottis.

A sack covered the prisoner's face, shutting out the light. He stood there as Marwood climbed off, checked all was ready, and wrenched a lever to send Fagan charging out of life. The body's steady swing indicated that death had come without a struggle.

But now there came a surprise. Somehow the cap suddenly blew off, exposing Fagan's face. Eyewitnesses said it showed 'only in the slightest degree' the nature of his terrible death.

An hour later at the inquest, the press could see that the lips were blue and swollen, and the back of the neck similarly distended, they thought from pressure of the rope, but possibly from rupture of the spinal cord. Fagan joined his fellows beneath lifted flagstones.

Thomas Caffrey was fixed to die on 2 June. His defence – that he did not know why he was in the park before the deed – was widely believed, even by the British press, and of course he had pleaded guilty. The London *Times* declared in a pang of conscience: 'in his case it would certainly not displease if the sentence were commuted to penal servitude'.

No commutation came however, even though by 21 May it was reported that Patrick Delaney, who pleaded guilty on the same day as Caffrey, had been reprieved. Lord Spencer had evidently been influenced by the claim that Delaney intentionally attracted the attention of one of Judge Lawson's guards to avoid obeying an order to shoot him.

Caffrey, a former army deserter, was the father of one child and a widower; even though he was aged only twenty-six. He chose to write his last letter to his mother:

Kilmainham Gaol, June 1st, 1883, half-past 8 o'clock, p.m.
Dear Mother,
I write you these few lines for the last time in this world, and hope you will offer up all your sorrows along with my sufferings in atonement for my crime, and for all the sins of my past life.

I hope you will forgive all those who have done me harm in this world, as I forgive them from the bottom of my heart, as I expect to get forgiveness from my merciful Father in heaven.

Dear mother, I am just after receiving the holy sacrament, and I am quite prepared, with the help of God, to go before the judgment seat of justice. Make sure to mind your religion, yourself and the child, and I hope to meet you one day in heaven, where there will be no more parting for all eternity. There, in the company of our blessed Mother and all the saints, we will praise our blessed Redeemer for ever more.

Tell all enquiring friends that I hope no-one will ever throw a slur on any child or anyone belonging to me for the death I had to suffer; and I hope you will never have cause to blush when my name is spoken, as I am paying the full penalty of my crime in this world, and I hope I will not have to suffer in the next.

Whenever you see this letter, pray for me. No more in this world from your loving son,
Thomas Caffrey

There were scarcely 150 spectators, including officials, outside the jail for Caffrey's execution, the numbers depressed because the prisoner had admitted 'guilt' in the crime. Some memorial cards would subsequently leave Caffrey's name off the list of those Invincibles who had 'died for Ireland' as a result of that confession.

Caffrey stood to be pinioned in the outer yard, and caught sight of the scaffold for the first time. An involuntary tremor overcame his frame, but the shuddering soon ceased and he regained control. A few moments later he was on the platform, asking the clergymen to shake his hand – and they had to stoop to where his arm was bound in order to do so.

The condemned dock porter thanked them for their ministrations. He said he died in the sure hope of forgiveness in the next world. The rope came around his neck, followed by the white bag. And then Marwood pulled the bolt.

Caffrey shot into space. His body jolted, but his neck did not break; instead he slowly asphyxiated. 'Death was not instantaneous, but sensibility was lost immediately and death was painless', it was reported from the inquest. He choked while unconscious.

And then it was the turn of Tim Kelly. Telegrams begging for a reprieve had been sent to Prime Minister Gladstone, but there was no reply. A Mr Varian of the Political Aid Society waited on the lord lieutenant on the eve of execution and laid a number of facts before his excellency, among them that Kelly had been present at a meeting of the society at 8 p.m. on the night of the assassinations. Spencer was unmoved.

Posters had gone up in Liverpool that day, declaring: 'Tomorrow Tim Kelly dies. Show your respect to Ireland by wearing crêpe on your hat or your arm'. The prisoner, who had asked to be transferred to Joe Brady's death cell for his last day, was visited there by his family. They brought flowers and souvenirs of affection.

His mother made it a request that he should leave no statement or letter, and he replied that he would not. At length they left, and darkness fell. Kelly was alone with his thoughts – and his ever-watching pair of warders.

That night before his execution Kelly spent in song. The chorister's 'strong, resonant voice' rang out along the corridors amid the silence of his fellow prisoners. They listened to the strains of the hymn he had so often sung in the Franciscan chapel, *Salve Regina*, with its concluding sentiment, 'pray for the sinner, pray for me'.

Other airs he favoured were from the operas of Balfe and Wallace, notably *I Dreamt I Dwelt in Marble Halls* from *The Bohemian Girl*. When the night was far through a warder implored him, 'Mr. Kelly, would you not lie down to take a sleep against the morning?'

The lad smiled, and said, 'I will, but let me sing one more song'. Then he burst forth into a beautiful rendition of Balfe's *The Memory of the Past*, and at last lay still to sleep.

The chief warder, Mr Searle, visited him an hour or two later. Kelly rose at five that Saturday morning, completed his toilet, and brushed his hair into its carefully shaped style, forming an angle over either temple. He wore a dark suit and a pair of jail slippers.

The two clergy, Canon Kennedy and Fr Bernard O'Reilly, arrived at the cell at half past six, and a small procession made its way down to the chapel for Mass. An hour later, the prisoner was conducted towards the yard, Marwood appearing and putting up his finger with an air of gravity to signal a halt.

Whispering in the youth's ear, the executioner got Kelly to raise his arms. A belt with two exterior loops now circled the waist. One by one, his arms were placed in the loops and tightened there. Kelly's shirt collar was taken off. They went outside.

There Kelly saw not just the rude wooden structure designed to kill him, but a large black crow perched on the chimney shaft close to the flagstaff. It had alighted there at twenty minutes to eight o'clock, causing no little wonder and murmuring among the 2,000 people gathered outside for the final vigil.

It was two minutes to eight when the small party began crossing the yard. The crow did not fly away as the humans approached, nor even when Kelly climbed the nine steps to his last earthly foothold. The governor, sub-sheriff and doctor remained below, but the priests and head warder joined Marwood and his victim on the platform.

The prisoner was shuffled onto pencil marks which had been drawn to indicate the place for his feet. He was now standing on boards weighed underneath with sandbags to ensure their speedy collapse. The legs were pinioned and Marwood dispassionately prepared the white cap.

Just before it was put on, Kelly cried: 'Won't you let me kiss the crucifix?' and Fr O'Reilly held a cross to his lips. It was withdrawn, and the sack came on.

The executioner adjusted the knot under the chin to the left, towards the angle of the jaw, then applied a leather washer to test the subsequent strain on the rope. Kelly's muffled praying could be heard to the last.

Then Marwood stepped back, withdrew the safety bolt, and looked up to make sure the rope was clear. His next action had the 'rapidity of a lightning flash', and Kelly disappeared from view. The crow at that moment rose and flew away, cawing.

The black flag chased it up the flagpole, 'to announce the vindication of justice', and Kelly's mother and father howled in anguish and sank to their knees outside. 'People who witnessed the painful scene raised their hats in deference to the awful happening, partly in respect to the poignant grief of the suffering innocent, and silently passed away, leaving the stricken parents still absorbed in their sorrow'.

Retribution

'On Saturday morning at eight o'clock, Timothy Kelly, the last of the Invincibles sentenced to death for the murder of Lord Frederick Cavendish and Mr Burke, was executed', the *Illustrated London News* declared in epilogue on June 16th, 1883.

'The executioner, Marwood, did his terrible work in the usual manner', said the magazine, taking the opportunity to print an illustration of the gallows, and explaining that 'hanging is effected by suddenly letting down the platform upon which the condemned man stands, when his body falls the length of the rope, disappearing into the pit'.

The *Times* noted with satisfaction the completion of the capital penalties in Dublin, despite widespread public dismay in Ireland that Kelly had been obliged to join their number. The soulful choirboy may have made an appealing impression, but readers were reminded that 'he was old enough to strike at the heart of a high-minded and devoted servant of the country', and thus 'must pay the penalty of his crimes in company with his associates'.

Even the *Freeman's Journal* said there could be 'no quarrel with the justice which declined to stop short of his execution', although *United Ireland* fancied he was 'a mere boy, in law still an infant'. Across the Atlantic, among the more rabid nationalist publications, the *Irish World* claimed his countrymen would ever remember and revere Kelly's name. 'A beardless boy, a youthful enthusiast, an unflinching patriot has received the martyr's crown in the sacred cause of Ireland.

If the Irish newspapers had to straddle a position between support for the upkeep of the law and certain yearnings among many

233

of their readers, they were broadly able to accomplish the feat by heaping odium and bile on the figure of James Carey.

It could be said that Carey was a scapegoat in the classical sense, since all could agree – whether radical nationalist or inflexible supporter of the Castle – that the informer's conduct towards his former comrades was reprehensible and despicable in the extreme.

The public mood can be gauged by penny ballad sheets, whose sale proliferated on street corners, and which were careful to reflect the tastes of the buying public. Some could not bring themselves to name Carey (there was no need in any case), making do with a dash:

> Now Joseph Brady's as harmless a young man as ever you did see,
> Till this cruel wretch _____ has proved his destiny
> Swore upon the Sixth of May, before that it was dark
> 'Twas he that murdered Mr Burke, all in the Phoenix Park.

There were '*Lamentable Lines on Joe Brady & Dan Curley*', and similar lines written on the occasion of every execution, a particular ballad for Tim Kelly concluding: 'With His just rod, may Heaven's God, James Carey soon chastise. And grant this boy / eternal joy, in the realms beyond the skies'.

Again and again the balladeers turned to the same simple target, many of their composers perhaps mindful of censorship and confiscation if their pens wandered with too much vitriol in the direction of the crown.

Lines Written on the Condemned Men for the Phoenix Park Murders contained this verse:

> Accused be you _____ wherever you may go
> By your duping and your treachery,
> You're the cause of all this woe.
> May the sun in the heavens deny its light
> May the stars on you refuse to shine
> May the grass wither beneath your feet
> On this earth no peace you will e'er find.

P. J. Tynan, the fringe player in the Invincibles who escaped to the safety of America, noted a few years later: 'The police, detectives, and the machinery of alien rule had a white elephant on their hands in the person of James Carey.

'His protection was necessary for British prestige. The English, no matter what their feelings toward Carey might be, knew that the duty of safely guarding him was imperative. On his person was concentrated the vengeful feelings of the Irish people instead of being hurled on the enemy'.

Of course, there was a string of others who had turned queen's evidence, with Joseph Hanlon being grateful that a little extra testimony had been needed for Kelly's third trial. He joined Robert Farrell, Michael Kavanagh, Peter Carey and Joseph Smith in protective custody.

Carey was anxious to recoup what he could of his reputation. In an 'interview,' smuggled out of Kilmainham by his wife, he had ringed 'yes' or 'no' answers to suggestions supplied on sheets of foolscap, such that the *Freeman's Journal* later claimed that Carey had a total abhorrence of informers and would never have 'peached' had not others attempted to offer him up to serve their own ends.

He attempted to demonstrate that he had saved lives by giving limited information. Mrs Frank Byrne, wife of the secretary to the British branch of the Land League, had been arrested at her home in Gothic Villas, Avondale Road, Peckham. She was sent to Dublin under heavy escort.

Carey had told investigators how a woman identified to him as Mrs Byrne brought knives, rifles and revolvers from London, hidden in her cloak. Her husband had already fled abroad, first to France, where there was an abortive Scotland Yard attempt to kidnap him to Britain, and then to the United States.

Now Carey swore in the Dublin Police Court that he did not know the woman in the dock, and that it was not she who had brought the munitions. Mrs Byrne was discharged, the British momentarily confused as to whether Carey's supplier could have been her sister, and she promptly returned home, packed, and left to join her husband's exile.

By 1885 she was being introduced at a special 6 May commemoration in New York as 'a brave little woman, whose memorable courage in connection with the victory in the Phoenix Park three years ago is known to all of us'.

Magistrate John Curran saw and questioned Carey as to what he meant by his conduct. His reply was 'Of course, Mr Curran, I knew and recognised her and swore I did not. But you must remember that I shall not always be here, but expect to go out once more a free man, so I had to do something to soften the people outside, who feel resentment against me and who are sore at my having given evidence'.

Carey was becoming bolder. He brought eviction proceedings in the police court against a number of his tenants who refused to pay rent. The cases came up on June 12th, but Carey did not appear, and they fell through.

Two days later he wrote a letter to John Beveridge, town clerk, from Kilmainham Jail, asking for the notice paper for the next meeting of the municipal council 'as it is my intention to attend at the same, regretting the cause of my unavoidable absence from my corporate duties'. He signed himself 'James Carey TC', even though his seat had been taken in March when Dr Robert Wade was declared elected for the Trinity ward.

It now appeared that the council did not have the power to unseat Carey, as he had not been convicted of any criminal offence. Still, his towering cheek and declared intention to return to local politics was embarrassing for the council, 'who never expected to have the pleasure of seeing him again in his civic robes'.

One day that early summer, Carey asked to see Curran in Kilmainham, whereupon he suggested that since he had 'gone through a great strain' he felt he was entitled to some form of relaxation and would like a short trip. Curran pretended to agree, and told him he should ask that Mr Mallon be sent with him. Carey said he believed that Killarney would be a nice trip.

'Mr Mallon came to me afterwards very indignant at the proposition, and was very considerably eased in his mind when I told him that I had no such intention, and that I was only laughing at Carey when I made the suggestion', Curran wrote. It was not the imminent danger of such a trip that alarmed Mr Mallon; 'it was pure disgust at the companionship'.

There were reports that Carey, who wanted to remain residing in Dublin, had been let out of Kilmainham with a special guard for several days under temporary release. The newspapers suggested that he had been lodging in the neighbourhood of either Rathgar or Harold's Cross, but his residence having been discovered, he was returned to the walled jail-fort opposite the Phoenix Park

Whether this happened or not, it was nonetheless clear that Carey had to be settled somewhere, and he and his family could not be released into Irish society. The journal *United Ireland* antici-pated his forthcoming disappearance in June with a front-page sketch of the Carey family as a pack of rats cast off aboard a raft.

As Bussy said, 'not only was that Prince of Ruffians amply pro-vided for, but money was poured out like water to feed and clothe and protect his family for months'. The wife and children were kept in guarded lodgings for weeks, with one Sergeant Patrick MacIntyre charged with their every creature comfort. He did such a good job that Mrs Maggie Carey later presented him with her husband's gold watch chain as a memento.

It was eventually settled that they would all be re-housed in the colonies. The Carey family first disappeared to England, and then it was time to spirit Carey away. On 24 June, the authorities denied reports that Carey's departure from Ireland had already taken place, 'but he will certainly leave in a few days', it was added.

The issue of Carey's disappearance, or his promised regal appear-ance at the town council meeting on Monday 2 July, excited the country. There was a rumour that he would sail from Queens-town to the United States, 'and some eagerness was manifested on behalf of the general public to see the informer, the passengers who embarked on the transatlantic steamers being closely scrutinised'.

Superintendent John Mallon in fact first removed Carey by

four-wheeled cab from Kilmainham on Friday 29 June 1883. The informer carefully took down the medal and ribbon of the Sodality of the Sacred Heart which had hung over the bed in his cell, and packed up what little he had.

He was given further bags of clothes at the gate, and entered the vehicle with Mallon, who told Carey he was going first to detective headquarters in the Lower Castle Yard. As the cab made its way to the city centre, it moved through Thomas Street, where Mrs Jane Curley maintained her small shop. Carey, looking out the window for it, crossed himself as they passed the premises.

Chronicler Tighe Hopkins has Carey turning back from the window to exclaim aloud in all sincerity: 'God save the soul of Dan Curley!'

'Why, you villain,' returned his conductor. 'You're after helping to hang the man!'

They arrived at the Castle. Going to his safe, Mallon provided the arch-informer with money and a service revolver and box of ammunition. He gave him bare details of the forthcoming arrangements, by which Carey would travel incognito to London and meet up with his family on a steamer sailing from southern England. They would go first to South Africa and then, if they wished, to the Antipodes.

Within a quarter of an hour the cab was on its way again. Driving along the city quays towards Dublin port and his first steam packet, Carey perused the papers he had been issued, then idly examined his new weapon. He asked if it was loaded and was assured, according to Mallon's biographer, that it was.

'Then what's to prevent me shooting you stone dead, John Mallon, and getting revenge for all the trouble you have brought upon me?'

'I have my finger on the trigger of a revolver myself', replied Mallon, hitching up the pocket of his dustcoat and levelling it at his opponent. Carey smiled: 'Faith, I was only joking with you'. He returned the revolver to his bag. Both men knew that Mallon was bluffing too.

Carey had previously complied with advice to shave off his beard, and appeared clean-shaven on the morning of his removal from prison. 'His kinky hair was cut short and parted at the side instead of being divided down the centre as of old.

'The removal of moustache and beard disclosed a peculiarly animal mouth that added to the sinister, cut-throat suggestiveness of the whole. Indeed, even his spouse might well have received a shock if she had never seen her James before without his hirsute appendages'.

Mallon did not leave the cab when they reached the dockside rendezvous, although he consented to a final handshake. Carey climbed down into the company of a pair of armed and plainclothes detectives from both Dublin and Scotland Yard. They boarded the boat for the same crossing that had been made more than a year earlier by the coffin of Cavendish.

Once on board the steamer a person well acquainted with Carey immediately 'penetrated the disguise', it was later reported. Several persons on the steamer talked of his presence among them, although such rumours would have been flying on many sailings in any case.

For the rest of the voyage Carey kept below. At Holyhead, the two plainclothes detectives who accompanied him managed to get him onto the London train without exciting the observation of the other passengers.

When the train arrived at Willesden Junction, Carey and his escort took their departure together. The same night it was known, or at least reported in Westminster, that Carey had been lodged at Scotland Yard. The next day he was taken to Newgate, where he remained until he left the country.

Two days after he was removed from Dublin, the Irish authorities telegraphed to Scotland Yard the news that a brother of Joe Brady had booked passage across the Irish Sea from the North Wall. Brady's sibling was watched from the moment of his arrival at Euston, but the strict surveillance was unnecessary, as he had nothing but peaceable intent.

Carey had meanwhile given a letter to a friend before leaving

Ireland, addressed to the lord mayor, Charles Dawson. It apologised for missing the meeting, adding characteristically: 'In conclusion I might draw your attention to the old and trite saying (nevertheless true) that a certain gentleman is not as black as he is painted. When I give my account to council, my conduct will stand in its true light'.

An attempt to retrospectively remove Carey's right to be called a councillor had meanwhile hastily begun through a prosecution by the corporation for his non-payment of rates, in the amount of £95, going back several years. No bankrupt could hold a seat.

Before leaving, Carey had transferred his property portfolio to a Mr Meade, his former employer, and his own house in Denzille Street and a dwelling in Harmony Row to a brother-in-law and nephew respectively. This was done 'in consideration of mutual love and affection, and a sum of five shillings'.

Carey left behind a legal row over his 'fraudulent deed' of transfer and a demand that the two houses be sold to raise the money towards his civic debts. Meade eventually kept his houses and Mr Wade the seat on the council.

In London, Carey suggested several positions for which he thought he was exceptionally qualified. Among them could have been gaoler or chief warder in a convict prison. He said he would also be content with an appointment in Malta or Egypt, and he grumbled bitterly at his treatment by the government, which appeared to be unreasonably delaying his reunion with his wife and family.

He may have had a day out, accompanied by his escort. He might have gone to see his own effigy in Madam Tussaud's, which was being advertised in all the newspapers. On 23 July it was reported by the *Times* that Carey had been seen 'a few days ago' in Richmond, Surrey, by the ubiquitous 'citizen of Dublin to whom he was known'.

'The Invincible informer was boating on the river Thames, accompanied by two detectives, one of them a member of the Dublin branch of the Criminal Investigation Department, and the other from Scotland Yard.

'Finding themselves recognised, Carey and his protectors hurriedly rowed ashore, but remained in the neighbourhood of Richmond for some hours, returning to London by train shortly before six o'clock and alighting at the Edgware Road station, whence they drove in a four-wheeled cab to Parliament Street'.

The personal appearance of Carey had altered, the paper reported. 'His beard has been shaved off and the scant side whiskers which are allowed to remain are dyed a dark brown colour. He is dressed in mourning attire and wears crêpe on his hat, a contrast to the costume usually affected by him.

'He is said to be temporarily lodged in one of the metropolitan prisons or in its neighbourhood, and is accompanied by his family. His ultimate destination is not yet settled, but it is stated that he has been offered a position as an official in one of the penal establishments'. Farrell, the original informer, had also been recognised in London, the paper said.

But Carey had not been boating on the Thames in late July, being instead on board a ship on the high seas. A third-class passage had been booked in London for him under the name of Power as early as 21 June. He was to travel in the *Kinfauns Castle* to Cape Town.

Passage for Mrs Carey and the children in the same vessel was booked in Messrs Donald Currie & Co. offices on 30 June, again under the name of Power. Two days later, on the eve of sailing, one Patrick O'Donnell booked second-class cabins for himself and his wife on the same steamer.

The *Kinfauns Castle* left London late on 3 July, under the command of Captain Winchester, and carrying Mrs Margaret Carey and her children. The vessel arrived at Dartmouth at noon on 5 July, where James Carey was smuggled aboard and brought into the bosom of his loved ones.

The initial voyage was uneventful, and the informer must have relished his escape from notoriety, savouring the sea air and playing with his children as land slipped out of sight. He had his entire family with him, a sum of spending money, and a cheque for £100 in his pocket.

Within a few days the voyage had become tedious, even if he was pleased to be finally out of the clutches of the police. He had his loaded pistol, manufactured by Weeks of Dublin, but the passengers looked a listless and uninteresting lot and clearly posed no threat. They all seemed English, Scottish or South African, apart from that Donegal fellow, O'Donnell, who was really the pick of the bunch.

O'Donnell said he was going out to try his fortune in the diamond mines and explained that he was an experienced mining engineer who had simply become fed up with life in America. James 'Power' replied that it seemed to be all Scots who did well in the colonies, and that he should change his name to McDonald. Thereafter Power, formerly Carey, continuously referred to O'Donnell as McDonald.

The two men 'chummed' together, frequently playing cards. Another Irishman named Kelly, from Wexford, was discovered to be aboard the *Kinfauns Castle*, but Mrs Power and her husband were suspicious of him and did not want to make his acquaintance.

The ship stopped at Madeira to replenish provisions and the passengers all went ashore for some sightseeing. But this pleasant interlude was soon out of the way, to be replaced by the endless, heaving sea. O'Donnell's wife was frequently seasick, this being her first sea voyage, and he was often forced to tend to her in their cabin.

At last, after more than three weeks, the *Kinfauns Castle* put in at Cape Town. It was four o'clock in the morning of Friday, 27 July 1883. When the sun came up most of the passengers disembarked.

O'Donnell and wife had been due to get off here too, as the Wexford man did. The Powers, however, were not disembarking. They were going up the coast, they said, joining the few passengers for Port Elizabeth and Durban being transferred to the *Melrose*, a vessel of just 839 tons and a speed of only nine knots. She lay conveniently alongside at the quay.

'McDonald' thought he and his wife might as well come along

Kinfauns Castle

too. Carey was delighted, having argued for much of the trip that the opportunities were much better in Natal. They all slept aboard ship that night while the O'Donnells rebooked on the smaller vessel for the trudge up the east coast of South Africa.

Their baggage was transferred the next morning and the *Melrose* departed that evening. It was the day after departure from Cape Town, on Sunday 29 July, some twenty-five miles south-west of Mossel Bay, that Patrick O'Donnell shot James Carey dead.

The two had been drinking together in the saloon when suddenly O'Donnell reached into his pocket, took out a revolver and shot Carey from a few feet away. Carey, hit in the neck, spewed blood and shuddered in surprise. He turned and tried to leave the saloon. O'Donnell followed him, firing twice more, hitting Carey in the back.

Mrs Carey came rushing in from an adjoining cabin. Carey cried: 'Oh, Maggie! McDonald has shot me!' and collapsed into her arms. A steward immediately disarmed O'Donnell, who had lowered his gun on Mrs Carey's arrival. She cried: 'Why did you shoot my husband?' and O'Donnell simply answered: 'I had to do it'.

The assailant gave himself up at once, was shoved to one area of the saloon and held down while Carey was attended. An effort was made to staunch the wound in his neck, but it was as grievous as that of Thomas Henry Burke in the same area, and the informer was already unconscious. In fifteen minutes James Carey had expired.

Captain James Rose had O'Donnell clapped in irons and taken below. The shooting had taken place twelve miles from land between Cape Barracouta and Mossel Bay (in Lat. 34° 33' S; Long. 21° 55' E), but he had no means of communicating with shore. The alarm could only be raised at Port Elizabeth.

O'Donnell's baggage was searched and a mysterious-looking electrical device found. It was at once consigned to the sea, the fear being that it was a bomb or 'infernal machine'.

On the arrival of the *Melrose* at Port Elizabeth at 2 p.m. the next day (Monday 30 July) news was swiftly conveyed to the authorities and a police launch went out to meet the ship. The prisoner and the stretcher-borne body of his victim were both taken ashore, O'Donnell being handcuffed to the rails of the launch, with a policeman on either side.

An immense crowd assembled to see the assassin land, 'the news having spread with the utmost celerity, and he was received with mingled groans and cheers'. O'Donnell was described as a 'tall, powerfully-built man, with an expression of determined fierceness in his features, standing fully six feet, and with a rather unusually high forehead, narrowing at the sides.

'His nose is straight and well-shaped, his eyes are grey, his hair dark, and he is apparently about 44 years of age'.

O'Donnell was taken as quickly as possible into the magistrates courthouse, and the doors closed – the most stringent precautions being adopted to prevent any possibility of a rescue.

The evidence of witnesses was taken during the next few days.

From the *Port Elizabeth Telegraph*, 4 August 1883:
James Carey's Funeral
The interment of the remains of James Carey took place on Wednesday (August 1st, 1883), at a little after four o'clock, in the burial ground a few hundred yards in the rear of the North-end prison.

The District Surgeon, Dr [Frederick] Ensor, was greatly distressed at the bare idea of the body being committed to the ground without any funeral service, and on consideration resolved to say a few words on the occasion.

The assistant magistrate (Mr H. Halse) proceeded to the gaol at three o'clock for the purpose of superintending the arrangements for sepulture and Dr Ensor accompanied him. As no notice of the burial had got abroad, very few people had any idea what was about to take place, but the fact of three or four cabs standing at the gaol door attracted a few idlers.

Mr Jones, the undertaker, arrived with a coffin at 3.45, and his assistants conveyed it to the mortuary. There lay the body of James Carey; the features composed in death. The corpse was placed in the coffin and the latter was conveyed to a vehicle outside, the distance to the grave being nearly half a mile.

Mrs Carey and her children were in the gaoler's quarters, and although efforts were made to dissuade her from following the remains of her deceased husband, she resolved on so doing, and with her baby and her son occupied the first cab, Dr Ensor following in the second cab and the assistant Magistrate in the third.

The cortege then moved slowly off to the grave, on arriving at which the body was lowered by the undertaker's men. The most perfect silence prevailed, although a good many coloured people and children, attracted by the procession, had assembled.

When the body was lowered into the grave, Dr Ensor, who for some time previously laboured under strong emotion, spoke in a clear and distinct voice as follows:

'Friends, in the absence of any official Minister, I think it is only right that a few words should be said over the grave of this poor man. Let us pray'. Every head was immediately uncovered, and Dr Ensor proceeded thus:

'O thou omnipotent, omnipresent and omniscient Ruler of the Universe, we restore, as it is fit, the mortal remains of our weak and erring brother to his mother earth. His immortal part, we are certain, is also under Thy guidance and control. We bow to the omnipotent. Yet we would at the same time remember that mercy is the attribute of God Himself.

'In mercy, then, look down on these, the widow and the helpless orphans, as they stand beside this open grave. Grant that time, the consoler as well as the avenger, may throw a thick veil over their past. Grant, Lord, that in all their future they may seek and find Thee to be a very present help in time of trouble and the comforter of the widow and orphans in their affliction. Amen'.

Earth was then thrown onto the coffin, and thus terminated the funeral obsequies of James Carey.

Sensation

CAREY'S GRAVE

'James Carey has been shot dead on the deck of a steamship off the coast of South Africa'. The cry which went up last evening in the thoroughfares of Dublin from the *Evening Telegraph* newsboys awakened only one query from the mouth of everyone. That query was: Is it true?'

So reported the *Freeman's Journal* as the breathtaking news broke. But although a dramatic and deadly development, 'nobody was horrified, nobody pretended to be sorry, [and] nobody was even surprised.

The pervading feeling was that, if the report were true, an event that the great bulk of the public looked upon as a foregone conclusion had occurred with something approaching precipitancy'.

The news created great excitement in the House of Commons when first made known, and it was the one topic of conversation among MPs who rushed to buy the Stop Press edition of an evening newspaper. It was at first disbelieved, the news being, as one prominent Irish member put it, 'too good to be true'.

But soon thereafter came news to the government by way of a telegram from the shipping line of Messrs Donald Currie & Co, South Africa, and the tidings were put beyond all doubt.

Members of the House 'entertained little doubt that Carey was followed from Dublin and believed that the Fenians had laid the most elaborate precautions to prevent the informer from escaping their clutches', it was reported next day.

A 'disconsolate feeling' had however been produced among ministers, who deplored the crime as showing that the 'Irish conspiracy has not been quashed through the execution of those whom the informer brought to justice'.

The immediate reaction of the mass of the Irish public, for whom the Invincibles had become virtual martyrs through Carey's infamy, was to celebrate with abandon.

Carey's death was received in Cork at first with incredulity, but soon provoked 'manifestations of popular rejoicing'. An effigy was burned in Cornmarket Street in the city and at Queenstown that night there were scenes of unrestrained jubilation.

News of Carey's death 'excites feelings of lively satisfaction among a large number of people', wrote one Dublin correspondent. 'Bonfires were lighted and mobs gathered around them, cheering for the Phoenix Park murders and execrating the name of Carey and the other informers. Effigies of Carey were burned, and the blazing remains carried about the streets until they were consumed.

'In the neighbourhood of Abbey Street and Temple Bar scenes of great disorder were witnessed. A few of the bonfires failing, a number of roughs rushed into the adjoining houses and carried away bedding and furniture, which they flung in the fires. The crowds were at length dispersed by the police'.

There were also bonfires and disorder in Clarendon Street, Mary Street, Cole's Lane, Golden Lane, Marlborough Street, George's Quay and Townsend Street, the latter being the last address of the informer Kavanagh, with crates and barrels of tar being used to feed the flames.

In one parade, in Chatham Street, the effigy of Carey managed to knock over an old woman named Whyte, fracturing her forearm.

There were dozens of arrests. In the Northern Divisional Court, forty-seven people were charged with having lit bonfires in the street on the Tuesday night, and each was fined ten shillings, or seven days in lieu. In the Southern Divisional Court, forty-five people were charged with the same offence. And the bonfires continued the night after, and the night after again.

In West Clare bonfires were lit on hilltops 'in congratulation of the murder', including one at Tullycrine, the homeland of Carey's parents. There it was remembered that Carey's father had been a crown witness in a case where a man was hanged at Naas – and his grandfather in one in which a man suffered the harshest penalty of the law in Mullingar.

His mother had run a boarding house in James Street, they remembered, where she passed on to the police the choice boasts of the petty criminals who lodged there, leading to the arrest of many of what the police would come to term 'Mother Carey's Chickens.' She was well paid for her information.

'His life has ended almost mercifully for himself,' said the *Freeman's Journal*. 'There are well-known lines picturing the terror in which Frankenstein lived for the monster he had made. Those lines might represent the life of Carey:

Like one who on a lonely road
Doth walk in fear and dread
And having once turned round, walks on
And turns no more his head
Because he knows a frightful fiend
Doth close behind him tread.

'One of the bloodiest and most appalling tragedies recorded in the history of any country has had an ending sensational beyond the power of fiction'.

In Claremorris, Co. Mayo, a mock wake was arranged, and afterwards a funeral procession marched through the town amid groans and catcalls for Carey. Guys and scarecrows of the informer were burnt in Limerick, Galway, and other places. Public saloons were packed, raucous singing ensued and jeering crowds gathered outside police stations and army barracks.

Only in Madam Tussaud's famous waxwork emporium in the heart of London was any graven image of James Carey left unscathed. Indifference to the approver's fate in England and Scotland and Wales was said to be 'mingled with regret that the Government could not give surer protection to its witnesses'.

The *Graphic* reported that while the news had been received with 'savage exultation' in Irish nationalist circles, it was also being boasted that the agents of the secret societies had never lost sight of Carey and his family, 'though the authorities believe that his death is due as much to his own reckless imprudence as to the vigilance of the assassins'.

It was immediately reported in the British press that O'Donnell had joined the Fenians in their rising of 1867, and had held a command at the Battle of Tallaght. After the arrest of the Invincibles, it was claimed that he was 'sent over from New York as chief of a number of men told to watch the course of events'.

Another account had it that 'before sailing he told some friends in London that he was going to Africa on an important mission'.

A decade later, the exiled P. J. Tynan (the 'Number 1' identified by Carey) published a book claiming that Carey's first intended destination had been learned by Fenian spies, only for the leak to be realised and the country changed to New Zealand. 'A man, still living, volunteered to go to New Zealand, and was sent on the first part of his journey', he claimed.

'When information came that Cape Town was Carey's destination, Patrick O'Donnell, an Irishman not in any way connected with Irish politics in London, took passage in the *Kinfauns Castle*. The tracking of Mrs Carey and her family was easy …'

Tynan maintained the Fenians had not expected Carey and his kin to be on the same boat. They had in fact separately communicated with 'a certain resident of South Africa' to be ready to trace Mrs Carey to her final destination, which was expected to be the Orange Free State.

It is easy to see through this shamming. O'Donnell was not involved in the 1867 rising and Battle of Tallaght, having emigrated to the United States as a teenager some twelve years earlier. While British intelligence initially believed the assassin could have been someone else using the alias of O'Donnell, they soon established that he had lived in New York and the mining area of Pennsylvania (where an Irish secret society named the Molly Maguires was active in industrial unrest). His story on the *Melrose* was correct in the detail related by Mrs Carey to investigators.

O'Donnell had gone out west and worked in the mines of Butte, Montana, where there was a significant Irish community and a rabid nationalist press to serve it. He also worked in the silver mines of California and Nevada, Ohio, and as far east as Toronto. There was no trace of any political involvement in any of the areas he had been, and no arrest sheets.

The prisoner was being extensively interviewed in Port Elizabeth, and his wife kept clamouring to see him. Dr Ensor, who had carried out the post mortem on Carey, went to see the killer and asked him if it were true that he had a relative with him. O'Donnell agreed, and claimed the woman was his niece, asking that she be cared for. Ensor said he would ask the Catholic Church locally to see to her needs, with the prisoner replying: 'That is all I care for'.

The doctor also discovered that O'Donnell was not sleeping and was being fed only on bread and water. He insisted that the man should be placed forthwith on a proper diet, and saw that it was done. He also prescribed barbiturates to enable him to rest.

The story that O'Donnell was telling was that he was not sent to carry out the act. He had done it on the spur of the moment, realising he was in the presence of a man who had betrayed his country, he said. The feared bomb found in his effects was not an 'infernal machine', but an electrical stimulus for treating a partially paralysed left hand.

O'Donnell said he was from the village of Derrybeg on the Gweedore coast of Co. Donegal. He had left New York on 19 May 1883, intending to visit home before going on to the diamond mines in Kimberley, South Africa to make a new life. He had been married in the United States, but the relationship had failed and he wanted to make a clean break.

Members of the Royal Irish Constabulary at length verified that O'Donnell had visited his mother and brother in Derrybeg in the midst of the Invincible executions. He learned all about the iniquity of Carey, which seemed to cast the other prisoners in the light of relative nobility.

At the beginning of June, O'Donnell went to Derry in the company of a young woman from his native parish, aged eighteen or twenty, named Susan Gallaher – the very one he was now claiming as his niece. Although less than half his age, they signed aboard an Allan liner for Liverpool as Mr and Mrs O'Donnell. A month later, in London, the pair booked passage for Cape Town.

O'Donnell made another court appearance in Port Elizabeth, the route being thronged with well-wishers whose cheers, rather than jeers, alarmed the authorities. But it allowed Tynan to gush: 'The marvellous Irish race, which covers the globe with its patriotic love for the land of its sires, was to be found on the dark continent with the same revengeful feelings against British rule in Ireland'.

It was resolved at the hearing that the prisoner would be sent back to Cape Town for trial, this being the same port where O'Donnell was now claiming he had first learned that the passenger 'James Power' was Carey. That arose because of an incident at the City Hotel, on Waterkant Street, on the day the *Kinfauns Castle* docked.

Carey had gone off for a drink with two of his fellow passengers, one of whom was named Williams and the other dubbed 'Scotty' in the same manner of the 'McDonald' nickname for O'Donnell, who on this occasion was nowhere to be seen. The barman duly set up the requested drinks and took a keen interest in the new arrivals.

The conversation eventually turned to Irish politics, probably steered in that direction by the ever combative informer, especially since he was becoming the worse for wear. Carey said the English were a people 'too base to live with', and if he had his way, he would 'exterminate every one of them'.

The barman watched and remembered this by-now heated discussion. Carey allegedly declared, 'Ireland for the Irish, that's my motto', causing the nettled Scotty to make the angry rejoinder that if the island were left to the Irish alone, the savages would 'eat one another up'.

Carey rounded on his companion and shoved his hand to his throat. 'Do you mean to say we are cannibals', he shouted, in a remark hardly tempered to dispel argument with the cold force of reason. Williams and the barman had to intervene quickly.

A short time after this incident, the three friends having been asked to leave, another passenger named Robert Cubitt followed the group up to the City Hotel. He was remaining in Cape Town, but now the shipmates he sought were nowhere to be seen.

Cubitt fell into conversation with the barman, who told him in detail what had happened. This attendant turned out to be Irish himself, which is why he had pricked up his ears to the discussion – and what's more, he had come to a stunning conclusion. Within minutes of slinging out the troublemakers, the counterman had consulted an old copy of the *Weekly Freeman* that had recently been sent to him. It happened to be the issue of 5 May, with a centrefold colour portrait of one James Carey.

It all now fell into place for the barman, as it did for Cubitt. The aggressive drinker, the man named Power, was none other than James Carey. No wonder he was pushing extremist views!

Cubitt fell back to the ship with his mind spinning. There he met Patrick O'Donnell, to whom he told the electrifying tale – and he had brought the paper to prove it.

O'Donnell, stunned, quickly perused its pages, coming across the portrait. It was indeed that of James Power, the beard taken away. He said that if satisfied of the man's identity he would 'soon let daylight into his damned carcass'.

The next morning, sailing day Saturday, the story had developed further. The *Cape Argus* carried speculation that a man named Power, who had arrived by the *Kinfauns Castle*, was none other than the notorious informer. It also reported that he was booked aboard the *Melrose*.

It was an open invitation to the curious.

That morning, as Carey stood on the upper deck of the second vessel, some men wandered down the quay and began staring. Carey was unsettled, and asked his fifteen-year-old son Thomas to see if they were looking at him, taking himself across to another area. The men continued to point, and the boy was obliged to confirm to his father that he was indeed the object of their fascination. The pair hurried below.

The news raced around a select group of the ship's complement, although naturally none of it came to the ears of any members of the Power family. The *Melrose* sailed at five o'clock.

Their Donegal friend was aggrieved that he had been fooled thus far. He had asked Cubitt for the picture, and actually persuaded him to hand it over. He stared at it repeatedly, and showed it to his companion. Susan Gallaher agreed that Power and Carey were the same man.

'I'll shoot him', he had told Cubitt, who clearly enjoyed his role as the herald of amazing news. The latter said later that he attached 'absolutely no importance' to such a fierce remark.

But O'Donnell had actually done what he promised, and the next day. A steward then remembered that O'Donnell had exclaimed in a similar snatched conversation: 'If I had known he was on board the ship, I would have swung for him'.

The steward thought the expression meant to swing a punch. He had missed another interpretation – that Carey's fellow Irishman could have been content to swing on the gallows for the man's murder.

Wild rumours continued in the Irish and British press for a few days. It was reported that O'Donnell had attempted to blow up the Mansion House 'two or three years ago', but escaped to France and thence to New York. On the contrary, asserted another report, his actual identity was that of Phelan, a professional killer from Chicago.

It was also rumoured, more benevolently, that O'Donnell had acted in London as a booking agent for public lectures by well-known personalities, among them Samuel Longhorn Clemens (Mark Twain). Felix Lynch, an Irishman of Rochester, New York, claimed he had been ordered to Quebec by the Invincibles to kill Carey if he landed there. The organisation had sent photographs of Carey all around the world to similar contacts and volunteers, he said, adding that O'Donnell was a member of the New York branch of the Ancient Order of Hibernians.

The renewed hysteria gradually petered out, the *Freeman's Journal* reflecting eventually that Carey's death had 'only added more blood to an already gore-drenched undertaking'.

The British government had meanwhile determined not to risk a trial in the colonies, the inhabitants being 'more liberal in their ideas than those who dwell in their native land', while the Irish and Dutch elements were in full sympathy with O'Donnell.

The colonies had a three-mile coastal limit, and the British flagged *Melrose* had been twelve miles offshore, even if plying between South African ports. The Cape and Natal administrations were ordered to send both the prisoner and the Carey family home – in separate ships.

'Putting legal technicalities aside, it would seem more natural that O'Donnell should have been tried, and if found guilty, put to death in the Cape Colony', murmured *The Graphic*. 'It must be assumed that the authorities are correct in their interpretation of the law', it added, while bemoaning the expense and trouble of bringing the prisoner and witnesses halfway around the world.

'We cannot feel sure of anything in this connection, knowing how grossly the Government blundered (for they cannot escape responsibility by laying the blame on the Dublin police) in their attempt to smuggle Carey out of Ireland', it sniffed, before turning its attention to the attitude of Parnellite MPs and their electorate towards O'Donnell: 'This man, who seems in the judgment of ordinary persons to have committed a peculiarly cold-blooded murder, is regarded across St George's Channel as a hero, and a possible martyr. It is this sympathy with violent and bloody deeds – this utter abnegation of all morals when their political passions are aroused – that makes the law-abiding Briton almost despair of the Irish'.

In South Africa, the *Natal Witness* was also generalising, suggesting that O'Donnell had acted 'in one of those extraordinary fits of Don Quixotism which frequently characterise some sections of the Irish people'.

Patrick O'Donnell was sent to London under a strong escort aboard the *Athenian*. 'Every precaution was taken to prevent the faintest chance of escape', and a whole company of soldiers guarded him at Cape Town. At Madeira, Portuguese soldiers lined the beach and native boatmen were ordered not to go within hailing distance of the steamer.

The same precautions were taken at Funchal when the *Garth Castle*, carrying Mrs Carey and family, replenished there. The *Athenian* arrived in Plymouth sound on 17 September, followed a week later by witnesses and the bereaved. O'Donnell was taken to London in a bristling train carriage, and conveyed to Millbank convict prison in an even greater show of force.

Meanwhile, unbeknownst to all but a few, the slain archinformer's brother, had sailed for sanctuary from Belfast on the 'loyal' twelfth of July aboard the Dominion liner *Montreal*. A little over a week later he landed at the port of the same name. A steerage passenger, Peter Carey travelled under the alias of 'O'Neill', and neither he nor his family was ever seen again.

Robert Cubitt

Weekley Freeman picture of Carey

O'Donnell on board
the *Athenian* off
Maderia

Endgame

The trial of Patrick O'Donnell, forty-eight, opened in the Central Criminal Court in London on 30 November before Mr Justice Denman, charging the wilful murder of James Carey in a British ship on the high seas, within the jurisdiction of the admiralty of England.

There was a very large attendance of spectators, with admission by special card. The prosecution was led by the attorney general (Sir Henry James), while Charles Russell, QC, and A. M. Sullivan acted as counsel for the defence, in consultation with General Pryor of the United States Bar, who attendance was paid for by readers of the *Irish World*.

O'Donnell was placed in the dock shortly after ten o'clock in the custody of five warders. He was well dressed, with a healthy and bronzed appearance. He entered a plea of not guilty.

The attorney general, opening the case, said it concerned the murder of one James Carey, 'and it would be affectation for me to suggest that you have not, every one of you, heard much of that man, of his conduct, and of his career.

'It is unnecessary for me to make any statement in defence of that man's conduct. Just before his death all that he had done had been the topic of conversation among most men in this kingdom, and it would be sufficient to say, without asking you to pass any judgement, that it had been found necessary for his personal safety that he should be removed from the presence of those likely to recognise him'.

The witness Cubitt, who had lately offered to come to England, would tell of taking Carey's likeness to the quay from which the *Melrose* was about to depart. He saw the prisoner there and both he and O'Donnell concluded that Power was Carey.

O'Donnell took the illustration, making use of the term 'I will shoot him'. When arrested, the picture was found in his trunk.

The attorney said he would now call witnesses as to the circumstances of the killing, but briefly the facts were that O'Donnell, seeing Mrs Carey in the saloon, had asked where her husband was, and suggested that they should have some drink together. The Carey boy was sent on deck to bring his father down. A bottle of ale was procured and in a few minutes James Carey was talking and drinking.

The persons in the saloon were O'Donnell, Mrs O'Donnell, and the murdered man, but also fifteen-year-old Thomas Carey, and the bosun, Thomas Jones, who was playing with Carey's young daughter at the bottom of the stairs. Mrs Carey had then gone to her berth, out of sight of what was taking place, because the baby was crying.

An important witness was a crewman aboard named James Parish, whose cabin was in the forepeak. As he walked out of there he entered the saloon, facing towards the stairs and the back of the settee where the O'Donnells were sitting facing Carey, who was standing.

The woman had her arm around O'Donnell's neck and apparently was talking to him. Everything seemed to be quiet and peaceful. Only a few feet away Carey leaned against a bulkhead. He was smiling, and the conversation seemed to be of a friendly character.

'I was in the act of coming out of my cabin when I heard and saw the first shot fired,' Parish said. 'I noticed O'Donnell taking his hand from his pocket and holding it towards the deceased. He fired and hit him in the neck. Power turned round and cried "Oh, Maggie, I am shot!" and, having got about two yards away, the prisoner fired two more shots, hitting him in the back'.

O'Donnell had remained sitting, with Parish only five yards further back. Mrs Carey came out of her cabin and caught the deceased as he was falling, they both falling together. 'I rushed past the defendant to the deceased and put my finger in his neck to stop the bleeding, and remained there until the doctor came.

'As I passed the prisoner, I saw him putting the pistol into his left side coat pocket. I did not rush forward as I thought I might get shot myself. I was afraid he might shoot at me as I was passing.'

Dr Everett attended Carey, who died within a quarter of an hour. Parish timed the first shot at about a quarter to four in the afternoon.

Thomas Jones, bosun, said he had seen Carey and the prisoner 'lifting their glasses as if drinking each other's health' just before the killing. Afterwards he took a revolver from O'Donnell's pocket and gave it to the second officer, Beecher. The prisoner did not say anything.

'I first saw Mrs Carey after I had taken the pistol. She went to the prisoner, who held out his hand saying, "Shake hands, Mrs Carey, I did not do it". I believe she put her hand in his'.

Jones said he heard at the Cape that Mrs Carey claimed O'Donnell had said 'I was sent to do it,' but he was 'almost sure' that O'Donnell said 'I did not do it'. It could have been 'I had to do it', or 'I could not help it', he agreed in cross-examination.

Thomas Carey, fifteen, said his mother and sisters slept in the second-class cabin 'and my father and three of us boys in the steer-age'.

When the shooting happened, 'I ran towards my mother's cabin to get my father's revolver. I took the revolver from the bag. I had seen him with the revolver when he came aboard at Dartmouth and I saw it when my father went ashore at Madeira. I had seen the revolver afterwards, when some money was taken out of the bag.

'I wanted to give the revolver to my father. I put the pistol in my pocket. I did not give it to my father because I saw he would not be able to use it. I saw my mother go towards O'Donnell, who put out his hand and said, "Shake hands, Mrs Carey. Your name is not Power", or something like that.

'I am not sure whether O'Donnell said, "I was sent to do it" or "I had to do it". I am not sure of the words used'. His mother refused to shake hands, whereupon Mrs O'Donnell said to her husband, 'No matter, O'Donnell; you are no informer'.

'I had seen O'Donnell using the pistol on the voyage. He was shooting flying fish with it', the fifteen-year-old testified.

'My father and O'Donnell were great friends on the way out. While we were at the Cape on the *Melrose*, some men came on shore and pointed at my father, who was on deck. But up to that time no one had suspected that my father was Carey'.

Mrs Margaret Carey took the stand, dressed in deep black that the jury could not fail to notice. She said she and her husband had become very friendly on the outward voyage with the prisoner and a woman 'who passed for his wife'.

O'Donnell had asked her husband to have a bottle of ale. James Carey first took the baby from his wife and put it in her cabin, 'but it awoke and I went to it. Before I went away I saw the men with ale before them. In five or ten minutes I heard something like the popping of a cork.

'My son was rushing into the berth as I was coming out'.

Passenger Nathan Marks said he was reading an English news-paper on deck when Carey asked to see it. When he was looking at it, hunting for news of himself, the boy came up and spoke to him, and they went below. 'I followed him down to the saloon to get some beer, but did not get it.'

In the brief time he was there, he noticed O'Donnell was talking in a very confidential way, but Carey was once more gesticulating, 'as if laying down the law'.

Cubitt gave evidence of receiving the portrait from the Cape Town barkeeper, and of not attributing any evil intent to O'Donnell's words before departure. He corroborated Carey's son's evidence about seeing O'Donnell fire his revolver at fish and birds.

Beecher, second officer, said he was on the bridge when the first shot was fired and he immediately went down to the saloon. The prisoner was sitting on the table. He laid hold of his wrist and saw Bosun Jones take the revolver from O'Donnell's pocket. The prisoner said, 'Do not be frightened, I am not going to hurt anybody'. Three chambers were full and three had been discharged. They searched him and found a further cartridge in his waistcoat pocket.

'Afterwards I searched young Carey and found upon him a bulldog pistol'. This gun, it turned out, was unloaded.

Beecher did not know the device found in O'Donnell's effects had been a 'galvanic battery' used to treat a partially paralysed left arm. 'We did not like the look of it'.

James Rose, master of the *Melrose*, said he had the prisoner searched while the deceased was still bleeding copiously. O'Donnell was secured in irons and his cabin and trunk searched. They found an old revolver and a leather belt with cartridges for a small revolver.

Chief Inspector Cherry of the Port Elizabeth police deposed that the prisoner's purse in the trunk held the portrait of Carey given to him by Cubitt. There was also a clipping from a newspaper; the article headed *Irish Revolutionists in America*.

The attorney general argued that an extract should be read as bearing upon what was the defendant's view of such cases as this, in which murder was not only justified but patriotic. After legal argument, the application was rejected as prejudicial to a fair trial.

Dr Frederick Ensor said he saw three bullet wounds on the body of Carey, as well as black powder marks on his face from the proximity of the muzzle. The first wound was in the neck, a little to the left of the centre of the windpipe. The bullet had made its way out at the side of the neck and struck the coat.

The two other wounds were to the back. One was in the upper portion, two inches from the spine, and the second at the lower angle of the shoulder blade. The upper shot (the second one fired) traversed the lung and made its way out of the chest between the fourth and fifth ribs, lodging itself in the skin just below the right nipple.

The third bullet had penetrated the lowest part of the lung, wounded the diaphragm, descended the stomach, and nearly cut the left kidney in two. All were serious wounds, but the third was the cause of death.

The first shot was upperward, the second nearly horizontal, as if the firer had stood, while the third took a slightly downward course.

Witness also deposed that the defendant's left arm had been wasted from disuse owing to an old injury. The fingers of the left hand were partially paralysed, he confirmed.

Detective Superintendent Mallon of the Dublin police was called, thus seeing an epoch-making saga to its conclusion. He swore that he had given a Weeks revolver similar to the one taken from young Carey to the elder Carey. His dealings with the informer had led him to regard Carey as 'a desperate man, regardless of human life'.

He had heard James Carey express regret at the murder of Lord Frederick Cavendish, he admitted in cross-examination, but not at other murders.

The court heard an allegation that O'Donnell had said at Port Elizabeth: 'I am not guilty of murder. What I did was in self-defence. Mr Carey pulled the revolver out of his pocket. I snatched it out of his hand'.

The crown case concluded, and the defence offered no evidence except a claim of self-defence. O'Donnell did not enter the witness box, and everything depended on the address of Charles Russell, QC, to the jury: 'It has been stated in the press, and nothing could be more reprehensible,' he began, 'that O'Donnell had gone aboard the *Kinfauns Castle* as the emissary of others, tracking Carey like a sleuthhound'. He wished to demonstrate the groundlessness of such an assertion.

The crown had brought forward no evidence of premeditation on the part of O'Donnell. This was despite the fact that they had, with their great detective power, followed the career of the defendant through the wilds of Donegal and America to expose from beginning to end the life and incidents of the prisoner down to the moment of his taking passage to South Africa.

They would have explained, if they could have done, the statement irresponsibly put forward, that O'Donnell knew Carey was to be a passenger on the *Kinfauns Castle*.

He hated to disturb the slumbering ashes of the dead, but it could not be dispensed with, and he wished to present them with something of a portraiture of James Carey.

Mallon had said that Carey in all his acts had taken care to protect his own person. When he found himself face to face with one of his own countrymen, who had named him, he would not have hesitated, coward as he was, to shoot the man, particularly as he knew that in those circumstances he could have done so with practical impunity.

When the mask was torn from his face, Carey became a desperate man. That the man was utterly regardless of human life was shown by the part he took in the Phoenix Park murders.

Was it likely that, without any previous quarrel, O'Donnell would have selected a time [for the murder] when there were several persons present, and when he was within forty-eight hours of Natal and the security and secrecy of the bush?

The defence claimed that Carey himself had pointed out that there was more chance of employment for O'Donnell in Natal, and that the defendant had finally agreed to go there.

After he learned Power's real identity, O'Donnell resolved to ignore the man, his counsel insisted, and had told Carey in the saloon: 'I want to have nothing to do with an informer'

'What do you mean?' Carey replied.

'You are James Carey, the damned Irish informer,' O'Donnell said.

On this, Carey sprang to his feet and produced a weapon, but O'Donnell was quicker in pulling his out, and he shot at Carey. That was the prisoner's account of the matter, said Russell, and they must see how it fitted with that given by crown witnesses.

'What was the most likely thing for a coward like Carey to do, armed as he was with a weapon the Government had furnished him with? Of course it would be to produce it, either for the purpose of a show of violence to deter the man from further acts, or for the purpose of deadly use'.

He suggested that Carey's own weapon had then been picked up off the floor by his son, who had then hidden it. Russell here appeared to insinuate revenge upon revenge, that the boy Carey might have hoped to avenge his father in turn.

He told the jury that if the circumstances justified O'Donnell firing the first shot, which would reduce the crime to manslaughter, then it required no argument to show that he could not be found guilty by reason of the other shots in quick succession, as these were part of the same act.

The remark made to Cubitt, 'I'll shoot him', was an expression of idle bravado, uttered while the man was laughing, and no importance had been attached to it. It was against human experience that a man should form a deliberate intent to murder and then talk about it.

Furthermore, the prisoner would, from his physical infirmities, have been at a great disadvantage in any conflict with Carey. Would he therefore have sought any such encounter?

Was it not more likely that Carey rushed to his feet when suddenly called an Irish informer, drawing his pistol, and that O'Donnell, being the quicker of the two, fired first?

Carey found himself on a vessel with strangers, among men of his own class with strong feelings, and capable of giving effect to them. And yet they were asked to believe that this was the time he would select for hiding away in his bag the weapon that was his only safeguard.

Russell pointed out that one of the passengers told second officer Beecher that young Carey had a pistol, but when he was searched he denied the possession, and it was not until a second search had been made that it was found in his trouser pocket.

'If there was an honest doubt in honest minds, the defendant was entitled to a verdict of acquittal. If they took the other part, then he was entitled to be relieved of the graver penalty of the law'.

Described as a 'brilliant and sustained address', lasting over three hours, at the close of the defence speech there was a burst of applause – which was only with difficulty suppressed.

The attorney general replied that it was an imaginary incident that the lad had picked up the revolver from the saloon floor and put it in his own pocket in order to secrete the fact that his father had possessed and possibly presented the weapon.

He asked the jurors to note especially that Mrs O'Donnell did not for a moment suggest self-defence, but justification, because she turned to the prisoner in seeming commendation, saying, 'Never mind, O'Donnell, you are no informer'.

Then there was the evidence of the witness Cubitt: that the man who said he would shoot Carey was actually the man who did, in the end, shoot him. The attorney sat down.

The judge, in summing up, drew attention to Dr Ensor's evidence that the third shot was the fatal one. It was most important. The law laid down that it was just as much murder to hasten a man's death who might have died within an hour as to kill a man who otherwise might have lived for forty years.

In the majority of cases where a plea of self-defence was raised there were witnesses to support it, but in the present case there were no witnesses other than those who had been examined by the prosecution.

The jury retired a few minutes before seven o'clock. After an interval of an hour, they sent a communication asking for clarification on a point of law. They wanted to know whether a stand-off between two armed men, one shooting the other in fear of being shot himself, should be construed as murder or manslaughter.

Mr Justice Denman suggested it might be neither. They could take the view that it was self-defence. Or they could instead decide that such a story was 'an idle tale'. He emphasised the importance of the three shots in this case, the last two of which were in the back.

The jury returned after a further three quarters of an hour, asking for the meaning of 'malice aforethought'. They then retired again, and after a total absence of nearly two hours, it being nearly nine o'clock, they sent word that they had reached a verdict.

'Do you find the prisoner at the bar, Patrick O'Donnell, guilty or not guilty of the crime of murder with which he stands charged?'

'Guilty'.

'And is that the verdict of you all?'

'It is'.

The convict was asked if he had anything to say as to why sentence of death should not be passed upon him. He merely bowed his head. Mr Justice Denman assumed the black cap and ordered that he be returned to his last place of confinement, Newgate prison, and there, on 17 December, 1883, be hanged by the neck until he be dead, and may the Lord have mercy on your soul'.

O'Donnell woke up to what was happening. He began 'execrating England and her laws', shouting imprecations, railing loudly against his fate until he was bundled below by a large party of police and warders. He declared himself the victim of an infamous plot, and called for cheers for 'old Ireland and her liberty'.

The *Times* described it as a 'violent tirade', which only 'served to lessen the sympathy which many had felt for the prisoner'.

Tranquil again some time later in the cells, O'Donnell again protested his innocence of murder, adding that the evident hesitation of the jury had inspired him with the hope that he would escape the extreme penalty.

The steamer *British Princess* arrived at Cork harbour from Philadelphia on Sunday, 9 December, with O'Donnell's lawful wife on board. She proceeded in the steamer to Liverpool and in London went to see her condemned husband, the man who had deserted her years before.

The US house of representatives meanwhile adopted a resolution pointing out the sentenced man's American citizenship, with congressmen calling on President Chester Arthur to intercede urgently with the British authorities.

The startling argument was also made that the O'Donnell jury should have comprised six British subjects and six aliens, under standing precedent for alleged cases of murder on the high seas.

The president of the USA personally conveyed a request to Lord Granville, the British ambassador, that the sentence be delayed to enable counsel for the defence to raise errors claimed to have been made during the trial on points of law.

But O'Donnell was hung at eight o'clock on Monday 17 December 1883. His brother, waiting in the throng outside the prison, told the press that 'a jury of Chinese' on the evidence before them would not and could not have convicted O'Donnell.

A crowd of considerable dimensions had collected outside the walls. The morning was damp and cheerless. Ten minutes before the time appointed for the execution the bells of St Sepulchre's commenced tolling, 'the muffled and subdued sound adding solemnity to the dismal proceedings'.

Bartholomew Binns, the crown executioner who had succeeded Marwood (the latter having died suddenly from 'inflammation of the lungs'), went through the process of pinioning the convict's arms. The man about to die smiled as it was done and was comparatively cheerful. It was observed that O'Donnell had allowed his beard to grow and was somewhat altered in appearance since the trial.

The procession began, Fr Fleming of Moorfields walking by the condemned man's side, reading some prayers. The tall Donegal man nodded his responses.

On gaining the platform, and the noose and cap being put over the prisoner, the clergyman withdrew to one side and Binns stepped forward. Touching a lever, 'the body of the unhappy man disappeared from sight. It fell with tremendous force and velocity, and in the opinion of the prison surgeon death must have been instantaneous.

'The rope, which had made a cutting sound as it passed through the air, quivered for a second or two and then became perfectly still and motionless'. A warder on the roof of the jail hoisted the black flag, and the bell of St Sepulchre's ceased to resonate. The flag was received by the crowd with a murmur, although no open sympathy for the prisoner was evinced.

O'Donnell's brother, who had taken to a doorway to avoid the curiosity of the crowd, declared to journalists: 'My brother has died as bravely as any man ever did'. He was later admitted to the prison, although permission to see the body was refused, and given some personal effects in accordance with the dead man's bequest. He emerged to express his intention of returning to Ireland as soon as possible.

The body of Patrick O'Donnell was buried within the precincts of the prison in a narrow paved passage with high walls on either side, 'where Muller, Wainwright, the Flowery Land pirates and other notorious offenders executed in Newgate lie buried'.

O'Donnell had embarked on the *Kinfauns Castle* at the suggestion of a German shipping agent, his counsel, A. M. Sullivan, later revealed in a letter to the *Dublin Weekly News*, printed in January 1884.

O'Donnell's self-defence story was 'probable and natural, and almost self-evident', he wrote firmly. Carey had drawn a pistol, and O'Donnell dashed it from his hand at the same instant that he fired his own. He followed up with two other shots as he saw the Phoenix Park assassinations plotter stoop towards the fallen pistol.

'Carey must have had that pistol there and then, and young Carey picked it off the floor'.

Susan Gallaher, or 'Mrs O'Donnell', was legally debarred as his presumed lawful wife from appearing as a witness at the trial, Sullivan pointed out, or she could have corroborated this version of events. O'Donnell intended to marry Gallaher, a native of his own parish, in South Africa, he added. A priest in London on whom they waited refused to marry them and they then proceeded to the Cape.

General Pryor met Gallaher in advance of the trial and elicited a statement as to what happened, Sullivan now told. The girl said Carey was a bully and always irritable, and Patrick had wanted to shake him off on finally finding out who he was.

Carey tackled O'Donnell about something on the *Melrose*, while she was laying her head against him, feeling seasick. The informer had interrogated O'Donnell and then went away, returning quickly afterwards. She was in a drowsy state with her eyes closed. She remembered hearing a sudden burst of angry words, 'damned informer', some stir of feet, and a shot.

Questioned as to whether she saw Carey with a pistol, she replied that she saw no firing and no pistol. 'Just before the shot I heard some stamps, a noise on the floor; it might be feet'.

'Did you see a pistol in Carey's hand or on the floor?'

'Oh, oh, if only'.

If she had said that she saw a pistol and that it was knocked out of Carey's hand, who would there have been to contradict her, Sullivan asked? 'The people of Donegal need not blush for Patrick O'Donnell, the victim of passion and provocation, and they may claim with pride the humble heroine of religion and truth, Susan Gallaher,' he finished.

A 'Patriot's' Epitaph
To the Editor of the *Times*:

Sir,

In the chief Roman Catholic cemetery of Ireland, a cenotaph bears the following inscription:

'In memory of Patrick O'Donnell, who heroically gave up his life for Ireland in London, England, on 17th December, 1883. Not tears, but prayers, for the dead who died for Ireland'.

This monument was erected by the grateful admirers of his heroism in the United States of America through the *Irish World*, and forwarded by a ladies committee of New York: Mrs F. Byrne, Mrs Maggie Halvie, Helen A. Ford.

O'Donnell was hanged for the murder of James Carey, the approver on whose evidence Mrs Francis Byrne's accomplices in the Phoenix Park assassinations were brought to justice. Her grateful admiration for the 'hero' who avenged them is natural enough. But what are we to think of the conduct of the cemetery's committee? All designs for monuments and all inscriptions to be placed in the cemetery are submitted for their approval. All monuments are actually put up by their servants and workmen.

The names of the present members of the committee are stated in Thom's official directory. They are all persons of character and position in the Roman Catholic community of Dublin. There are ten Justices of the Peace among them, a couple of doctors of medicine, and a Very Rev canon. These gentlemen themselves can hardly think the assassination of Crown witnesses a fit subject for ostentatious commemoration.

Why do they suffer this monument, reared by a confessed murderess to a convicted murderer, avowedly in honour of his crime, to pollute the consecrated ground where the mangled body of one of his victims rests?

I am, Sir,
Your obedient servant,
Exul.

(The *Times*, 16 April 1887)

Flotsam

The steamer *Pathan*, from London and Plymouth, arrived in Adelaide, South Australia, on 30 July after a voyage of a few weeks. Among her passengers were reported to be 'some notable Irish characters'.

The news angered and astonished the government of Victoria, her next port of call. Rumours at the end of May that the imperial government was taking steps for the deportation to Australia of certain approvers in the Phoenix Park murders had caused consternation.

The protest of Victoria had been communicated all the way to the lord lieutenant of Ireland. Certain assurances were given, and it seemed the story might have been a ruse 'to cover the secret departure of the men in some other direction'.

But here was the ship, with Adelaide telegraphing that it was intended to land certain persons at Melbourne. The state parliament was outraged, and Prime Minister James Service promised no such individuals would be allowed ashore.

'We in Australia resent,' he said, 'and in self-respect we must continue to resent, the very notion that our communities are a fit place of deposit for the refuse of other populations'.

On the arrival of the *Pathan* at Port Phillip Heads outside Melbourne, several local detectives boarded her 'with a view to settling the question of identity'. They quickly established that the passenger claiming to be 'Peter Murphy' was in fact the car man Michael Kavanagh, and that another would-be immigrant was Joseph Hanlon, who had finally ensured the conviction of Tim Kelly.

These two admitted their identities and said that another man, who went by 'Kiernan', was actually Joe Smith, the man brought to the Phoenix Park to identify the under secretary.

Smith at first denied himself, but finally admitted the truth to the detectives. He said Dublin Castle had separately obtained his ticket for Sydney, a detective accompanying him on board in England.

Kavanagh and Hanlon were annoyed that a separate approver had been packed onto the same voyage. Another detective, Simmons, who handed Kavanagh a bank draft for £96 and Hanlon one for £50, had arranged their passage.

The car man complained that George Bolton, crown solicitor, 'told me there would be no fear of me in any of the Crown colonies, and that is why I consented to come'. Superintendent Mallon had added that if they went to Melbourne they would have the protection of the crown, while the government had provided for their safety.

'We did not know Smith was coming on the same steamer; we would have objected had we known that he was to be a passenger'.

Prime Minister Service later wrote to London: 'By a convenient though lamentable coincidence, the tidings of the murder of Carey reached us almost simultaneously with the arrival of the *Pathan*'. The approvers were quickly made aware of their plight.

Hanlon penned a letter asking the local authorities to 'entosceade [*sic*] on my behalf to the Government for the porpose of having me sent quietly from hear to the port of Calceta (Calcutta)' and Kavanagh was of a like mind.

These letters were helpful, and a contract was entered into with Captain Rowley to retain the trio on board for the remainder of the voyage. The *Pathan* arrived in Sydney eight days later on 9 August, but instructions had now been received by telegraph from London, and the men were taken on board the ironclad HMS *Nelson*. They were eventually taken home again.

All that is known of their subsequent careers is that one 'made a comfortable fortune in a corner of the globe where he is never likely to be traced', while 'others are not too badly housed elsewhere'.

Michael Kavanagh reportedly died within three years, 'poisoned by drink' according to Tighe Hopkins, in a lunatic asylum in London.

Records show that Robert Farrell received a payment of £1,000 'in consideration of the fact that he came forward to inform the authorities before he was arrested', thus becoming the first tongue.

Among the witnesses, little Alice Carroll was paid a princely £500. Huxley, the garrulous gardener, got £100. There were other rewards or compensation, the largest being the £3,500 paid to Denis J. Field for the injuries inflicted on him near his home after he had done his duty as a juror.

The second car man, James 'Skin the Goat' Fitzharris, was convicted at his second trial of aiding and abetting. Notwithstanding an enormous reward of £10,000 offered to him for his full compliance by the government, Fitzharris had remained silent.

This fact, coupled with his nickname, ensured him a lasting place in the pantheon of Dublin characters, and he was immortalised again as the keeper of a cabman's shelter in the Eumaeus episode of *Ulysses*, even if Joyce twice referred to the Phoenix Park murders taking place in 1881 instead of 1882, the year of the author's birth.

Sentenced to penal servitude for life, Skin the Goat was released from Maryborough [Portaloise] prison having served sixteen years. He tried to enter America but was deported by the United States government.

Destitute, he was arrested again in October 1900 to prevent him from appearing at the Roscommon Music Hall, Everton, where he had been announced as a 'star turn'. The authorities made in clear they would not tolerate him attempting to make money by speaking about the Phoenix Park killings.

During the latter years of his life, as Joyce relates, Fitzharris had a small appointment as night watchman under the Dublin corporation. He 'led a most exemplary life' thereafter, the *Times* admitted in a brief obituary, in 1910, following his death in the South Dublin Union Infirmary, which 'removes almost the last of those who were personally concerned in the murders'.

Fitzharris and Laurence Hanlon had been the last two released, and then only on licence. Hanlon was condemned for the attempted murder of Denis Field, along with co-defendant Joe Mullet, the latter released only a few weeks before his fellow Invincibles.

The magistrate of the Star Chamber, John Adye Curran, received a telegram from the attorney general soon after the trials telling him that the position of chief justice in Jamaica, worth £2,500 a year, was vacant, and offering him the post.

He consulted his wife 'who was very nervous and anxious as to my personal safety', and instead took a seat on the County Court Bench.

In 1892, Detective Superintendent Mallon, who had been given a small monetary 'prize' for his efforts, called at the house of politician Tim Healy. Gladstone had come into office again, and Mallon was asking for influence toward his promotion. 'He told me the usual tale of the boycotting of Catholics by Dublin Castle, and said he had been shut out from advancement'.

Healy was astounded at the treatment of such a famous figure. Others had earned the credit of his work, Mallon explained, and he had no hope of getting the vacant job of assistant commissioner of police unless under a Liberal government. As it transpired, John Morley became chief secretary, and Mallon got the post he wanted.

Healy had also been canvassed by someone else, several years earlier – 'A knock came to the door. I found a stern-faced woman outside. "I want to speak to you," she said.

'"Who are you, ma'am?" I asked.

'"The mother of Joe Brady," she replied.

'I as little expected the Witch of Endor. Sensing tragedy, I said, "Come in."

'All was dark, and she sat down in my shuttered study. I had had no time to let in the light before she knocked. "The hangman," she began, "took the ivory cross from my son's neck which Lady

Frederick Cavendish sent to him. I want it back. It's unfair that the only thing given to my dead boy is kept from me."

'She then produced a prayer book of her son, with writings on the fly-leaf. I examined it, and found this script: *Joseph Brady, condemned to death by the perjured traitor, Carey.* Underneath in a different hand (evidently Carey's) was – *James Carey was no traitor. He gave evidence only when he had been betrayed himself. He saved the lives of innocent men, and one woman.*

'While I read this, Mrs. Brady fastened her eyes on me. "I have not shed a tear since he was hanged struggling against the English, but I would like to get the cross he got as a keepsake from Lady Cavendish".'

'I was unable to help her, and sorrowfully she went away'.

In Yorkshire, at the Bolton Abbey estate of the Cavendish family, there is a memorial fountain to their fallen son. There is also an obelisk modelled on the Wellington Monument in the Phoenix Park across the sea.

Opposite the place where Thomas Burke's remains are laid is a handsome pillar designed by Sir Thomas Drew, Architect, and surmounted by a facsimile of the Cross of Cong. It was raised by a group of friends 'in appreciation of his high character and eminent public service'.

At the base of Burke's gravestone [ZB 75] is the inscription 'murdered in the Phoenix Park'.

Not far away, also in Prospect Cemetery, Glasnevin, is the memorial to Patrick O'Donnell. Within a further stone's throw is a slab erected over the grave of Skin the Goat [VH 159] with a plaque by Lorcan Leonard that commemorates Fitzharris and his Invincible comrades, stating that those executed 'died for Ireland'.

A similar plaque in Kilmainham Jail, fixed to the grey stone wall where the scaffold was erected, names the five men executed there in May and June 1883. An inscription in Irish says their bones lie beneath the flags of the yard below.

And in the Phoenix Park itself, etched into the grassy roadside bank below the path, between a milestone and a lamp standard, there is a simple cross.

It faces directly towards Áras an Uachtaráin, and flowers appear there every year on the sixth day of May.

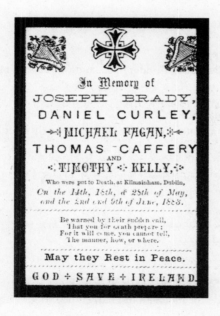

In Memory of
JOSEPH BRADY,
DANIEL CURLEY,
MICHAEL FAGAN,
THOMAS CAFFERY
AND
TIMOTHY KELLY,

Who were put to Death, at Kilmainham, Dublin,
On the 14th, 18th, & 28th of May,
and the 2nd and 9th of June, 1883.

Be warned by their sudden call,
That you for death prepare;
For it will come, you cannot tell,
The manner, how, or where.

May they Rest in Peace.

GOD ÷ SAVE ÷ IRELAND.

List of Invincibles

Joe Brady
(26), 22 North Anne Street; Stonecutter. Hanged 14 May 1883.

Thomas Caffrey
(26), 45 Upper Rutland Street; Labourer. Hanged 2 June 1883.

James Carey – *Approver*
(45), 19A Denzille Street; Builder and Landlord. Assassinated 29 July 1883.

Peter Carey – *Approver*
(32), 7 South Gloucester Street; Bricklayer. Secretly resettled.

Daniel Curley
(35), 2 Love Lane, Mount Street; Carpenter. Hanged 18 May 1883.

Daniel Delaney
(40), 49 Lower Clanbrassil Street; Carpenter. Ten years penal servitude. Released 1891.

Patrick Delaney
(32), 123 Cork Street; Carpenter. Sentence of death commuted to penal servitude for life, then discharged due to ill health.

Peter Doyle
(35), 14 Wexford Street; Coachbuilder. Discharged on continuing bail.

Thomas Doyle
(40), Cross Kevin Street, Coachbuilder. Five years penal servitude. Released 1887.

John Dwyer

(19), 6 Chatham Street, Tailor. Discharged for ill health, died 1883.

Michael Fagan

(24), 36 Artisan Buildings, Buckingham Street; Blacksmith. Hanged 28 May 1883.

Robert Farrell – *Approver*

(24), 12 Kennedy's Lane; Van driver. Secretly resettled.

James 'Skin the Goat' Fitzharris

(53), Lime Street; Car driver. Penal servitude for life. Released 1899, died September 1910.

Joseph Hanlon – *Approver*

(23), 29 Lower Camden Street; Carpenter. Secretly resettled.

Laurence Hanlon

(22), 29 Lower Camden Street; Carpenter. Penal servitude for life. Released 1899.

Michael Kavanagh - *Approver*

(23), 9 Townsend Street; Car driver. Died in Britain 1886.

Timothy Kelly

(20), 12 Redmond's Hill; Coachbuilder. Hanged 9 June 1883.

Thomas Martin

(30), St John's Tce, Fontenoy Street; Compositor. Discharged on own recognisances.

Edward McCaffrey

(40), 21 Peter Street, Mineral water distributor. Ten years penal servitude. Released 1891.

William Moroney

(40), 19 Bride Street; Shoemaker. Ten years penal servitude. Released 1890.

James Mullett

(35), 12 Lower Bridge Street; Publican. Ten years penal servitude. Released 1891.

Joe Mullett

(35), 6 Temple Cottages; Clerk. Penal servitude for life. Released 1899.

Edward O'Brien

(40), 14 Old Kilmainham; Shoemaker. Ten years penal servitude. Released 1891.

Henry Rowles

(50), 11 Fishamble Street; Tailor. Died before trial.

George Smith

(21), O'Brien's Cottages, Haddington Road; Bricklayer. Discharged on own recognisances.

Joseph Smith – *Approver*

(24), South King Street; Office of Public Works employee. Secretly resettled.

Patrick Whelan

(30), St James' Terrace, Dolphin's Barn; Clerk. Discharged.

FLIGHT OF THE ASSASSINS

Select Bibliography

Anonymous, *Phoenix Park Murders: Depositions of Witnesses* (Dublin, 1883).

Anonymous, *Phoenix Park Murders: Report of the Trials* (Dublin, Thom, 1883).

Anonymous, *The Mysteries of Ireland, giving a graphic and faithful account of Irish Secret Societies and Their Plots* (London, 1883).

Bussy, Frederick Moir – *Irish Conspiracies: Recollections of John Mallon, the Great Irish Detective* (London, Everett, 1910).

Corfe, Tom – *The Phoenix Park Murders: Conflict Compromise and Tragedy in Ireland 1879–1882* (London, Hodder & Stoughton, 1968).

Curran, John Adye – *Reminiscences* (London, Edward Arnold, 1915).

Davitt, Michael – *Leaves From a Prison Diary* (London, Chapman & Hall, 1885).

Hopkins, Tighe – *Kilmainham Memories* (Dublin, 1886).

Moriarty, Tomás – *An examination of reaction to the Phoenix Park murders and the subsequent Invincible trials and executions* (Dublin, MA thesis, 2003).

Tynan, P. J. P. – *The Irish National Invincibles and Their Times* (London, Chatham & Co., 1894).

Newspaper and periodicals include but are not confined to: *Belfast Newsletter, Cape Argus, Evening Telegraph, Freeman's Journal, Irish Times, Irish World, History Ireland, Hue & Cry, Natal Witness, The Times, The Graphic, The Illustrated London News, United Ireland, Weekly Freeman.*

There are multiple manuscripts on the crime and its investigation in the National Library, National Museum and National Archives.

Assassination scene, Phoenix Park 6 May 2006

Acknowledgments

Charles Callan, David Carter, Northants Record Society; Joanna Finnegan, National Library; Hughie Geraghty, John Heuston, Seamus Moriarty, Tomás Moriarty, Niamh O'Sullivan, archivist, Kilmainham Jail.

PICTURE CREDITS
p. 6 *Illustrated London News* x 2
p. 7 *The Graphic* x 2
p. 8 *Ibid.*
p. 9 *Ibid.*
p. 26 *Illustrated London News*
p. 32 *Ibid.*
p. 42 *Penny Illustrated*
p. 54 *Illustrated London News*
p. 61 *The Graphic*
p. 74 *Ibid*
p. 91 *Ibid.*
p. 96 *Illustrated London News*
p. 108 *The Graphic*
p. 114 *Ibid.*
p. 123 *Ibid.*
p. 133 *Illustrated London News*
p. 135 *Ibid.*
p. 138 *The Graphic*
p. 149 *Ibid.*
p. 155 *Penny Illustrated*, left. *Freeman's Journal*, right
p. 163 *Penny Illustrated*
p. 167 *The Graphic*
p. 176 *Illustrated London News*
p. 185 *Ibid.*
p. 195 *Ibid.*
p. 198 *Ibid.*

p. 208 *The Graphic*
p. 219 *Ibid.*
p. 245 *Penny Illustrated*
p. 247 *Ibid.*
p. 257 *The Graphic*, top left, *Weekly Freeman*, top right, *Penny Illustrated*, middle, *The Graphic*, bottom.
p. 258 *The Graphic*
p. 272 Kilmainham Jail
p. 277 Author
p. 280 *The Graphic*
p. 282 Author
p. 285 *Penny Illustrated*

Picture Insert Section 1
p. 1 Cavendish and Burke, Author collection; *Illustrated London News*
p. 2 *L'Ilustration* top; Author collection, National Museum.
p. 3 National Library top, *Illustrated London News* bottom left, Tighe Hopkins, bottom right
p. 4 National Library
p. 5 *The Graphic*, top x 3, *Illustrated London News* bottom.
p. 6 *Penny Illustrated* x 2, top left. National Library, top right; *The Graphic*, bottom left, *Illustrated London News* bottom right.
p. 7 *Illustrated London News* top left. *The Graphic* x 3, *Illustrated London News* bottom.
p. 8 Edward Arnold, top left; National Library, top right & inset, middle left. National Museum, middle right. *The Graphic*.

Section 2
p. 1 Kilmainham Jail
p. 2 Author Carte De Visite top left, Mansell collection top right, Kilmainham Jail, National Library.
p. 3 Kilmainham Jail, National Library, National Archives, National Library x 2
p. 4 Kilmainham Jail x 2, middle left to right: *Penny Illustrated*, *Weekly Freeman*, *Illustrated London News*, *Ibid.* bottom left, Hopkins bottom right, inset *Weekly Freeman*
p. 5 National Library, Kilmainham Jail x 3
p. 6 Kilmainham Jail x 2, mid left *The Graphic*, mid right and bottom left *Weekly Freeman*, bottom right *The Graphic*.
p. 7 National Library, Kilmainham Jail x 4.
p. 8 Kilaminham Jail x 2, top. *The Graphic* x 3, middle. *Weekly Freeman*, bottom left, *The Graphic*, bottom right.

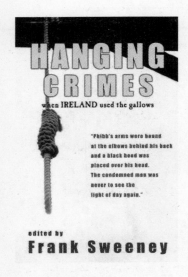

MERCIER PRESS

WHAT YOU NEED TO READ

HANGING CRIMES
When Ireland Used the Gallows

Frank Sweeney (ed.)

ISBN 1 85635 462 8

From a time when the ultimate punishment in criminal cases in Ireland was the gallows, *Hanging Crimes* brings us ten spellbinding stories of rape, murder, love and betrayal from around the country.

In all of these stories the murder or rape shook the entire community, exposing fears, disloyalties, treachery and, often, an appetite for vengeance.

The authors of these pieces have trawled through the archives to bring alive these crimes, the resulting courtcases and the final dispensation of justice.

MERCIER PRESS
WHAT YOU NEED TO READ

RESTLESS SPIRIT
The Story of Rose Quinn

Margaret Hawkins

ISBN 1 85635 496 2

Rose Quinn died in an asylum less than a year after being committed by her brother for refusing to live with the man she had been forced to marry. Such was the stigma attached to having had a relative in the asylum that the story remained a family secret until it was revealed three generations later to Rose's great-niece, Patricia.

The news catapulted Patricia into a dedicated search to find out more about the woman she never knew existed. Shocking coincidences were uncovered and an unexpected spiritual connection in the family surfaced. This was to result in finding Rose's burial place – a plot behind the asylum, now known as St Senan's Hospital.

For almost 100 years Rose's fate had been kept secret, but her spirit never died. This is the story of that restless spirit.

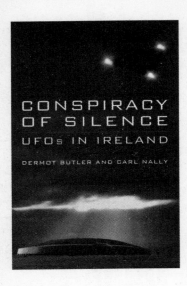

MERCIER PRESS
WHAT YOU NEED TO READ

CONSPIRACY OF SILENCE
UFOs in Ireland

Dermot Butler and Carl Nally

ISBN 1 85635 509 8

UFOs have been sighted in Ireland for over one hundred years. People who have no previous interest in such phenomena have reported bizarre experiences and encounters with the paranormal in almost every county in Ireland, from Derry to Cork, Dublin to Galway.

Here for the first time Nally and Butler present the eye-witness reports, together with their own investigations and interviews with pilots and flight engineers who have, until now, been loathe to talk of their experiences. Certain locations are closely examined, such as Newgrange, where paranormal activity is recorded more often than anywhere else in the country, and the history and official response to UFO activity is explored.

The time is right for the truth about UFOs in Ireland to come out.

This is the story so far ...

he·roes (hē´-rōz), *n. and v.* a male person manually propelling a watercraft with oars. *"He oughta be fit, 'cuz **heroes** that boat for two hours every morning."*

her·o·in (her´-ə-win), *n. and v.* the predicted triumph of a long-eared mammal of the family Leporidae. *"You gotta be on drugs if you think a **heroin** a race against a tortoise."*

hide·away (hīd´-ə-wā), *n. and v.* the speaker's speculation on a future method or course of action. *"If **hideaway** to be a pro baseball player, hide do it."*

high-speed (hī´-spēd), *n. and v.* the speaker when moving at a velocity beyond the posted limit. *"I drive slow when I see a cop, but if I don't see none, **high-speed**."*

Hol·ly·wood (hȯl´-ē-wüd), *n., pron., and v.* speculation connecting an august institution or a part of a building to possible future action. *"Twenty bucks says if Pete Rose got into the **Hollywood** still bet on baseball."*

horny (hȯrn´-ē), *n. and pron.* a phrase connecting a male to either a brass wind instrument or a protuberance of keratinized skin projecting outward from the skull of an animal. *"When he grabbed that bull by the **horny** got more than he'd bargained for."*

hun·ger (həng´-ər), *v. and adj.* the suspending of a female's possession from a fixed object so that it does not touch the ground. *"We just about lost it when she **hunger** bra on the clothesline."*

hys·te·ria (hi-ster´-ē-ə), *n. and v.* a male person achieving intimidation using a concentrated and unblinking ocular technique. *"Don't make eye contact with that dude—**hysteria** down."*